THROUGH THE
PILLARS OF HERAKLES

This is the first study in over 50 years of the Greek and Roman civilizations' explorations through the Pillars of Herakles into the Atlantic.

Although the Greco-Roman world was centered on the Mediterranean, and classical scholarship often confined to these topographical boundaries marked by the pillars themselves, from *c*700BC into the Roman period a series of explorers were to discover the entire Atlantic coast, north to Iceland, Scandinavia and the Baltic, and south into the African tropics. With the Carthaginians' own discoveries – including the British Isles, the coast of Africa and the Atlantic islands – the world of classical antiquity reached from Iceland to Viet Nam.

In this long-overdue project, Duane W. Roller chronicles a detailed account of these early pioneers and their discoveries and in doing so contributes a new chapter to the history of exploration.

Discussing for the first time in detail the relevance of Iceland and the Arctic to Greco-Roman culture, and examining the impact of the Greeks and Romans themselves on the world beyond the Mediterranean, this book is essential reading for students and scholars of classical, and indeed global, history.

Duane W. Roller is Professor of Greek and Latin at The Ohio State University. His previous publications include *The Building Program of Herod the Great* (University of California Press, 1998) and *The World of Juba II and Kleopatra Selene* (Routledge, 2003).

THROUGH THE PILLARS OF HERAKLES

Greco-Roman exploration of the Atlantic

Duane W. Roller

Routledge
Taylor & Francis Group

NEW YORK AND LONDON

G
84
R65
2006

60715009

5-7-07

c. 1

First published 2006
by Routledge
270 Madison Ave, New York, NY 10016

Simultaneously published in the UK
by Routledge
2 Park Square, Milton Park, Abingdon, Oxon OX14 4RN

Routledge is an imprint of the Taylor & Francis Group

© 2006 Duane W. Roller

Typeset in Garamond by Bookcraft Ltd, Stroud, Gloucestershire
Printed and bound in Great Britain by The Cromwell Press,
Trowbridge, Wiltshire

All rights reserved. No part of this book may be reprinted or reproduced or
utilized in any form or by any electronic, mechanical, or other means, now
known or hereafter invented, including photocopying and recording, or in
any information storage or retrieval system, without permission in writing
from the publishers.

British Library Cataloguing in Publication Data
A catalogue record for this book is available from the British Library

Library of Congress Cataloging in Publication Data
Roller, Duane W.
Through the pillars of Herakles : Greco-Roman exploration of the
Atlantic Ocean/Duane W. Roller.
p. cm.
Includes bibliographical references.
1. Atlantic Ocean–Discovery and exploration–Greek. 2. Atlantic
Ocean–Discovery and exploration–Roman. 3. Classical geography.
I. Title.
G84.R65 2005
910'.938–dc22   2005016469

ISBN10: 0-415-37287-9

ISBN13: 9-78-0-415-37287-9

CONTENTS

ILLUSTRATIONS

Figures

Maps

ACKNOWLEDGEMENTS

The author would like to thank the libraries of The Ohio State University, the University of California at Berkeley, Stanford University, and the Harvard College Library, the primary places where the research for this book was performed. Thanks are also due to the Center for Hellenic Studies and its library. Several grants and leaves from The Ohio State University were of major assistance. Field research included a Fulbright Senior Lecturing Award to Poland in 2000, which allowed exploration of the southern Baltic and the northern frontier reaches of the Greco-Roman world, as well as numerous other trips to sites mentioned in the text. For supplying photographs and the permission to use them, the author would like to thank Donna Martin, the late Duane H. D. Roller, Letitia K. Roller, and Susan Weinger. Among those who assisted in the completion of this work are Charles Babcock, Barry Cunliffe, James S. Romm, Richard Stoneman and many others at Routledge, A. E. K. Vail, and Wendy Watkins and the Center for Epigraphical Studies at The Ohio State University.

ABBREVIATIONS

AAntHung	*Acta Antiqua* Academiae Scientiarum Hungaricae
AbbGött	*Abhandlungen der Akademie der Wissenschaften in Göttingen*
ACF	*Annuaire du Collège de France*
AFLM	*Annali della Facoltà di Lettere e Filosofia*, Università di Macerata
AJA	*American Journal of Archaeology*
AMal	*Analecta Malacitana*
AncS	*Ancient Society*
AncW	*The Ancient World*
AnnBr	*Annales de Bretagne*
ANRW	*Aufstieg und Niedergang der römischen Welt*
AntAfr	*Antiquités africaines*
AntCl	*L'Antiquité classique*
BAC	*Bulletin archéologique du Comité des travaux historiques et scientifiques*
BAGRW	*Barrington Atlas of the Greek and Roman World*, ed. Richard J. Talbert, Princeton: Princeton University Press, 2000
BAMaroc	*Bulletin d'archéologie Marocaine*
BAR	British Archaeological Reports
BAssBudé	*Bulletin de l'Association Guillaume Budé*
BCH	*Bulletin de correspondance hellénique*
BÉFEO	*Bulletin de l'École française d'Extrème-Orient*
BIFAN	*Bulletin de l'Institut Fondamental d'Afrique Noire*
BollClass	*Bollettino dei classici*
CAH	*The Cambridge Ancient History*
Carpenter, *Beyond*	Rhys Carpenter, *Beyond the Pillars of Heracles*, n.p.: Delacorte Press, 1966
Cary and Warmington	Max Cary and E. H. Warmington, *The Ancient Explorers*, revised edition, Baltimore: Penguin, 1963
CÉFR	*Collection de l'École française de Rome*
CHA	*Cambridge History of Africa*
CISA	*Contributi dell'Istituto di Storia Antica*
CJ	*Classical Journal*
ClMed	*Classica et Mediaevalia*
CP	*Classical Philology*
CQ	*The Classical Quarterly*
CR	*The Classical Review*

CRAI	*Comptes rendus des séances de l'Académie des inscriptions et belles-lettres*
Desanges, Recherches	Jehan Desanges, *Recherches sur l'activité des Mediterranéens aux confins de l'Afrique, CÉFR* 38, 1978
DSB	*Dictionary of Scientific Biography*
EClás	*Estudios clásicos*
ÉtCl	*Les études classiques*
FGrHist	Felix Jacoby, *Fragmente der griechischen Historiker*, Berlin 1923–
GaR	*Greece and Rome*
GeoAnt	*Geographia Antiqua*
GGM	*Geographi graeci minores*, Paris 1855
GJ	*The Geographical Journal*
GRBS	*Greek, Roman and Byzantine Studies*
Hennig	Richard Hennig, *Terrae Incognitae*, second edition, Leiden: Brill 1944
HispAnt	*Hispania Antiqua*
HRR	Hermann Peter, *Historicum romanorum reliquae*, reprint, Stuttgart: Teubner, 1967
HSCP	*Harvard Studies in Classical Philology*
JAH	*Journal of African History*
JHS	*Journal of Hellenic Studies*
JN	*Journal of Navigation*
JRAS-C	*Journal of the Royal Asiatic Society: Ceylon Branch*
JRIC	*Journal of the Royal Institution of Cornwall*
JRS	*Journal of Roman Studies*
LibAE	*Libyca Archéologie-Épigraphie*
LSJ	H. G. Liddell, R. Scott, and H. Stuart Jones, *Greek–English Lexicon*, ninth edition, Oxford: Clarendon Press, 1940
MCV	*Mélanges de la Casa de Velázquez*
MélBeyrouth	*Mélanges de l'Université Saint-Joseph, Beyrouth*
MHA	*Memorias de historia antigua*
MM	*Madrider Mitteilungen*
MSE	*Miscellanea di storia delle explorazioni*
MusHelv	*Museum Helveticum*
NumAntCl	*Numismatica e antichità classiche*
OJA	*Oxford Journal of Archaeology*
OrSue	*Orientalia Suecana*
OT	*Orbis terrarum*
PCPS	*Proceedings of the Cambridge Philological Society*
PECS	*Princeton Encyclopedia of Classical Sites*, Princeton: Princeton University Press, 1976
PP	*La parola del passato*
ProcBritAc	*Proceedings of the British Academy*
ProcRIA	*Proceedings of the Royal Irish Academy*
RE	Pauly-Wissowa, *Real-Encyclopädie der klassischen Altertumswissenschaft*
RÉA	*Revue des études anciennes*
RÉL	*Revue des études latines*
RGA	*Reallexikon der germanischen Altertumskunde*
RHist	*Revue historique*
RhM	*Rheinisches Museum für Philologie*

RivFil	*Rivista di Filologia*
RivStorAnt	*Rivista storica dell'antichità*
Roller, *Juba*	Duane W. Roller, *The World of Juba II and Kleopatra Selene: Royal Scholarship on Rome's African Frontier*, London: Routledge, 2003
Romm, *Edges*	James S. Romm, *The Edges of the Earth in Ancient Thought*, Princeton: Princeton University Press, 1992
RPFE	*Revue philosophique de la France et de l'étranger*
RPhil	*Revue de philologie, de littérature et d'histoire anciennes*
RStFen	*Rivista di studi fenici*
RStLig	*Rivista di studi liguri*
SchwMbll	*Schweizer Münzblätter*
SCO	*Studi classici e orientali*
SS	*Skandinavskii Sbornik*
StIt	*Studi italiani di filologia classica*
TAPA	*Transactions of the American Philological Association*
Thomson	J. Oliver Thomson, *History of Ancient Geography*, Cambridge: Cambridge University Press, 1948
TI	*Terrae incognitae*
TIBG	Transactions of the Institute of British Geographers
TTEMA	*Trade, Travel, and Exploration in the Middle Ages*, ed. John Block Friedman and Kristen Mossler Figg, New York: Garland Publishing, 2000
UJA	*Ulster Journal of Archaeology*
YCS	*Yale Classical Studies*
ZfA	*Zeitschrift für Archäologie*
ZPE	*Zeitschrift für Papyrologie und Epigraphik*

PREFACE

Sometime in the 320s BC, a Greek explorer and scientist stood at the northern end of Scotland. It was midwinter, and he determined that the sun only rose four *peches* above the horizon (somewhat less than two meters), an observation that eventually yielded him the latitude. Then he headed north into the Atlantic, recording phenomena that were completely alien to anyone from the Mediterranean. Before he returned home to Massalia, this traveller, Pytheas, had seen the frozen ocean and the midnight sun, and had theorized about the tides and determined the location of the celestial pole. Yet like many explorers to exotic places in both ancient and modern times, his reputation came to be derided and dismissed.

Greco-Roman culture is so centered on the Mediterranean and its world that it is easy to forget the wide reach of Greek and Roman travellers and explorers. Over the thousand years from the time of Homer to the later Roman Empire, much of the southern and western coasts of the eastern hemisphere were explored. Greeks went into the Arctic and the Baltic, and may have determined how to travel overland from the Baltic to the Black Sea. They also sailed along the coasts of Africa – here building on Carthaginian knowledge – at least as far as the Niger delta, perhaps beyond.

India came into Mediterranean knowledge as a result of the travels of Alexander the Great, and in the following century diplomatic relations were established between the Indian and Hellenistic kings. The sea routes to India were explored, as well as the east coast of Africa at least as far as Zanzibar. Geographical theorists began to see the entire southern half of the world as a connected unit, and it came to be believed that a way to India was through the Pillars of Herakles. Whether this was ever empirically demonstrated is uncertain, but it had a profound influence on the explorers of early modern times.

Romans continued Greek exploration. Political and mercantile interests resulted in greater knowledge of the North Sea and Baltic, and, in the opposite direction, merchants rounded the Indian peninsula and learned about China, sending an embassy in the latter second century AC to the Chinese court. Roman trade goods and Antonine coins have also been found at Oc-èo in the Mekong delta, but whether the Romans themselves actually reached this point is debatable.[1]

Thus the world of classical antiquity reached from Iceland to Viet Nam. As an essential part of the Greco-Roman cultural identity, travels to these far regions affected not only exploration itself, but the natural and physical sciences, mathematics and astronomy, ethnography, and trade and commerce. By exposing Greeks and Romans to environments unlike their own, theorization about the complexity and diversity of the world became possible. No longer could the cosmos be defined merely by the limited phenomena of the Mediterranean.

The following study focuses on the western half of ancient exploration, that of the Atlantic. This was the only part of the great encircling ocean that could be accessed with ease from the Mediterranean, through the Pillars of Herakles. At some early date, perhaps not long after 1000BC, Greek sailors left the Mediterranean and entered the Atlantic. Eventually they explored almost all its eastern coast from lower Scandinavia to tropical West Africa, perhaps even circumnavigating that continent. That the Atlantic was in some way connected to India became conventional wisdom.

Study of Greek and Roman knowledge of the Atlantic falls literally at the margins of classical scholarship. But the margins are as important as the center. The classics are still driven by the vestiges of the medieval and early modern reading list: a glance at the session topics of the national meetings demonstrates this. Homer, Sophokles, and Vergil are essential to an understanding of the classical world, but they are not the essence of it. In many ways their impact was greater on the post-antique world than on antiquity itself. Obviously the vicissitudes of survival of ancient literature influenced what has been canonized in modern times, yet the increasing evidence from epigraphy and archaeology, to say the least, has begun to limit the importance of the traditional reading list. One need only to peruse the thousand fragmentary historians in Jacoby's *Fragmente der griechischen Historiker* to realize not only how much was lost, but how much is out there that is never studied.

At the academic level, one finds endless courses on Homer or Horace but rarely one on Strabo or Pliny the Elder. Indeed, the very fact that curricula still tend to be structured by authors is itself revealing. Moreover, excessive compartmentalization of the discipline has played a nefarious role: one is identified as an archaeologist or philosopher or philologist, as a Hellenist or Latinist, but rarely as a classicist. Placement of a scholar within one of these sub-disciplines often presumes that he or she has no competence in the others. This emphasis on specialization has made study of the diversity of the ancient world difficult: the entirety of polymaths such as Eratosthenes of Kyrene remains unexplored because they cannot be fitted into the compartments. The idea that a Greek scientist stood on the shores of Iceland and

---

1 The excavations at Oc-èo are discussed by Louis Malleret, "Les fouilles d'Oc-èo (1944): rapport préliminaire," *BÉFEO* 45, 1951, 75–88. For the Roman presence in the Far East, see Mortimer Wheeler, *Rome Beyond the Imperial Frontiers*, London: G. Bell and Sons, 1954, pp. 172–5; see also John Ferguson, "China and Rome," *ANRW* 9.2, 1978, 581–603.

created some of the first coherent tidal theories seems as central to the classics as the sublime beauty of Vergil. This work moves to the edges of ancient knowledge, in both geographical and academic senses, with the hope that it may become the center.

This book evolved from the author's previous examination of Juba II and Kleopatra Selene of Mauretania and their interest in the extremities of the world. As a player in Greco-Roman exploration of the Atlantic, both personally and academically, Juba helped to define knowledge of the southern half of the earth from West Africa to India.

The present work moves beyond Juba's world to the entire Atlantic coast. Autopsy has played a significant role in the preparation of these pages: gone are the days when scholars could write about the landscape of antiquity without leaving the comfort of their studies. Although the present author cannot claim to have visited every place mentioned in the pages that follow, most of them have been personally examined, from Iceland and the interior Baltic to the coasts of northwest Africa. This book would have been impossible without that field research.

INTRODUCTION

The first explorers were the gods and heroes. The Homeric *Hymn to Dionysos* records that, at an early age, the god was captured by pirates, thus beginning his life as a traveller. His captors already associated him with the Hyperboreans, the people of the far north. It was Dionysos who brought grape vines from Lydia to Greece, travelling by a circuitous route that included Media and Arabia.[1] The other significant divine traveller, often mentioned in tandem with Dionysos, was Herakles, whose labors describe wandering from his eastern Peloponnesian home to northwest Africa, the location of the final labor, the Apples of the Hesperides.[2] Ancestor of many of the remote peoples of the world, Herakles left his mark on the toponymic map of the Mediterranean, with dozens of places named after him.[3] Indeed, all remote places came to be connected with the hero.[4]

With such a distinguished and divine ancestry in travel and exploration, it was difficult for mortals to follow, and, more importantly, for the accounts of their travels to be believed. From ancient to modern times there always has been a large degree of skepticism toward travellers' reports. The travellers themselves are often no help, because they can be secretive and uninformative. State-sponsored travel was usually not for public dissemination. Since travellers to remote places inevitably encounter unusual phenomena, disbelief is easier than acceptance. Moreover, only one actual traveller's account survives from antiquity, that of the Carthaginian Hanno, existing only in a translation several removes from its original. All the other travellers discussed in the pages that follow are known only through highly derivative sources, often several centuries later. The *Ora maritima* of Avienus is the outstanding example of this type of source: its date of the fourth century AC and its translation into Latin of Greek accounts that are themselves derivative do not inspire confidence as to the accuracy of its information on Phokaian exploration of a thousand years earlier. Yet to reject it totally serves little purpose in any attempt to understand early knowledge: cautious use of its data seems a wiser choice.[5] At the same time one must not diminish the element of literary creativity that is an essential part of all travel literature from Homer

---

1 Euripides, *Bakchai* 1–31.
2 Pliny, *Natural History* 5.1–3.
3 See the index to *BAGRW*, which has over 50 places named after the hero.
4 For example, Tacitus, *Germania* 34.
5 See further, infra, pp. 9–12.

and Herodotos onward. Geographical writing as literature is a valid and interesting topic,[6] but it is not the subject of this book. Rather the pages that follow are about the travellers themselves: where they went and why they did so, with skepticism about the sources as limited as seems reasonably possible.

Nonetheless there is a whole genre of fantasy literature about travel to remote places, beginning with the *Odyssey*. These accounts often mixed in actual data, and so can be valuable sources that may be difficult to untangle. In modern times it is perhaps easier to be more dismissive of promiscuous red-haired men with tails[7] than a frozen ocean,[8] yet in antiquity the former was believed rather than the latter. Fantasy writers, even today, are always skillful in mixing the real and the unreal, and siting their tales just beyond the limits of human knowledge, whether in the western Mediterranean or on a remote planet. Now that essentially the entire surface of the earth is known, it is possible to be topographically astute in a way that ancient scholars could not be, but the tradition of disbelief is deep. Just as Strabo rejected Pytheas' frozen sea, nineteenth-century critics rejected the geysers and mudpots of northwest Wyoming as "fantaisies ridicules."[9] Herodotos still has his skeptics. No traveller's account is totally accurate: explorers are often dependent on local informants, whose language may be imperfectly understood. Especially in the pre-industrial age, travellers' views were limited to their immediate sight lines. They may have had little comprehension or understanding of what they were seeing: continental coasts could be misunderstood as islands, bays as the open ocean. The essential nature of the surface of the earth was not well understood. Places once found could not easily be located again. And there was always the subtle connection with the first travellers, the gods and heroes, whose exploits were well known and who became unfortunate role models.

The Greeks and Romans had no specific terms that correspond to the modern "exploration." Latin "exploro" and its related words are military in context, connected with the concept of reconnaissance. "Exploratores" were essentially spies: Caesar sent them to find a place for a camp in hostile country;[10] Turnus used them to spy on Aeneas.[11] The modern sense of the word seems absent. The Greeks also had no word for exploration. Kolaios of Samos was merely driven off course,[12] a common way to begin travels to remote places, betraying Homeric connections. Herodotos' travels were research,[13] as were those of Pytheas.[14] Hanno merely "sailed."[15] Eudoxos of Kyzikos "tested the land,"[16] which does suggest exploration. Polybios was more

---

6 This is best set forth by Romm, *Edges*.
7 Pausanias 1.23.5–6.
8 Strabo 1.4.2–3.
9 Merrill J. Mattes, *Colter's Hell and Jackson's Hole*, Yellowstone National Park: Yellowstone Library and Museum Association, 1962, p. 11.
10 Caesar, *Bellum gallicum* 2.17.
11 Vergil, *Aeneid* 11.511–14.
12 Herodotos 4.152: ἀπηνείχθη.
13 Herodotos 1.1: ἱστορίη.
14 Strabo 7.3.1.
15 Hanno 1: πλεῖν.
16 Strabo 2.3.4: πειρᾶσθαι τῆς γῆς.

explicit: he "reconnoitered the land."[17] a phrase with military overtones that perhaps reflects his Roman environment but is the closest to a modern statement of intent to explore. Yet, all in all, there is no consistent ancient sense of exploration, in the view that has been predominant since the Renaissance. Ancient travellers set forth for a variety of reasons: research, military purposes, economics, even (allegedly) by accident. Yet the results of their travels were profound and influenced ancient and indeed modern knowledge of the world.

The travellers

Around 630BC, a certain Kolaios of Samos ended up in the Atlantic Ocean. Claiming, as sailors from ancient to modern times have, that he was merely driven off course, he brought news of far western riches back to East Greece, and thus was a participant in – if not the catalyst for – the infusion of wealth that marked the Archaic Greek world. Kolaios is the first documented example of a long series of Greeks and Romans who penetrated the Atlantic Ocean, eventually making its entire eastern coast, from the Arctic to southern Africa, known to the ancient world.

Kolaios' endeavors stimulated Phokaian exploration of the west: even before his day they had begun to seek out the western Mediterranean, and with their founding of Massalia in the early sixth century BC, a western outpost was established that allowed exploration of the outer coasts of Europe perhaps as far as the British Isles. An elusive search for western wealth may have been the ostensible reason for these voyages, but their most apparent by-product was the expansion of geographical knowledge and the first Greek experience of the harsh world of the open ocean. Massalians also attempted to go south of the Pillars of Herakles but, because this entered the Carthaginian zone, Greeks were less than welcome. Nevertheless, one Massalian, Euthymenes, managed to reach the West African tropics around 500BC.

After this time, Greek activity beyond the Pillars diminished sharply in the face of Carthaginian pressure. The Carthaginians themselves had already been heavily involved in westward exploration, again, it seems, searching for wealth, particularly sources of metals. The twin voyages of Himilco and Hanno, perhaps around or just after 500BC, were the peak of Carthaginian exploration. Himilco went north, perhaps as far as Britain, and possibly well out into the Atlantic; Hanno entered the West African tropics. Hints of these voyages became known to the Greeks, and a summary of Hanno's report was promptly translated into Greek. The Carthaginians also reached some of the Atlantic islands, certainly the Madeiras and Canaries and possibly the Azores and Cape Verdes. However, Greek knowledge of their activities was limited and confused, although at least one Greek visited the Carthaginian West African outposts in the fourth century BC.

Another issue was whether or not Africa could be circumnavigated. The continent had long been known to be unique because of its access to the external Ocean. As early as 600BC there were attempts at circumnavigation, by Phoenicians or

---

17 Polybios 3.48.12: τοὺς δὲ τόπους κατωπτευκέναι.

Carthaginians. A century later Hanno may have been commissioned to make the journey, but does not seem to have done so. Yet reports of these and other voyages became increasingly tangled with the literary genre of the geographical fantasy, which had its origins as early as the time of Homer. Evolving scientific knowledge about the size and shape of the earth also led to theorization as to whether the Atlantic could be crossed and who might live on the other side. All this became tangled with the actual explorers' accounts so that it was difficult to separate them from either fantasy or scientific theory. Yet the many reports about ancient crossings of the Atlantic all seem spurious.

Increasing scientific knowledge had its greatest impact on exploration with the journey of Pytheas of Massalia, who set forth in the 330s BC on a voyage that took him to and around Britain and into the Arctic, and eventually to the Baltic. He became the first Greek to observe the midnight sun and frozen ocean, and was an astute observer and recorder of the alien Arctic phenomena and tidal activity, perhaps the only actual explorer whose theories entered the mainstream of scientific thought. He also discovered Thoule, ever thereafter an elusive goal for northern explorers.

Pytheas reflected the expanding horizons, both intellectual and geographical, of the world of Aristotle and Alexander. The travels of the latter focused Greek interest on the east: the Arabian peninsula, East Africa, and the routes to India entered Greek knowledge at this time. The writings of Eratosthenes of Kyrene in the latter half of the third century BC synthesized geographical knowledge and theory. Yet interest in the Atlantic languished in the generations after Pytheas, although Carthaginian decline and increasing knowledge of East Africa reawakened some curiosity about West Africa.

Early in 146BC Carthage fell to Rome. Access to the Carthaginian records had a dramatic effect on the conquerors and their Greek advisors. The historian Polybios took the lead in analyzing Carthaginian data about remote places, and this led him to the Massalian explorers, who were as yet little known. Polybios made several voyages of reconnaissance to confirm his information, along the coast of West Africa and into northwest Europe, and even wrote a scientific treatise about the tropical climate.

By the second century BC geographical knowledge had reached the point that it was possible to connect the various discrete parts of the southern half of the world. Even Aristotle had suggested that India could be reached through the Pillars of Herakles, an idea later stressed by Eratosthenes. This was to be tested at the end of the century by the charismatic Eudoxos of Kyzikos, who pioneered the route from Alexandria to India, and then, because of Ptolemaic interference, sought several times to reach India through the Pillars. Although lost at sea before he was able definitively to prove his theory, he was an inspiration to later generations, especially Columbus and Vasco da Gama. It remained for the scholarly King Juba II of Mauretania, writing in the Augustan period, to draw all the knowledge of the southern half of the world together in a pair of treatises that covered the entire extent from the Pillars to India. Nothing more was to be added until the fifteenth century.

North of the Pillars was another matter. Pytheas' definitive report sank into obscurity, although his scientific conclusions entered the mainstream of thought. Yet those who synthesized the accounts of his travels – Poseidonios and Strabo – did so only to disparage him, ranking him as one of the most creative of geographical fantasists. It remained for the Romans to re-explore some of the areas that Pytheas had reached, from Britain to the Baltic, and to provide the first detailed information about the coasts of the North Sea. This was all in the context of military operations: Julius Caesar in Britain, and Drusus and his son Germanicus farther north. The amber trade generated interest in the Baltic: the eternal search for Pytheas' Thoule led Romans into the north, but nowhere near as far as the Massalian had reached. Yet Roman activities were not without disaster, and more than once the unforgiving Ocean hindered their operations. By late in the first century AC, further attempts to sail on the Ocean were abandoned. It was not until the rise of the Vikings that the northern Atlantic came to be explored again.

Ancient and modern sources

The ancient sources are extremely scattered. No treatise on Greek or Roman exploration survives: perversely, the only extant report of an actual explorer is the fifth-century BC Greek translation of the expedition of the Carthaginian, Hanno. Moreover, with the exception of the *Geography* of Strabo, none of the Hellenistic geographical works that synthesized explorers' reports has been preserved. Thus one must rely heavily on Strabo's *Geography* and the *Natural History* of Pliny, where the bulk of references to ancient exploration occur. There are a few existing *periplooi* – coastal sailing itineraries – some of which, like the *Periplous of the Erythraian Sea* (first century AC) are primary data, and others, like the *Ora maritima* of Avienus (fourth century AC), and even that preserved under the name of Skylax (fourth century BC), are composite derivative works, incorporating material hundreds of years old. Yet much of ancient literature, from Homer, Herodotos, and the dramatists to the late antique encyclopedias, includes information on ancient exploration. The evidence crosses a wide range of disciplines, which has made understanding difficult. Often the age, reliability, and method of transmission of the data are matters of great dispute, not assisted by the negative way in which the extant sources, especially Strabo, presented the reports of ancient explorers.

There has been no comprehensive study of ancient exploration in well over half a century. The most thorough modern account is M. Cary and E. H. Warmington's *The Ancient Explorers*, originally published in 1929 with a revised edition in 1963, although most of the changes were merely bibliographic. Rhys Carpenter's *Beyond the Pillars of Heracles* (1966) is interesting but excessively idiosyncratic. Richard Hennig's *Terrae incognitae* (1944) is valuable but essentially a catalogue. Another important study, J. Oliver Thomson's *History of Ancient Geography* (1948) is more concerned with the evolution of the discipline of geography than exploration, and can be astonishingly dismissive about the accomplishments of ancient explorers. James S. Romm's essential *The Edges of the Earth in Ancient Thought* (1992) is about geography as

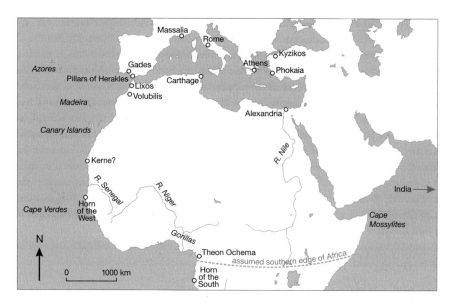

Map 1 Exploration south of the Pillars of Herakles

literature. Barry Cunliffe's *Facing the Ocean* (2001) is a broad study, not limited to antiquity, and with little to say about the world south of the Pillars. Other works, cited in the pages that follow, focus on specific explorers or regions. Often, however, there is a strong nationalistic bias among modern authors, which can impede analysis of the data.

Transliteration and units of measurement

Ancient toponyms have, as much as possible, been transliterated directly from their extant source. This is not as easy as it seems, however, since the texts are usually highly derivative. Hanno's report, for example, is preserved in a Greek summary which may not have fully comprehended – or properly translated – the Punic original. Latin sources often betray Greek signatures in their handling of toponyms: this is especially apparent in the *Natural History* of Pliny, where names often retain Greek case endings while being reduced to latinized spellings. And, of course, virtually all toponyms, whether preserved in Greek or Latin, are themselves derived from indigenous terms that may not have been understood or recorded correctly. Sometimes the toponym may have been translated – for example, Pytheas' "Bed of the Sun" or Hanno's "Chariot of the Gods" – and at other times forced into Greek or Latin terminology, or simply rendered in Greek or Latin, but not necessarily correctly. Examples include Hanno's Thymiaterion, a Greek word, perhaps translated from Punic, or used because it sounded like the Punic original, and Hierne – Ireland – which became the Sacred Island – Hiera Nesos – in some accounts.

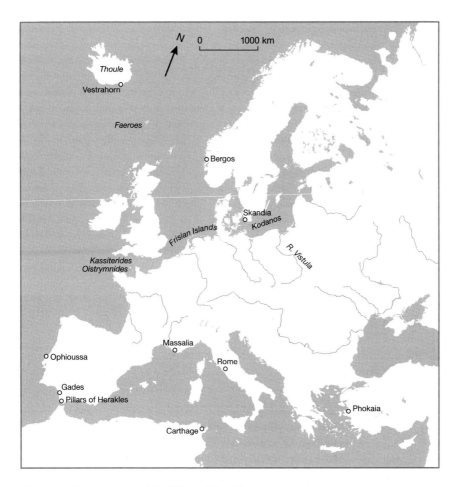

Map 2 Exploration north of the Pillars of Herakles

Ancient units of measurement are a persistent problem to the modern topographer, and can be used (or misused) to support theories of toponym location. In what follows the measurements represent those of the source, generally Greek stadia or Roman miles. The length of the Roman mile is not in dispute (1,480m or 4,865 feet – but the stadion varied considerably. Although always 600 feet, it was the foot length that was not constant; these erratic stadia lengths have been the source of many topographical problems. Generally a stadion would be about 180m, but this is merely an average, and especially with the distances of tens of thousands of stadia used in global measurements, the variations can produce enormous differences. All that can be said is that caution is advisable. Modern distances are provided in metric units, except that those over the ocean are in nautical miles and tidal heights are in feet.

1

GREEK EXPLORATION
BEFORE 500BC

To the Greeks the sea now called the Mediterranean was the Great Sea,[1] or, more tell-ingly, the Internal Sea or the Inside Sea,[2] since at first it seemed to have no outlet. In fact there were two. To the northeast was the long narrow treacherous channel of the Hellespont and Bosphoros, leading to another enclosed sea, the Euxeinos – perhaps Persian *aesaena*, "dark" or "sombre" – or Black Sea,[3] which, although not mentioned in Greek literature until Herodotos,[4] was probably first explored a little after 700BC. Greeks discovered the western outlet at about the same time, sailing far beyond the Greek heartland.[5] At the westernmost extremity of the Great Sea were two prominent mountains, which at an early date came to be called the Stelai, or Pillars, of Herakles (Figure 1), so named because it was believed that this was the farthest point that the hero had reached.[6] Although there was some confusion as to exactly what constituted the Pillars, they are generally thought to be the two prominent peaks flanking the Mediterranean that today bear Islamic names: to the south Jebel Musa (862m eleva-tion), and 30 miles to the north Gibraltar, corrupted from Jebel Tariq (423m eleva-tion). These mark the entrance to a long passage, the Herakleian or Gadeian Strait (Figure 2).[7] It was as narrow as seven miles across and ran somewhat south of west for 35 miles. Sailors passing through the straits would find the water turning from blue to

1 Hekataios (*FGrHist* #1), fr. 26.
2 Aristotle, *Meteorologika* 2.1.
3 Stephanie West, "'The Most Marvellous of All Seas': The Greek Encounter With the Euxine," *GaR* 50, 2003, 151–67; see also Georges I. Bratianu, *La mer noire*, *Acta Historica* 9, 1969, 43–6.
4 Herodotos 3.93, etc.
5 The longest distances in the Mediterranean are in the area bounded by the Peloponnesos, Sicily, and the coast of Libya, where one can be 250 miles from land, as Odysseus well knew. Anywhere else, a sailor cannot be more than 200 miles from shore, and, west of Italy, never more than 100 miles, although local weather conditions, the flatness of a given coast – especially in eastern North Africa – and other natural phenomena could substantially reduce visual distance.
6 Strabo 3.5.5. They may have been mentioned by Homer (*Odyssey* 1.53–4, 24.11–13); see also Luca Antonelli, "Aviénus et les Colonnes d'Hercule," *MCV* 31, 1995, 77–83. On the Pillars generally, see Michele R. Cautaudella, "Quante erano le Colonne d'Ercole?" *AFLM* 22–23, 1989–1990, 315–27; on their role as the end of the earth, Gabriella Amiotti, "Le Colonne d'Ercole e i limiti dell'ecumene," in *Il confine nel mondo classico*. ed. Marta Sordi, *CISA* 13, 1987, pp. 13–20.
7 Plutarch, *Sertorius* 8.1; Pliny, *Natural History* 3.3.

Figure 1 The Pillars of Herakles. View east toward the Mediterranean.

Photograph by Duane W. Roller.

a less benign green, and increased swell and tidal phenomena.[8] Eventually they would be outside the Internal Sea and in a different world, where one could not only be out of sight of land, but be so forever, eternally lost in the great Ocean that encircled the world, on which sea travel was not advisable.[9] The Ocean could not be crossed,[10] for the gods would not allow it.[11]

It is not known exactly when the first Greek ventured beyond the Pillars into that portion of the Ocean that came to be named after Atlas.[12] There was a tradition that Odysseus had reached Spain, but this is not documented before Roman times.[13] Yet

8 On the straits, see M. Ponsich, "La navigation antique dans le détroit de Gibraltar," in *Littérature gréco-romaine et géographie historique, Mélanges offerts à Roger Dion* (*Caesarodunum* 9bis, Paris 1974, pp. 257–73, and Otto Jessen, *Die Strasse von Gibraltar*, Berlin: Dietrich Reimer, 1927, especially the essay in this volume by Adolf Schulten, "Die Säulen des Herakles" (pp. 174–206).

9 Pindar, *Olympian* 3.42–5; *Nemean* 3.21–2. One may contrast, however, the optimism of Sophokles (*Antigone* 332–41).

10 Pindar, *Nemean* 4.69.

11 Euripides, *Hippolytos* 742–7. In a somewhat later context, a certain Albinovanus Pedo, who served with Germanicus on his northern expedition of AD15, wrote a poem on the campaign, some of which described the terrors and dangers of the open sea (see further, infra, pp. 120, 125–7).

12 The name "Atlantic," as applied to the Western Ocean, is first cited in extant literature by Herodotos (1.203: to him it was somewhat unfamiliar). Hekataios seems to have known the Ocean simply as "outside the Great Sea" (*FGrHist* #1, fr. 26). But the tale of Atlas in the *Odyssey* (1.51–4; see also Aischylos, *Prometheus Bound* 349–52) connects him with the Atlantic, remarking on his knowledge of all the depth of the seas and making reference to his pillars, those later to be named after Herakles. For a thorough study of pre-Classical Greek movements into the Atlantic, see Luca Antonelli, *I Greci oltre Gibilterra, Hesperìa* 8, 1997.

13 Strabo 3.2.13, 3.4.3–4; see also A. T. Fear, "Odysseus and Spain," *Prometheus* 18, 1992, 19–26.

Figure 2 The Herakleian Strait. View from Africa to Europe.
Photograph by Duane W. Roller.

Homeric references to strange celestial phenomena may be among the first reports of the far reaches of the world – the close day and night of the Laistrygonians[14] and the eternal darkness of the Kimmerians[15] – although both passages are shrouded in obscurity and may be nothing more than a description of the mythical world beyond human knowledge where everything is reversed. Similar are the Fortunate Islands or Islands of the Blessed, the legendary place of reward for those given an eternity of bliss, which steadily moved west just ahead of seamen's knowledge. They are first mentioned in Greek literature by Hesiod, already outside the Pillars of Herakles.[16] Although mythical, they were a strong force in Greco-Roman conceptions of and interest in the Atlantic, and they influenced patterns of exploration well into Roman times.

The first Greek documented to have gone beyond the Pillars is Kolaios of Samos.[17] His story, known solely from Herodotos, was one of the most excessive examples of a voyage badly gone off course. Kolaios was a merchant captain on the Samos–Egypt

14 Homer, *Odyssey* 10.86.
15 Homer, *Odyssey* 11.13–19. For this passage, and early Greek views of the remote north, see Lutz Käppel, "Bilder des Nordens im frühen antiken Griechenland," in *Ultima Thule*, ed. Annelore Engel-Braunschmidt *et al.*, Frankfurt, 2001, pp. 11–27.
16 Hesiod, *Works and Days* 170–5; see also *Theogony* 215–16; Homer, *Odyssey* 4.561–9.
17 Herodotos 4.152; see also Hennig, vol. 1, pp. 51–9; Rhys Carpenter, "Phoenicians in the West," *AJA* 62, 1958, 49–51. Early Greek explorers in the Atlantic are summarized by M. L. Allain, "Greek Explorers in the Atlantic Ocean of the Seventh and Sixth Centuries BC. (M. A. thesis, The Ohio State University, 1971); see also Paul Fabre, "Les grecs à la découverte de l'Atlantique," *RÉA* 94, 1992, 11–21. On earlier Phoenician penetration into the Atlantic, see C. R. Whittaker, "The Western Phoenicians: Colonisation and Assimilation," *PCPS* 200, 1971, 58–79.

run who was blown to Platea, east of Kyrene. In attempting to return to his route he was driven by a constant easterly wind so far that he passed through the Pillars – some 1,100 miles to the west – and ended up in the district of Tartessos on the southwestern coast of Spain, which Greeks allegedly had never previously visited, although it was vaguely known to them.[18] Kolaios returned home with 60 talents' worth of wealth.[19] His voyage can be fairly precisely dated to around 630BC because it was contemporary with the founding of Kyrene.[20]

There is something suspicious about the journey. It is difficult to imagine a constant east wind for the days or weeks necessary, too remindful of the storm that assailed Odysseus for nine straight days.[21] It is striking that Kolaios made no attempt to reconnoiter during the frequent times that he must have been in sight of land. Moreover, his original detour to Platea was remarkably convenient, removing him from the areas in which he was known and bringing him into contact with another adventurous seaman, one Korobios, who may have told Kolaios about the riches of Tartessos. Despite Herodotos' assertion that no Greek had previously visited Tartessos, this may be what he was told by his Samian sources in an attempt to give themselves priority. The wealth of Tartessos was probably already known to the Greek world, perhaps from the Phoenicians,[22] and it seems that Kolaios knew exactly where he was going and why, but attributed his trip to an accident,[23] one of the earliest examples of the familiar theme of a momentous discovery that was credited to being off course but which had an aura of premeditation.[24]

18 As early as the 640s BC, the Sikyonian Treasury at Delphi had doors of Tartessian bronze (Pausanias 6.19.2–3). Whether this predated Kolaios' voyage, or was a result of it, cannot be determined.

19 A constant theme of these early Greek voyages to the west is the search for metals: see the detailed analysis by Michail Yu. Treister, *The Role of Metals in Ancient Greek History, Mnemosyne Supp.* 156, 1996, pp. 21–287.

20 The enigmatic Sostratos of Aigina, whom Herodotos described as even more successful than Kolaios, is much later, if this is the Sostratos who made a dedication at Gravisca in Etruria around 500BC (Piero Alfredo Gianfrotta, "Le àncore votive di Sostrato di Egina e di Faillo di Crotone," *PP* 30, 1975, pp. 311–18; F. David Harvey, "Sostratos of Aigina," *PP* 31, 1976, pp. 206–14). Herodotos' comparison was in profits made, not place visited or date, although a journey to Tartessos may be implied.

21 Homer, *Odyssey* 9.82–4. For an interesting study of the problems of ancient navigation, see E. G. R. Taylor, *The Haven-Finding Art: A History of Navigation From Odysseus to Captain Cook*, London: Hollis and Carter: 1956, especially pp. 35–64.

22 A tradition of far-western wealth had existed in prehistoric times, perhaps surviving into the Iron Age and reinforced when the Greeks became aware of the earliest Phoenician explorations. See C. F. C. Hawkes, "Archaeology and Ancient Ideas of a Plenteous West," *UJA* 38, 1975, 1–11.

23 Greek material from the seventh century BC has been discovered in southwest Spain, most notably a Corinthian helmet from Jerez dating to 700–650BC; see John Boardman, *The Greeks Overseas*, fourth edition, London: Thames and Hudson, 1999, pp. 213–15. This gives weight to the premeditation of Kolaios' journey.

24 "Accidental" famous discoveries by seamen, often attributed to a storm, are a formula from Odysseus into early modern times. Examples include not only Kolaios but Eudoxos of Kyzikos in the late second century BC (infra, pp.107–11), and, more recently, Bjarni Herjolfsson, the first Norseman to sight the American continent, in the late tenth century (*Grænlendinga Saga* 2), Pedro Cabral, the discoverer of Brazil in 1500 (infra, pp. 55–6), and to some extent, even Columbus. It seems too frequent to be as accidental as sailors have claimed.

Figure 3 Phokaia. View of site.
Photograph by Duane H. D. Roller.

Tartessos was a mineral-rich district of southwestern Spain whose primary products were tin and silver.[25] The Phoenicians had established a trading post at nearby Gadir – Gadeira or Gades, modern Cadiz – allegedly shortly after the Trojan War, although archaeological evidence suggests that the foundation was not until the eighth century BC.[26] Tartessos became a prosperous trading center, and knowledge of it and its wealth penetrated east: the earliest reference may be to biblical Tarshish, one of the sources of the riches of Solomon.[27] The lyric poet Stesichoros, of the early sixth century BC, seems to have been the first in Greek literature to cite it by name, although Strabo believed that Tartaros, the deepest reaches of the underworld, had been so named by Homer because he had heard of Tartessos.[28]

25 On Tartessos, see *Tartessos: Arqueología protohistória del bajo Guadalquivir* (ed. María Eugenia Aubet Semmler, Barcelona: Editorial AUSA, n. d.; A. Trevor Hodge, *Ancient Greek France*, Philadelphia: University of Pennsylvania Press: 1999, pp. 167–9.

26 Velleius 1.2.3; Pomponius Mela 3.46. On Gades, see María Eugenia Aubet, *The Phoenicians and the West*, second edition, tr. Mary Turton, Cambridge: Cambridge University Press, 2001, pp. 257–91.

27 Genesis 10.4; I Kings 10.22. On the complexities of this evidence, see James D. Muhly, "Copper, Tin, Silver and Iron: the Search For Metallic Ores as an Incentive For Foreign Expansion," in *Mediterranean Peoples in Transition*, ed. Seymour Gitin *et al.*, Jerusalem 1998, pp. 314–29, and J. A. Charles, "Where Is the Tin?" *Antiquity* 49, 1975, 19–24.

28 Stesichoros, fr. 184 (= Strabo 3.2.11–12). Stesichoros may have been influenced by Kolaios' travels, but this would require the Samian seaman to have travelled around 660BC, a generation earlier than usually supposed: see Hodge (supra n. 25), p. 277. Pindar's reference to "flowers of gold" on the Blessed Islands (*Olympian* 2.72) may also be an awareness of western wealth.

Kolaios' return home to Samos and his deposit of a tenth of his profits in the Heraion made the wealth of Tartessos well known in the East Greek world.[29] It was the Ionian city of Phokaia that was to exploit this knowledge, becoming the first Greek state to make long sea journeys.[30] The Phokaians were believed to be Central Greek in origin – perhaps only because of the similarity of the name Phokis[31] – and had settled in Ionia with Athenian help, perhaps as early as the ninth century BC.[32] Their city was located on a small bay at the end of the peninsula that defines the north side of the Hermaian Gulf (Figure 3), at whose head is Smyrna. The site of Phokaia is marked by a promontory at the end of the peninsula, on which stood a temple to Athene.[33] Before the city was destroyed by the Persians, it was one of the most impressive of Greek cities. The city walls had been constructed with money from Tartessos and became a conspicuous and enduring reminder of the western wealth.[34] These walls, which are still visible, had made Phokaia one of the largest cities in the world.[35] Excavation has also revealed remnants of a later temple, a theater of the fourth century BC, and tombs.[36] The town and its name have survived and today it is the pleasant resort village of Foça. The modern visitor can only marvel at the impact on world exploration of this quiet and unprepossessing site.

The Phokaians had begun to explore the Mediterranean as early as the beginning of the seventh century BC: Herodotos emphasized the shipbuilding technology that made this possible. They participated in the emergent Egyptian trade soon after the founding of Naukratis by Miletos, joining other cities in building the Helleneion, the Ionian religious and trading center.[37] The Phokaians also penetrated into the Black Sea.[38] But it was in the western Mediterranean that their efforts were most

29 Ivory may have been what Kolaios was seeking: see Brigitte Freyer-Schauenburg, "Kolaios und die west-phönizischen Elfenbeine," *MM* 7, 1960, 89–108.

30 Herodotos 1.163. A glimpse of the intensity and discipline of Phokaian seamanship is provided in the description of their training before the battle of Lade, which was too strenuous for the rest of the Ionians (Herodotos 6.11–12). On Phokaia, see Hodge (supra n. 25), pp. 7–15.

31 Pausanias 7.3.10.

32 Strabo 14.1.3.

33 Xenophon, *Hellenika* 1.3.1; Pausanias 2.31.6, 7.5.4.

34 Herodotos 1.163.

35 Ömer Özyiğit, "The City Walls of Phokaia," *RÉA* 96, 1994, pp. 77–109.

36 Ekrem Akurgal, *Ancient Civilizations and Ruins of Turkey*, tr. John Whybrow and Molly Emre, seventh edition, Izmir: Turistik Yayinlar, pp. 116–18.

37 Herodotos 2.178.

38 Phokaian city foundations on the Black Sea are cited in one of the texts in the *Minor Greek Geographers* (*GGM*). The text in question (vol. 1, pp. 196–243 [lines 917–20 for the foundations]) has no author attributed but was dedicated to a King Nikomedes (line 2), presumably one of the kings of Bithynia in the late second and early first century BC. In the seventeenth century the author was suggested to be Skymnos of Chios, but there is no strong evidence and this should be rejected (Aubrey Diller, *The Tradition of the Minor Greek Geographers, Philological Monographs Published by the American Philological Association* 14, 1952, pp. 20–1). Following Diller, the work will be titled hereinafter as *The Periplous Dedicated to King Nikomedes*. See also *Géographes grecs* 1, ed. Didier Marcotte, Paris: Les Belles Lettres, 2000, pp. 145–6, 257–9.

impressive.[39] As Herodotos recorded:[40] "they discovered Adria, Tyrrhenia, Iberia, and Tartessos," an impressive list that defines all the northwest quadrant of the Mediterranean as well as territory beyond the Pillars of Herakles. They were at Tartessos no later than the mid-sixth century BC, where they were befriended by the local king Arganthonios, who unsuccessfully attempted to persuade them to settle in his territory, and then financed the building of their city walls as defense against the Persians.[41]

The Phokaians founded many cities in the western Mediterranean, but none was as significant as Massalia. About 600BC, a Phokaian contingent led by a certain Euxenos discovered the site, having travelled over 1,000 miles from their homeland.[42] Euxenos and his companions would have been sailing north along the coast when they came to an entrance that led to the southeast, barely 100m across and flanked by two promontories 50m high. Sailing in, they would soon have turned from southeast back to slightly north of east, as the passage expanded into a spacious harbor that was not visible from the open sea (Figure 4). It extended inland for nearly a kilometer and was 400m across, with potential anchorages all around, but especially on the north side, where the city of Massalia would develop. Most impressive, however, was a northeastern extension of the harbor with several freshwater creeks and springs, particularly the one that the Phokaians were to call the Lakydon (Figure 5). This meant that the site provided not only a hidden anchorage but coastal freshwater: the spring is still visible today in its monumentalized form of the Roman period, and still seeps fresh water.[43] It was an ideal site for settlement, not only due to its inherent characteristics but because it was the last harbor before the marshes that marked the mouth of the Rhodanos (the Rhone, some 30–50km to the west), the main access to the interior. Massalia quickly became the dominant Greek city of the western Mediterranean, and even today, as Marseille, retains its image as the earliest city of western Europe: tourists now enjoy bouillabaisse where Euxenos' ships once landed. As Phokaia itself was depopulated during the Persian War,

39 Jean-Paul Morel, "Les Phocéens en Occident: certitudes et hypothèses," *PP* 21, 1966, 378–420, his "L'expansion phocéenne en Occident: dix années de recherches (1966–1975)," *BCH* 99, 1975, 853–96, and his "Les Phocéens d'Occident: nouvelles données, nouvelles approches," *PP* 37, 1982, 479–500; P. Bosch-Gimpera, "The Phokaians In the Far West: An Historical Reconstruction," *CQ* 38, 1944, 53–9.

40 Herodotos 1.163.

41 Arganthonios was said to have reigned 80 years: he had died by the time of the Persian attack on Phokaia in 540BC (Herodotos 1.165), so the Phokaian contact with him may have been as early as 620BC, not long after the time of Kolaios. His name may be derived from *argant*, the Keltic word for silver (Adolf Schulten, *Tartessos: Ein Beitrag zur ältesten Geschichte des Westens*, second edition, Hamburg: Cram, De Gruyter, 1950, p. 54). See also F. Cauer, "Arganthonios," *RE* 2, 1895, 686. On the Phokaians and Tartessos, see Jean-Paul Morel, "Les Phocéens dans l'extrême Occident: vus depuis Tartessos," *PP* 25, 1970, 285–9.

42 Athenaios 13.576a (= Aristotle, *Constitution of Massalia*); Justin 43.3. On the date of foundation, and the evidence for it, see H. G. Wackernagel, "Massalia," *RE* 14, 1930, 2130–1.

43 The visible physical evidence for ancient Massalia is summarized by James Bromwich, *The Roman Remains of Southern France: A Guidebook*, first paperback edition, London: Routledge, 1996, pp. 168–77. See also Boardman (supra n. 23), pp. 217–19; Hodge (supra n. 25), pp. 62–93; and Antoine Hermary *et al.*, *Marseille grecque 600–49 av. J.-C.: La cité phocéenne*, Paris: Errance, 1999, a handsome volume with many fine plans, photographs, and reconstructions.

Figure 4 Massalia. View of main harbor, looking northwest toward hidden entrance.
Photograph by Duane W. Roller.

Massalia took up the cause of westward expansion, founding cities of its own and exploring and trading far beyond the Pillars of Herakles.[44]

Before its decline, however, Phokaia continued to send its own explorers into the Atlantic. Evidence of these is largely through the surviving remnants of a new literary genre, the *periplous*, or coastal sailing itinerary, created as a direct result of the proliferation of Greek exploration. A *periplous* listed the features of a particular section of coast, generally from an offshore perspective.[45] It was primarily for the assistance of sailors, but as it tended to include topographical features and characteristics of the local inhabitants, the *periplous* soon took on geographical, commercial, and ethnographic overtones. The earliest known examples date from the latter sixth century BC.[46] Dareios I of Persia commissioned a certain Skylax of Karyanda to sail down the Indos to its mouth and then to return across the Indian Ocean to the head of the Red Sea, a journey that took

44 It is perhaps significant that a Massalian coin of the second century BC was discovered in extreme north-western France, on the coast of the English Channel in the department of Finistère: see Jean Bousquet, "Deux monnaies grecques: Massalia, Sestos," *AnnBr* 75, 1968, 277–9. On Massalian exploration generally, see Paul Fabre, "Les Massaliotes et l'Atlantique," in *Océan Atlantique et Péninsule Armoricaine: Ètude archéologiques, Actes du 107e Congrès National des Sociétés Savants, Brest 1982*, Paris 1985, pp. 25–49.

45 For a discussion of the genre, see O. A. W. Dilke, *Greek and Roman Maps*, Ithaca: Cornell University Press, 1985, pp. 130–44.

46 Francisco J. Gonzáles Ponce, "El corpus periplográfico grìego y sus integrantes más antiguos: épocas arcaica y clasíca," in *Los límites de la tierra: el espacio geográfico en las culturas mediterráneas*, ed. Aurelio Pérez Jiménez and Gonzalo Cruz Andreotti, Madrid 1998, pp. 41–75.

Figure 5 Massalia. View of Lakydon.
Photograph by Duane W. Roller.

two and a half years.[47] Skylax published an account of his voyage,[48] which was soon used by Hekataios, and eventually by Aristotle, Strabo, and others.[49]

Evidence for Phokaian *periplooi* of the Atlantic appears in the *Ora maritima* of Rufus (or Rufius) Festus Avienus, who wrote in the fourth century AC.[50] The work is a disjointed and jumbled poem that describes the coast between Massalia and Brittany.

47 Herodotos 4.44.
48 *FGrHist* #709.
49 Hekataios (*FGrHist* #1), fr. 294–99; Aristotle, *Politics* 7.13.1 (= Skylax, fr. 5); Strabo 12.4.8, 13.1.4 (= Skylax, fr. 11, 12). The existing text that bears Skylax's name (*GGM* vol. 1, pp. 15–96), hereinafter Pseudo-Skylax, is not by the explorer from Karyanda. This later work is a compilation from between 361–335BC, perhaps later rather than earlier in that period, and based on historical and geographical literature of that and the previous century. On the date, see Paul Fabre, "La date de la rédaction du périple de Scylax," *EtCl* 33, 1965, 353–66; M. L. Allain, "The Periplous of Skylax of Karyanda" (Ph. D. thesis, The Ohio State University 1977); Didier Marcotte, "Le periple dit de Scylax. Esquisse d'un commentaire épigraphique et archéologique," *BollClass* 3. ser. 7, 1986, 166–82; and Aurelio Peretti, "Dati storici e distanze marine nel *Periplo* di Scilace," *SCO* 38, 1988, 13–19. Nevertheless there has been a certain uncertainty – probably since antiquity – in identifying the genuine fragments of the *periplous* of the earlier writer. See further, Desanges, *Recherches*, pp. 91–4; F. J. González Ponce, "La posición del *Periplo* del Ps.-Escílax en el conjunto del género periplográfico," *RÉA* 103, 2001, 369–80.
50 On Avienus, see Carpenter, *Beyond*, pp. 199–213. There are many editions of the text, most notably those by Adolf Schulten (1922, second edition 1955), Dietrich Stichtenoth (1968), J. P. Murphy (1977), whose commentary is heavily topographic, F. J. González Ponce (*Avieno y el Periplo*, 1995), and Luca Antonelli (*Il periplo nascosto*, 1998).

Its sources range over several centuries: early in the poem there is a list of 11 authors of the sixth and fifth centuries BC, including familiar ones such as Herodotos and Thoukydides and obscurities such as Kleon of Sicily and Bakoris of Rhodes.[51] The list seems to bear little relationship to the poem itself – there is nothing overtly recognizable from either Herodotos or Thoukydides – and it was probably lifted from a Hellenistic geographical author. Later material also appears in the *Ora maritima*, such as the inscription at Gades honoring the duumvirate of Juba II of Mauretania, which Avienus probably saw.[52] But the ultimate source of most of the poem must be early *periplooi* that described the coast from Massalia to the English Channel.[53] Avienus' presentation is so chaotic that the exact sources and transmission of the material are impossible to determine, and, moreover, he seems to have reversed the direction of the account, for it is hard to imagine a *periplous* that began at the remote ends of the earth and ended up at home. All this calls into question the exact location of features. Avienus' immediate source was probably a Hellenistic geographical work in which various *periplooi* were embedded, but the author of this treatise cannot be determined. The Carthaginian Himilco, not in the list of 11, is cited by name three times,[54] but he cannot be the sole or even major source because the poem has Phokaian signatures.[55]

The descriptive section of the *Ora maritima* begins at the important feature known as the Oistrymnic Bay. In the bay were islands (96), and from here the locals sailed for

---

51 Avienus, *Ora maritima* 42–50. Bakoris of Rhodes is otherwise unknown. For suggestions as to the identity of Kleon, see F. Jacoby, "Kleon von Syrakus" (#8), *RE* 11, 1921, 718–9. Skylax of Karyanda is also listed, which might be dismissed were it not for the *Souda* ("Skylax"), which attributes to Skylax a *Periplous Beyond the Pillars of Herakles*. It is impossible to untangle all the material that exists today under the name of Skylax, who may have become proverbial as an author of early *periplooi*, confusing more than one author with the same name (F. J. González Ponce, "*Suda s. v.* Σκύλαξ. Sobre el título, el contenido y la unidad de *FGrHist* III C 709," *GeoAnt* 6, 1997, 37–51). The *Periplous Dedicated to King Nikomedes* may also have been a source for Avienus (see Serena Bianchetti, "Avieno, *Ora mar.* 80 ss.: le colonne d'Ercole e il vento del Nord," *Sileno* 16, 1990, 241–6).

52 Avienus, *Ora maritima* 275–83.

53 For an interpretation that finds Avienus more literary than historical, see F. J. González Ponce, "Sobre el valor histórico atribuible al contenido de *Ora maritima*: las citas de los Iberos y otros pueblos, como paradigma," *Faventia* 15.1, 1993, 45–60. Such a view seems simplistic and not in accordance with Avienus' technique. His career seems to have been devoted to creating Latin versions of Greek texts, as demonstrated by his other surviving works. One is the *Descriptio orbis terrae*, an adaptation – as a school text – of the geographical treatise of Dionysios Periegetes, which had been written in the early second century AC, itself based on the writings of Eratosthenes of Kyrene. Another is an astronomical poem, *Aratea phaenomena*, based on the *Phainomena* of Aratos of Soloi of the early third century BC. Neither of these works by Avienus is deeply creative, which leads to the presumption that the *Ora maritima* is also heavily derivative.

54 Avienus, *Ora maritima* 117, 383, 412; on Himilco, see infra, pp. 27–9.

55 Other sources may have emanated from Massalia, and the transmission may have included the historian Ephoros. See C. F. C. Hawkes, *Pytheas: Europe and the Greek Explorers*, n. d., n. p., pp. 19–20. There may also have been Phoenician material of the early sixth century BC: see María José Pena, "Avieno y las costas de Cataluña y Levante I. *Tyrichae*: *TYRIKAÍ, «¿la Tiria?»," *Faventia* 11.2, 1989, 9–21; and Pere Villalba i Varneda, "La «qüestió avienea»," *Faventia* 7.2, 1985, 61–7. Other possible sources are discussed by John Hind, "Pyrene and the Date of the 'Massaliot Sailing Manual'," *RivStorAnt* 2, 1972, 39–52.

two days to the land of the Hierni and Albiones (110–112), which indicates that the starting point of the text is probably in the vicinity of the western extremity of Brittany.[56] The account then moves south, eventually reaching the territory of Tartessos (225) and continuing to Gades (267), the Pillars of Herakles (341), and around the Mediterranean coast of Spain past Tarraco (519), the mouth of the Rhone (631), and eventually to Massalia (704). Throughout there are the diagnostic elements of a *periplous*: sailing times (108–9, 182), the winds (120, 176–7, 572–3), and the tides (623). The land is described from an offshore viewpoint (137–9), because features are said to "rise up" (*intumescit*, 183; *attollitur*, 545, 689). The rivers that empty into the sea (284–5) and the various coastal tribes (303) are noted. There are comments on the quality of landing places (319, 460–1). And, expectedly, as the description approaches Massalia, details become clearer and the account is less mystical and frightening.

The more remote sections, especially the portions off Brittany, display an early state of knowledge when sailors from the Mediterranean did not enter the English Channel and had only the vaguest knowledge of what lay beyond. Thus the poem is based on material originally composed around 600BC, when the Phokaians first ventured beyond the Pillars. Toponyms in an East Greek style point to Phokaian authorship of part of the original. These include Ophioussa (147) and Onoussa (491), descriptive terms ("snaky" and "donkey-like") that are distinctly Phokaian in form.[57] Both may refer to particular coastal features as viewed from out to sea. Ophioussa is the more remote – and farther north – and may indicate the limit of Phokaian penetration.[58] Although used generically for Spain, it is specifically a major promontory on the west coast, five days from the Pillars of Herakles, marking a division between the little-known lands to the north, where details are few and dangers great, and those to the south, where toponyms and ethnyms are frequent. Ophioussa has normally been equated with Cape Roca, near Lisbon, the western-most point of Europe.

It seems, then, that Phokaian exploration moved beyond Tartessos and up the west coast of Spain, but little was known of what lay beyond Ophioussa, where dangers outweighed practical information. As is normal with remote areas, terrors abounded, with monsters in the ocean (102) and even the locals living in a perpetual state of fear (139–42). There was some comprehension of Brittany and the British Isles, but the route was barely understood.[59] Equally poorly known was the journey between Spain and Brittany: it may be that seamen learned early on to cut across the Bay of Biscay, the "magnus sinus" (147), a distance of about 275 miles. As an indicator of how the

---

56 At this point there is a digression (129–45), which may describe the far northern reaches of the British Isles, not from any Phokaian source. See further, Carpenter, *Beyond*, pp. 208–11, and infra, pp. 28–9.

57 On the Phokaian use of toponyms ending in -oussa, see Schulten (supra n. 41), p. 51; Morel (*PP* 21, supra n. 39), pp. 385–7. About ten such names are known, extending from Pithekoussa – modern Ischia in the Bay of Naples – to those cited by Avienus.

58 Avienus, ed. Murphy, pp. 54–5.

59 On possible East Greek amphoras of 600BC from Britain, see Boardman (supra n. 23), p. 214.

Carthaginians would eventually come to control the knowledge of these regions, the voyage of Himilco seems better known to Avienus' source than these early Phokaians.

The final record of a Phokaian voyage beyond the Pillars is that of Midakritos. His nationality, to be sure, is not certain, but his early date and Ionian name suggest that he was indeed Phokaian.[60] Whether he wrote the *periplous* that ended up in Avienus' account cannot be determined. All that is known about him is a single sentence in the *Natural History* of Pliny:[61] he was the first to import *plumbum* from Kassiteris Island. Although *plumbum* can mean either lead or tin, the toponym, from Greek κασσίτερος, demonstrates that the latter is meant. Pliny's statement is so brief that it is difficult to place it in its proper context, and his source is not readily apparent, although it probably was the geographer Artemidoros of Ephesos (ca. 100BC), who wrote on the far west.[62] Tin was known to the Greek world from earliest times,[63] but the word κασσίτερος is of Elamite origin, indicating that the first supplies were from the east, not the west.

Kassiteris Island, or the Kassiterides, as they are usually known, has become a major problem in ancient topography.[64] Strangely, the islands became less well known and more mythical as exploration increased. Herodotos, the first to use the name,[65] discussed them in the context of far western Europe but wrote that he did not know anything about them. Later authors were equally vague. Diodoros merely located them off Spain.[66] Strabo, drawing on Poseidonios, placed them in the Ocean at approximately the latitude of Britain.[67] His detailed description states that they were ten in number and uninhabited, but with mines of tin and lead. The Phoenicians had originally traded there, and by Strabo's day the Romans had allegedly found them.[68] Later authors, such as Pomponius Mela and Pliny,[69] added little new about their location. Significantly, by the time of the Roman conquest of Britain the toponym seems forgotten, because Tacitus did not mention it.

Although some attempts have been made to suggest that the Kassiterides were purely mythical,[70] becoming vaguer – or more distant – as knowledge increased, this is simplistic. The name "Kassiterides," not a local toponym but from Greek, had to be applied to the islands by Greeks. Moreover, they do not need to have been islands,

---

60 Schulten (supra n. 41), p. 46. Attempts to turn him into a Phrygian Midas seem unreasonable: see Pliny, book 7 (ed. Schilling), pp. 241–2.
61 Pliny, *Natural History* 7.197.
62 Pliny, *Natural History* 1.7; see also 2.242.
63 Homer, *Iliad* 11.25, 18.474, 23.503.
64 F. Haverfield, "Κασσιτερίδες," *RE* 20, 1919, 2328–32; Roger Dion, "Le problème des Cassitérides," *Latomus* 11, 1952, 306–14; Jacques Ramin, *Le problème des Cassitérides*, Paris: A. and J. Picard, 1965.
65 Herodotos 3.115.
66 Diodoros 5.38.
67 Strabo 2.5.15, 2.5.30, 3.2.9, 3.5.11.
68 Infra, p. 116.
69 Pomponius Mela 3.47; Pliny, *Natural History* 4.119.
70 For example, see Malcolm Todd, *The South West to A. D. 1000*, London: Longman, 1987, pp. 185–7.

because the promontories of unfamiliar coasts are often first identified as islands.[71] Because the name went out of favor and was virtually forgotten by Classical times, perhaps as the actual local toponym became known, the name, but not the islands themselves, entered the realm of myth. They are difficult to locate, but existed nonetheless, because the problem is toponymic rather than geographical.[72] There are many islands off the coast of Brittany and the British Isles, but no group of ten. Traditionally, the most common candidate for the Kassiterides has been the Scillies – now 30 in number but perhaps fewer in antiquity – which may have produced some tin, although the limited amounts seem hardly to deserve the name "Tin Islands." Recent scholarship has become more vehement in rejecting them.[73] Diodoros, Pliny, and to some extent Strabo, placed the Kassiterides off the Spanish coast.[74] Yet this may only mean that the sailing direction to them was from Spain, and it is probable that the data have become confused beyond untangling, a victim of the desire of those trading with the islands to keep their location secret.[75]

Nevertheless, Midakritos' journey to Kassiteris Island marks the opening up of new western tin supplies. Assuming that he went as far as the Scillies – or perhaps the coast of Cornwall – he would have found tin deposits. Those in Cornwall may have been mined since 2000BC or earlier, and had reached the Aegean in the late Bronze Age.[76] But Midakritos' journey would not have been remembered had it not been notable, and thus it must have been something more than merely bringing western tin – which had long been available at Tartessos – to the eastern Mediterranean.[77] He must have found a new source of tin, or directly accessed supplies that had previously come only via Tartessos.[78] Thus he may have been the first Greek to go beyond Europe to the offshore islands, or to Cornwall, presumably sometime after Avienus' anonymous explorer, who

71 Cary and Warmington, p. 47, but see Stephen Mitchell, "Cornish Tin, Iulius Caesar, and the Invasion of Britain," in *Studies in Latin Literature and Roman History* 3, ed. Carl Deroux, *Collection Latomus* 180, 1983, p. 85.

72 On this problem, see Mitchell (supra n. 71), pp. 80–8. Ancient citations are summarized by A. L. F. Rivet and Colin Smith, *The Place Names of Roman Britain*, Princeton: Princeton University Press, 1979, p. 43.

73 Charles Thomas, *Exploration of a Drowned Landscape: Archaeology and History of the Isles of Scilly*, London: B. T. Batsford, 1985, pp. 149–51. R. D. Penhallurick, *Tin In Antiquity*, London: Institute of Metals, 1980, is perhaps the most emphatic: "Those who have sought to equate the Cassiterides with the Isles of Scilly clutch at straws" (p. 121). See also Paul Ashbee, *Ancient Scilly: From the First Farmers to the Early Christians*, Newton Abbot: David and Charles, 1974, pp. 277–8.

74 For specific possible islands off the Spanish coast, see Luis Monteagudo, "Casiterides," *Emerita* 18, 1950, 1–17, and his "Oestrymnides y Cassiterides en Galicia," *Emerita* 21, 1953, 241–8.

75 Of particular relevance is the story related by Strabo (3.5.11) of the Phoenician or Carthaginian sea captain who preferred to run his ship aground rather than to reveal the location of the islands to a following Roman ship, an event of perhaps the third century BC. Whatever the context of the tale (for problems, see infra, pp. 115–16), it demonstrates the obsessive possessiveness of those making discoveries.

76 J. D. Muhly, "Sources of Tin and the Beginning of Bronze Metallurgy," *AJA* 89, 1985, 287–8; see also Todd (supra n. 75), pp. 185–8.

77 Cary and Warmington, p. 45.

78 On the sources of tin see Barry Cunliffe, *Facing the Ocean*, Oxford: Oxford University Press, 2001, pp. 302–8.

functioned in a world where Greeks did not go beyond Europe. Midakritos would date to before 500BC, when the Carthaginians made Greek exploration in the Atlantic difficult, and, if he were Phokaian, probably before the Persian takeover, so a date of the first half of the sixth century BC is most likely. But by the following century, largely due to Carthaginian control of the west, the Kassiterides had become merely an unlocated and even mythical toponym, not re-entering Greco-Roman knowledge until the late Hellenistic period. Thus, by the latter sixth century BC the Phokaians had explored the European coast beyond Tartessos, and had detailed knowledge as far as Ophioussa. Beyond that point information was scanty: the interior of the Bay of Biscay seemed little known, but Brittany had been visited and contact made with the natives, who knew about the British Isles. At least one attempt was made to visit the offshore islands, or Britain proper, but the impact was minimal as Phokaia declined and Carthaginian power tended to exclude Greeks from the Atlantic.

As minimal as the information is for early Greek exploration northwest of the Pillars of Herakles, there is even less known about the areas to the southwest, along the African coast. Although there were early rumors about metals in this direction, these were much less specific than those that emanated from Tartessos.[79] Moreover, from early times, before Greeks showed interest, it was an area of Carthaginian exploration and settlement, so Greeks were probably unwelcome. Hints of their presence here before Hellenistic times are rare.[80]

In the Pseudo-Skylax *periplous* of the fourth century BC[81] there is a description of a journey south of the Pillars.[82] The information therein reflects knowledge of the late Classical period and is jumbled, but some of the toponyms are vestiges of early Greek voyages to the south. In particular there is the lake (or tidal inlet) known as Kephesias, not far from the Pillars. Nearby are the Gulf of Kotes and a village named Pontion. This cluster of names, all in the same area, is Central Greek in origin and may be the memory of an early colonizing voyage. Kephesias, in one form or another, is the name of two rivers of Central Greece, numerous members of the most prominent family of Tanagra in Boiotia,[83] and a common personal name throughout Boiotia. Kottes is one

---

79 See infra, pp. 41–2.

80 Archaeological evidence of early Greek activity on the African coast is scant. A Persian coin said to be of the third century BC was allegedly found in the 1950s at Idjil in northwest modern Mauritania (R. Mauny, "Monnaies antiques trouvées en Afrique au Sud du limes romain," *LibAE* 4, 1956, 253), although there is some difficulty in identifying it, since there was no official Persian coinage after the late fourth century BC (on this, see Barclay V. Head, *Historia Numorum: A Manual of Greek Numismatics*, new and enlarged edition, Oxford: Clarendon Press, 1911, pp. 828–9) and it may be from one of the Hellenistic dynasties in former Persian territory. A coin of Gades (no date specified) was said to have been discovered in 1940 on the beach at Temara just southwest of Rabat (René Rebuffat, "Vestiges antiques sur la côte occidentale de l'Afrique au sud de Rabat," *AntAfr* 8, 1974, 30). In addition, a Roman coin of 58 BC, minted in Gaul, was found at Rasseremt, also in northwestern modern Mauretania (Mauny, p. 253). Yet the circumstances of discovery of these coins make them almost worthless as artifacts.

81 On the date, see supra n. 49.

82 Pseudo-Skylax 112.

83 Duane W. Roller, *Tanagran Studies 2: The Prosopography of Tanagra in Boiotia*, Amsterdam: Gieben, 1989, p. 115.

Figure 6 Area of Lixos. View toward the ocean with the twisting Leukos River.
Photograph by Duane W. Roller.

of the Hekatoncheirai, known from the *Theogony* of the Boiotian poet Hesiod.[84] His brother was Briareos, who had once given his name to the Pillars later called those of Herakles.[85] Thus Boiotian toponyms abound in a small area of coastal northwest Africa.[86] It is possible that some Boiotians were lured by the tales of great wealth from Tartessos, and made their own journey in the late seventh century BC, somehow ending up on the African coast. But the trip had no lasting impact beyond a number of toponyms, because there are no reports of fantastic wealth returning to Boiotia.[87]

The first identifiable Greek to venture south of the Pillars was Euthymenes of Massalia.[88] Information about him is fragmentary and late, and his voyage does not

84 Hesiod, *Theogony* 149.
85 Aelian, *Diverse History* 5.3; Antonelli (supra n. 6), pp. 78–80.
86 For other Boiotian toponyms in the western Mediterranean, see Duane W. Roller, "Boiotians in Northwest Africa," to appear in the *Proceedings of the Tenth International Boiotian Congress.*
87 Modern commentators have tended to locate these toponyms just south of Cape Spartel, the northwest corner of Africa (Aurelio Peretti, *Il periplo di Scilace*, Pisa: Giardini, 1979, pp. 373–9). The names "Cotte" and "Cephisis" existed in this area in Roman Imperial times (Pliny, *Natural History* 5.2, 37.37). The best evidence for Lake Kephesias is the silted-in flats of the lower Leukos river, the site of ancient Lixos (Figure 6): see Michel Gras, "La mémoire de Lixus," in *Lixus, CÉFR* 166, 1992, 37–41.
88 F. Jacoby, "Euthymenes" (#4), *RE* 6, 1907, 1509–11; W. Aly, "Die Entdeckung des Westens," *Hermes* 62, 1927, 305–7; Hennig, vol. 1, pp. 80–5; Ch. Mourre, "Euthyménès de Marseille," *RStLig* 30, 1964, 133–9; Desanges, *Recherches*, pp. 17–27; Federica Cordano, *La geografia degli antichi*, Rome: Laterza, 1992, pp. 31–2; Serena Bianchetti, "Eutimene e Pitea di Massalia: geografia e storiografia," in *Storici greci d'Occidente*, ed. Riccardo Vattuone, Bologna, 2002, pp. 441–7, 480–1.

seem to have interested – or more likely, been available to – mainstream Hellenistic geographers. But Euthymenes was remembered not as an explorer but as a theorist about the flooding and source of the Nile, and the few scattered references to him appear in those authors treating the perennial intellectual problem of the peculiarities of the Nile. The earliest extant citation of Euthymenes by name is by Seneca, who seems to have quoted him directly, although probably through a Hellenistic geographical source. In Seneca's Latin, Euthymenes is credited with the following terse statement: "I sailed on the Atlantic ocean," although it is unlikely that he would have used the name "Atlantic."[89] But there are no details of where he went, or why he made his journey: merely that he believed that the Nile originated in the Atlantic, a theory based on winds, and that creatures in the Atlantic were similar to those in the Nile. Much the same material was presented, although to condemn it, by Aelius Aristeides, whose source was probably Ephoros.[90]

The lateness of sources means that the date of Euthymenes is uncertain. Hekataios was aware of the concept of a Nile flowing from the exterior Ocean, and Herodotos, probably critiquing Hekataios, as he often did, dismissed the idea.[91] Aetios, the doxographer of the latter first century AC, listed six scholars who theorized about the Nile, in seeming chronological order: Thales, Euthymenes, Anaxagoras, Demokritos, Herodotos, and Ephoros,[92] thus placing Euthymenes in the latter sixth or early fifth century BC. A later list, preserved in the text known as the *Anonymus Florentinus*,[93] gives seven scholars, eliminating Ephoros and substituting Kallisthenes and Oinopides. Euthymenes is fifth, after Demokritos and before Oinopides and Herodotos. Again this list seems chronological, with the exception of Kallisthenes, who, if this is the nephew of Aristotle, is badly misplaced between Anaxagoras and Demokritos. But he is the only person on either list who seems out of order, and thus there is strong circumstantial evidence that Euthymenes was active around 500BC or slightly earlier, a sensible hypothesis, as this was the peak period of Massalian exploration.[94] Because Euthymenes was remembered as a geographical theorist rather than as an explorer, information about his journey is scant. Whether he published a *periplous* cannot be determined, although Seneca seems to have had access, however derivatively, to his actual

---

89 Seneca, *Natural Questions* 4a.2.22: "navigavi Atlanticum mare."
90 Aristeides 36.85–95 (Keil). The source is Ephoros' Book 11, which includes a lengthy discussion of the Nile (*FGrHist* #70, fr. 65f), written seemingly in the context of the Athenian expedition to Egypt in 459 BC (G. L. Barber, *The Historian Ephorus*, Cambridge: Cambridge University Press, 1935, pp. 32), but this provides no solid information on Euthymenes' date.
91 Hekataios, fr. 302b; Herodotos 2.21. Dikaiarchos of Messana (fr. 126 Mirhady), in the late fourth century BC, reported the same theory of the source of the Nile, but no source has been preserved.
92 *FGrHist* #647, no. 2.
93 *FGrHist* #647, no. 1. On the text, see H. Oehler, *Paradoxographi florentini anonymi opusculum de acquis mirabilibus*, Tübingen: J. J. Heckenhauer, 1913.
94 Desanges, *Recherches*, pp. 24–7. It is debatable whether Hekataios knew of Euthymenes, although his toponym "Lizas" (*FGrHist* #1, fr. 355) is remindful of "Lixos." See further, infra, p. 30.

words.[95] The Massalians were never forthcoming about their explorers: the information they gathered and their very existence were considered state secrets for economic purposes. Poseidonios, the culmination of the Hellenistic geographical tradition, who probably spent time in Massalia,[96] knew nothing of Euthymenes, nor did Strabo.

Perhaps the most revealing statement surviving from whatever report Euthymenes submitted is that he came to a river so large that fresh water went well out to sea, and which contained crocodiles and hippopotami.[97] If he actually wrote "crocodile" and "hippopotamus," the latter even in its more common two-word form, he may have been the first to document the animals: Herodotos and Hanno are the first in extant literature.[98] No toponyms or other details are preserved,[99] and the remaining material about Euthymenes concerns his theory that strong onshore winds forced the river to flow upstream to the Nile.[100] This may seem bizarre today but should not be ridiculed, because it was reasonable within the limited geographical perspective in which Euthymenes lived, where little was known about oceanic phenomena: he may have seen a strong rising tide.[101] The presence of crocodiles and hippopotami added to the proof of his theory, because in his day Greeks knew them nowhere except the Nile.[102]

His river has been variously identified.[103] Suggestions range from the Dra'a, which enters the Atlantic in southern Morocco and which seems on occasion in recent times

---

95 Markianos of Herakleia, perhaps of the fourth or fifth century AC, who was one of the compilers of the Minor Greek Geographers, included Euthymenes in a list of authors of *periplooi* (*GGM* vol. 1, p. 565), but there is nothing actually in the corpus to support the claim. On Markianos, see Diller (supra n. 38), pp. 45–6.

96 Poseidonios (*FGrHist* #87), fr. 58a, 90 (= Strabo 3.4.13, 4.1.7)

97 This incited great criticism: Aristeides (36.85–95 Keil) was vehement in his belief that Euthymenes made up his tale. Yet his arguments were based more on literary rather than geographical concerns: see Romm, *Edges*, pp. 200–2.

98 Herodotos 2.68–71; Hanno 10. The West African hippopotamus (*Hippopotamus liberiensis*) is smaller than the Nile animal (*Hippopotamus amphibius*): see Otto Keller, *Die Antike Tierwelt*, Leipzig: Wilhelm Engelmann, 1909–1913, vol. 1, p. 407. Crocodiles and hippopotami are often mentioned together in ancient sources.

99 The river is not named in any of the extant material about Euthymenes, but it may have been the Chremetes, which Aristotle (*Meteorologika* 1.13) called "the major stream of the Nile." The same name appears in Hanno's report.

100 On this theory of the origin of the Nile, see Paul T. Keyser, "The Geographical Work of Dikaiarchos," in *Dicaearchus of Messana: Text, Translation, and Discussion*, ed. William W. Fortenbaugh and Eckart Schütrumpf, *Rutgers University Studies in Classical Humanities* 10, 2001, pp. 368–70.

101 One obscure source, *On the History of Philosophy* (88: see Hermann Diels, *Doxographi graeci*, Berlin: Walter de Gruyter, 1879, p. 634) in the corpus of Galen, names Euthymenes as a theorist about tides, and he did report on them, but any theorization is probably anachronistic and an error for Pytheas.

102 This is indirect proof of a date before the time of Alexander the Great, when the range of the animals became better known.

103 The rivers of West Africa were not untangled from the Nile until the nineteenth century, and all run remarkably close together: the Senegal and Niger (Figure 7) are only 60km apart, and affluents of the Niger and Nile are only 30km distant. See C. K. Meek, "The Niger and the Classics," *JAH* 1, 1960, 1–17. Thus Euthymenes (or any other explorer) could have gone across Africa from the mouth of the Senegal to Alexandria with less than 100km of overland travel.

Figure 7 Niger River at Mopti (Mali).

Photograph by Donna Martin.

to have had both crocodiles and hippopotami,[104] to the more probable Senegal, a large river that produces the phenomena Euthymenes observed.[105] The Senegal is the first significant river in the tropics, lying 850 miles beyond the Dra'a.[106]

If Euthymenes reached this point, his journey was profound, for he sailed along the lengthy Saharan coast, passing the Canary Islands, and perhaps becoming the first Greek to reach the western tropics and to report on strong tides.[107] The Massalian

104 Hennig, vol. 1, pp. 82. Today the Dra'a is completely separated from the ocean by a bar. In its vicinity the ocean is thick and muddy, due to sand blown off the desert (*Africa Pilot*, eleventh edition, London: Hydrographic Office, 1953–1954, vol. 1, p. 202), which may have been observed but not understood by Euthymenes.

105 Jacoby (supra n. 88), p. 1509; Desanges, *Recherches*, pp. 21–2; Paul Fabre, "Les grecs à la decouverte de 'Atlantique'," *RÉA* 94, 1992, 14.

106 Like the Dra'a, the Senegal is blocked today by a bar, but only during the dry season. Its mouth can easily be missed from the north, but whether this was the case in Euthymenes' day remains unproven. It can be navigated for 550 miles upstream, although only 180 miles in the driest years (*Africa Pilot* [supra n. 104], vol. 1, pp. 226–9).

107 The highest tidal ranges in West Africa are in the vicinity of Bissau, where there are many rivers flowing into the ocean. The 400 miles from Dakar to Conakry has no less than nine river mouths as well as numerous inlets and bays. The highest tides are at the mouth of the Geba River, where the range is 17.8 feet. Further north, toward the Senegal, it lessens, and is only 4.4 feet at St Louis, the mouth of the Senegal. See National Oceanic and Atmospheric Administration, *Tide Tables 1995: Europe and the West Coast of Africa*, Washington, 1994, p. 159. This might suggest that Euthymenes went beyond the Senegal to the well-watered coast of Guinea, where he developed a theory of a freshwater sea.

secretiveness that made his trip virtually unknown as a piece of geographical research does not hide its importance. Its purpose may have been reconnaissance, to learn about Carthaginian settlement in the region, concluding – encouraged by the Carthaginians no doubt – that there was nothing of interest to Massalia along the route, or that the Carthaginian presence was too extensive to justify further Massalian incursions.

Vestiges of Euthymenes' journey may appear in the jumbled African portion of the *periplous* of Pseudo-Skylax.[108] At least three different sources have been mixed together, describing the coast of Africa from the Pillars of Herakles to Kerne, a Carthaginian trading post that was the most important center on the West African coast. The distance from the Pillars to Kerne is given as 11 days and then as 12 days, and some toponyms are repeated, sometimes in different forms. The account also includes a lengthy excursus on the trading situation in the region of Kerne. It reflects a period of heavy Carthaginian involvement in the area after the exploratory journey of Hanno in the early fifth century BC.[109] Other toponyms embellish the account, including the Boiotian cluster previously mentioned, and Lixos, known to Hanno, which would become a significant coastal town in the Hellenistic and Roman periods. Other toponyms in the *periplous* are obscure. The source cannot be Hanno's own report, as Pseudo-Skylax's version contradicts Hanno in stating that it is no longer possible to sail beyond Kerne because the ocean is full of seaweed, shallow, and muddy – perhaps due to desert sand.[110]

The differences may be due, in part, to Carthaginian misinformation, but seem to echo some of the difficulties Euthymenes had with the winds and tides. Thus Pseudo-Skylax's account represents a world in which the Carthaginian presence and perhaps even their hostility toward the Greeks is well established, but the text itself is not derived from Carthaginian sources. Given that the *periplous* was written in the mid-fourth century BC, when Carthaginian power was still strong, Euthymenes, the only Greek known to have explored northwest Africa before this period, seems a probable source, but not the only one. The text was in part based on a report from someone who had visited Kerne, since nearly half the account is an ethnography of the "Ethiopians" who came to Kerne to trade, perhaps derived from a source close to the date of Pseudo-Skylax. Mention of Attic pottery as one of the trade items makes it probable that the author was a Greek. This interesting account of trade adds a number of topographical points: that there is a large city of the local inhabitants to which the Carthaginians sailed – obviously not Kerne itself and perhaps up a river – and that Africa could be circumnavigated. The large city implies a location beyond the barren desert coast and well into the tropics; the circumnavigability, although later than Herodotos' famous statement,[111] may represent an independent tradition learned

---

108 Pseudo-Skylax 112. On this chapter, see Aurelio Peretti, *Il periplo di Scilace*, Pisa: Giardini, 1979, pp. 373–417; Desanges, *Recherches*, pp. 87–120.

109 For Hanno, see infra, pp. 29–43.

110 *Africa Pilot* (supra n. 104) vol. 1, p. 202.

111 Herodotos 4.42.

locally. Both comments contradict the assertion already made that one could not go beyond Kerne. It would seem that perhaps by the mid-fourth century BC a Greek had managed to visit Kerne and see the trade in process, learning some things from the resident Carthaginians, who, at the same time, were careful to discourage the Greeks from their own exploration or even presence in the area.[112]

Perhaps at about the same time as Euthymenes' voyage was that of the Persian Sataspes.[113] Herodotos, the only source, learned about the event shortly afterward on Samos from one of Sataspes' eunuchs. Because it took place during the reign of Xerxes and presumably after Samos was relieved of Persian control, the trip can be precisely dated to between 479–465 BC.[114] Sataspes was forced to attempt to circumnavigate Africa as expiation for a crime. He obtained a vessel and crew in Egypt – their nationality is not specified – and went through the Pillars of Herakles and south along the African coast for many months. He found an area inhabited by small people who dressed in palm leaves and who ran away into the mountains at the Persians' approach. They raised animals for eating. But at this point Sataspes turned back, and told Xerxes that he was forced to do so because the ship could not move (ἐνίσχεσθαι), a reason that the king did not believe, and thereupon had Sataspes executed.[115]

This is the only specific report on Sataspes' journey. Other citations in Greek literature of an ocean on which it was impossible to move have been assumed, somewhat implausibly, to refer to his trip.[116] Plato, in his discussion of the disappearance of Atlantis, wrote that the ocean became impassable because of mud, a sentiment echoed somewhat more scientifically by Aristotle.[117] There was also an early awareness of thick and heavy plant matter in the external Ocean.[118] Yet these reports are vague and need not be connected with Sataspes, whose account, as reported by Herodotos, cited neither mud nor plants. It seems more probable that Sataspes encountered constant headwinds and adverse currents – which were perhaps coupled with a lack of enthusiasm – that made further progress impossible and even feared.[119]

---

112 D. B. Harden, "The Phoenicians on the West Coast of Africa," *Antiquity* 22, 1948, 141–50.

113 Herodotos 4.43; Desanges, *Recherches*, pp. 29–33; Cary and Warmington, pp. 119–21. Herodotos stated that this was a Carthaginian story, although his source was Samian. The Phoenician circumnavigation, mentioned immediately previously, is confused somewhat with Carthaginian exploration, indicative of the uncertainty as to who was responsible for the early trips around Africa. See further, infra, pp. 22–7.

114 Frédéric Colin, "Le recit de Sataspes s'inspire-t-il de sources egyptiennes?" *ZPE* 82, 1990, 288.

115 Xerxes' disbelief is echoed by some modern scholars: for example, Raymond Mauny – a strong proponent of a minimalist view of Greek and Carthaginian exploration of the West African coast – "Trans-Saharan Contacts and the Iron Age in West Africa," *CHA* 2, 1978, 296–7. He suggested that Sataspes simply hid out on the Moroccan coast, perhaps learning from his crew some bits of data about points farther south.

116 Hennig, vol. 1, pp. 133–7.

117 Plato, *Timaios* 25; Aristotle, *Meteorologika* 2.1.

118 Avienus 406–13 (from Himilco); Theophrastos, *Research on Plants* 4.6–7.

119 Herodotos used the word ἐρημία – desolation – to describe what frightened Sataspes. It is perhaps hard to imagine the effect that the Ocean had on early sailors, with its tides, swell, and limited coastline: see Romm, *Edges*, pp. 16–17.

The most interesting element of Sataspes' trip is his confrontation with "small men" (ἄνθρωποι σμικροί). Commentators have universally assumed these to be pygmies, who had been known to the Greek world (in the ethnym "Pygmaioi") since Homeric times,[120] and appear on the François Vase of the early sixth century BC. Yet the "small men" of west central Africa are not called pygmies by Herodotos, either in his account of Sataspes or in that of the journey of the Nasamonians,[121] who encountered "small men" in a large city on a great eastward flowing river in sub-Saharan Africa, probably the Niger in the vicinity of Timbuctu. The specific term "pygmy" seems to be Egyptian in origin, perhaps from as early as the Middle Kingdom.[122] Herodotos' only use of the word is in reference to a wall painting that he saw at Memphis.[123] Aristotle seems to be the first to locate them in central Africa.[124] The modern range of pygmy tribes does not extend northwest of Cameroon,[125] although the experience of the Nasamonians places them on the upper Niger, perhaps in Mali, in Sataspes' day. The Persian explorer may have gone as far as Cameroon, but it would seem that he reached at least the Niger delta.[126] In the interior Gulf of Guinea, especially beyond the mouth of the Niger, the combination of currents and winds would appear to cause a ship to become stuck.[127] Thus it seems that Sataspes went farther than Euthymenes, and because of Herodotos' Samian connections his story became better and earlier known. Yet the motivation is difficult to determine. Although it is from an era when the Persians and Carthaginians were drawn together because of mutual opposition to the Greek states, the ultimate reason for the journey may only have been Xerxes' desire to emulate the explorations of his father.[128]

By the early fifth century BC, then, Greeks knew about the coast of the Atlantic from the English Channel to perhaps the Gulf of Guinea. Much of the detail of these coasts was unknown, and myth and human experience were deeply intertwined. Precise knowledge was perhaps limited to the area between Cape Roca and the Atlas Mountains. Many things were not understood, especially the peculiarities of both the tropics and the Ocean itself. Yet after this promising beginning there was little Greek exploration outside the Pillars for many years.

---

120 Homer, *Iliad* 3.6. The word is usually derived from πυγμή ("fist": see *LSJ*), but the rationale is not strong and it may be purely an ethnym.

121 Herodotos 2.32.

122 Colin (supra n. 114), pp. 292–3.

123 Herodotos 3.37. Ancient references to pygmies are listed by Martin Gusinde, "Kenntnisse und Urteile über Pygmäen in Antike und Mittelalter," *Nova Acta Leopoldina* n. s. 25, no. 162, 1962, 1–12.

124 Aristotle, *History of Animals* 7 [8].12.

125 See the map in Luigi Luca Cavalli-Sforza, "Demographic Data," in *African Pygmies*, ed. Luigi Luca Cavalli-Sforza, Orlando: Academic Press, 1986, p. 24.

126 The "mountains" into which the locals fled at the approach of Sataspes and his companions are too vague a term to be geographically useful. It has also been suggested that he only reached Cape Palmas, the southernmost point before the coast turns east into the Gulf of Guinea: see Ciaran Branigan, "The Circumnavigation of Africa," *Classics Ireland* 1, 1994.

127 Thomson, p. 73; Carpenter, *Beyond*, pp. 80–1.

128 B. H. Warmington, *Carthage*, revised edition, New York: Praeger, 1969, pp. 68–9.

2

THE CARTHAGINIANS NORTH AND SOUTH OF THE PILLARS

In the early fifth century BC, Greek exploration of the Atlantic diminished sharply and that of the Carthaginians began to flourish.[1] They significantly expanded knowledge of both the north and south, and perhaps discovered some of the mid-Atlantic islands. The Carthaginian movement beyond the Pillars was in part inspired by earlier Phoenician activity. There is no evidence that the Phoenicians had gone any distance north beyond Gades, but they showed early interest in the African coast to the south. Sometime after the foundation of Gades, they began to explore along the Atlantic coast of Africa, settling at Lixos (Figure 6), Mogador (Figure 8), and perhaps elsewhere. Pottery from Lixos and Mogador demonstrates that those sites were first occupied in the late seventh or early sixth centuries BC and were dependent on Gades.[2] Mogador, 600 miles from Gades, may have been the farthest Phoenician penetration for settlement or trade, and by Hellenistic times many of these sites were abandoned.[3] Yet the Phoenicians had some knowledge beyond Mogador, since around 600 BC, according to various sources, they circumnavigated Africa, but, interestingly, in a clockwise direction.

That this could even be conceived is in part due to the uniqueness of Africa. From early times it was believed that the Ocean surrounded the earth: the image is most clearly depicted on the shield of Achilles, where the Ocean encircles the rim.[4] It was here that the sun rose and set, and the Ocean was defined as the limit of the earth.[5] All constellations except the Bear sank into it.[6] The only people known to live on its shores were the Ethiopians.[7] The Ocean could only be reached by sea along Africa: through the Pillars of Herakles or down the Red Sea. Moreover, the continent was so

---

1 The archaeological record in southwestern Spain shows that Greek finds are replaced by Carthaginian ones around 500BC: see Carpenter, *Beyond* 65; John Boardman, *The Greeks Overseas*, fourth edition, London: Thames and Hudson, 1999, p. 215.

2 María Eugenia Aubet, *The Phoenicians and the West*, tr. Mary Turton, second edition, Cambridge: Cambridge University Press, 2001, pp. 297–304.

3 Avienus, *Ora maritima* 440–3, 459–60.

4 Homer, *Iliad* 18.607–8.

5 Homer, *Iliad* 7.421–3; 8.485; 14.200–1, 301–2.

6 Homer, *Iliad* 18.485–9.

7 Homer, *Iliad* 1.423; 23.205–6. The term "Ethiopian" is consistently used in Greek and Roman literature to mean the people of sub-Saharan Africa.

Figure 8 Mogador (Essaouira).
Photograph by Duane W. Roller.

narrow that one could drag a ship across it.[8] Thus it was not difficult to believe that it could be encircled easily. Although this was Greek thought, others probably had similar ideas or were early exposed to these theories.

The circumnavigation of Africa is most famously described in a much disputed account by Herodotos.[9] The Egyptian king Necho (610–595 BC) commissioned Phoenicians to sail down the Red Sea, around Africa, and into the Mediterranean through the Pillars of Herakles.[10] They spent three years on the journey, stopping each autumn to plant and harvest crops. A century later, a certain Mago, presumably a Carthaginian, told the court of Gelon of Syracuse (ca. 491–478 BC) that he had circumnavigated the continent,[11] although if this is same person who claimed to have crossed the Sahara three times without drinking water, his veracity can hardly be presumed.[12] In addition, the *Periplous* of Pseudo-Skylax, another century later, alludes,

8 Hesiod, *Catalogue of Women and Eoiai*, fr. 45 (= Scholia to Apollonios of Rhodes 4.259). On ancient views of the shape of Africa, see Serena Bianchetti, "L'idea di Africa da Annone a Plinio," *Africa Romana* 7, 1990, 871–8.

9 Herodotos 4.42. For modern sources, see Hennig, vol. 1, pp. 63–7; Cary and Warmington, pp. 11–20; Thomson, pp. 71–4 – among the most disbelieving of modern commentators; Desanges, *Recherches*, pp. 7–16.

10 It has been suggested (Hennig, vol. 1, p. 67) that the journey took place at the end of Necho's reign, between 597–595BC, and that the death of the king, perhaps even before the expedition returned, may have contributed to its obscurity.

11 Strabo 2.3.4 (= Poseidonios, fr. 28), quoting the *Dialogues* of Herakleides of Pontos, who lived only a few years after Mago. The story is unclear and "Mago" may not be a personal name, but a Persian Magus; if so, the source may be Herakleides' *Zoroaster* (Plutarch, *Reply to Kolotes* 14).

12 Athenaios 2.44e. Here Mago is without question a personal name. He was probably a member of the important Magonid family, as, it seems, were all the great Carthaginian explorers.

vaguely, to the possibility of circumnavigation, but in a counter-clockwise direction from West Africa to the Red Sea.[13] Thus by the end of the Classical period there were three separate reports of such a journey: the Phoenicians commissioned by Necho, Mago of Carthage, and the unnamed explorer who started from West Africa.[14] The final allusion to an early voyage was by Pliny, who wrote that Hanno sailed from Gades to Arabia, something not supported either in previous accounts or in the extant report of the Carthaginian seaman, but which adds another version to the three already in existence.[15] These need not be mutually exclusive: Mago and Hanno may be the same – Hanno was of the Magonid family – and either could be the explorer of Pseudo-Skylax. But Herodotos' account stands alone both in its early date and its clockwise direction.

Despite these reports, by late Hellenistic times opinion turned against any circumnavigation. Polybios, an African explorer in his own right who had personal access to the Carthaginian records, believed that there was no evidence of such a journey.[16] Slightly later Poseidonios, although making note of both Mago and Herodotos' tale of the Phoenicians – and attributing it to Dareios of Persia, not Necho of Egypt[17] – felt that both voyages were unsubstantiated. This view was emphasized more vehemently by Strabo, who – whether he was quoting Poseidonios is not obvious – called Herodotos' account a "Bergaian" tale, a proverbial term for a fanciful story.[18] By the first century BC some even believed that circumnavigation was impossible, not because of human limitations but geographical ones, since theory of the period came to feel that the Indian Ocean was an enclosed sea, which would make going around Africa moot.[19] It was also

---

13 Pseudo-Skylax 112.

14 The alleged circumnavigation of Ophelas (Strabo 17.3.3) has too many difficulties of interpretation to place confidently. See further, infra, pp. 95–9.

15 Pliny, *Natural History* 2.169. Pomponius Mela (3.90), writing slightly earlier than Pliny, wrote rather ambiguously that Hanno circumnavigated the greater part of Africa ("magnam partam eius circumvectus"). The travels of Eudoxos of Kyzikos, in the late second century BC, although inevitably tangled into these Hellenistic and Roman critiques of earlier voyages, belong to a different environment from the Herodotean account, and are discussed infra, pp. 107–11.

16 Polybios 3.38.

17 Poseidonios, fr. 28 (= Strabo 2.3.4). The Persian commissioning of the voyage is generally considered an error on the part of Strabo or Poseidonios, but may hide a more plausible Persian role in circumnavigation, especially if it were a Magus and not Mago who claimed to have made a journey. The Persians at least had a consistent interest in exploration. See also Poseidonios, *Posidonius 2: The Commentary*, ed. I. G. Kidd, Cambridge: Cambridge University Press, pp. 240–2.

18 Strabo 2.3.5: the term comes from Antiphanes of Berga and the type of material that he wrote. Antiphanes is first mentioned in extant literature in the *Periplous Dedicated to King Nikomedes* (653–5), as an author of "truthless history and ridiculous tales." Strabo used his name several times to condemn what he saw as fanciful geography (see also 1.3.1, 2.4.2). See Susan A. Stephens and John J. Winkler (eds.), *The Ancient Greek Novels: The Fragments*, Princeton: Princeton University Press, 1995, pp. 104–5; G. Knaack, "Antiphanes von Berga," *RhM* n. s. 61, 1906, 135–8.

19 Hipparchos, *Geography*, fr. 4 (= Strabo 1.1.9); see also fr. 5 (= Pomponius Mela 3.70). This was accepted by the geographer Ptolemy (*Geography* 7.5.9).

believed that the heat of the tropics made that region uninhabitable, although this need not preclude exploration.[20] Much of the problem in analyzing the accounts is connected with the Hellenistic evolution of geography as a discipline and a growing skepticism toward reports of early travels, especially those at the extremities of the earth.[21] Even more recent explorers, such as Pytheas and Eudoxos, did not escape the criticism of Strabo, who is the major extant source for post-Herodotean discussion. Circumnavigation became an important political issue in the late Hellenistic and Roman period: it was an essential part of the foreign policy and political self-conception of Juba II, the geographer, explorer, and scholarly king of Mauretania in the Augustan period.[22]

Herodotos' report on the Phoenician journey is frustratingly vague, something that has been a problem since antiquity.[23] Lacking is the remarkable amount of detail normal for the historian. No personalities are mentioned by name, and there are no geographical or ethnographic specifics. There are only two significant facts: the sowing and harvesting of crops during the three-year journey, and the comment that the sun was on the right hand during part of the trip. The latter is by far the more significant, as it indicates movement well beyond the equator, and is the most telling memory of a voyage far to the south, although not necessarily a circumnavigation. The Tropic of Cancer would have been crossed before the explorers were halfway down the Red Sea, after which the summer sun would appear in the north. The equator is reached on the southern Somali coast. But Herodotos reported that the sun was on the right – not that it was in the north – which implies a lengthy westward journey, only possible for the 600 miles at the southern end of Africa or, further on, in the Gulf of Guinea.[24]

The sowing and harvesting of crops is interesting but not a problem with regard to the veracity of the voyage: Eudoxos of Kyzikos was to attempt the same around 100BC.[25] Although it has repeatedly been suggested to be implausible,[26] it is probably the only way that such an extended journey would have been possible for explorers who had no concept of what the resources were of the area that they were penetrating, and who had limited storage space. The results may not have been completely successful, although this does not mean that the expedition starved. Yet the three years for the total journey of approximately 13,000 miles is quite

20 Aristotle, *Meteorologika* 2.5; Pomponius Mela 1.4; see also Horace, *Odes* 1.22; Pliny, *Natural History* 6.199 (from Ephoros).
21 On this see Romm, *Edges*, pp. 172–5.
22 Roller, *Juba*, pp. 187–9, 230; infra, pp. 112–14.
23 Cary and Warmington, p. 114; see also John Ferguson, "Classical Contacts with West Africa," in *Africa in Classical Antiquity: Nine Studies*, ed. L. A. Thompson and John Ferguson, Ibadan 1969, p. 4.
24 Desanges, *Recherches*, p. 10–14.
25 Infra, p. 109.
26 See, for example, J. R. Masson, "Geographical Knowledge and Maps of Southern Africa Before 1500 A. D.," *TI* 18, 1986, 2–3: " … the Early Iron Age which brought cultivation and livestock rearing did not reach these parts for another five hundred years," which really does not address the issue.

reasonable. This would provide a raw average of about 12 miles per day, or 24 miles if half the days were spent in port.[27]

Modern scholars have tended to center their arguments on whether the journey was logistically possible, given the state of contemporary seamanship.[28] Yet this is somewhat of a distraction: the issue is not whether it was possible – of that there seems no doubt – but whether it actually happened. The most serious question remains its rationale. Assuming that it was Necho and not Dareios who commissioned the expedition, there is no obvious reason for him to have done so, other than his desire for grandiose projects, as demonstrated by his attempted Nile–Red Sea canal.[29] Yet the Egyptian world did not extend to the Atlantic. The Persians had greater interest in the western Mediterranean and were to send a reconnaissance there in the late sixth century BC,[30] and the confusion between Phoenicians and Persians in accounts of the tale may be significant. It is possible that circumnavigation was not the actual purpose of the trip; rather it may be seen as an exploration or perhaps even colonization – hence the supplies – into the wealthy areas of southern East Africa. By Roman times the Atlantic was believed to begin at Cape Mossylites, which is modern Cape Guardafui or Ras el-Asin, the eastern-most point of Africa where the coast turns sharply southwest.[31] It may be that a Phoeni-cian or Egyptian colonizing voyage into East Africa was thus thought to have reached the Atlantic, becoming confused with Carthaginian explorations outside the Pillars of Herakles. Herodotos may have conflated this voyage with that of Hanno, whom he did not mention by name but of whom he seems to have been aware.[32] This may be reflected in Pliny's assertion that it was in fact Hanno who made the circumnavigation.[33]

The question of a Phoenician circumnavigation remains unproven. It seems more plausible that Necho commissioned an exploration of East Africa, and this became mixed with other early reports of circumnavigation: Persian attempts, the mysterious Mago at Syracuse – who may have sailed with Hanno – and Hanno himself.[34] By Hellenistic times the information was so confused that it was easy for geographical

27 In the fifth century BC a ship could sail 70,000 *orgyiai* (ca. 70 miles) in a long day and 60,000 (ca. 60 miles) in a night (Herodotos 4.86), far above the necessary average, even allowing for lengthy stops and other problems. An *orgyia*, the spread of the outstretched arms, is slightly less than two meters. See Jacques Ramin, *Le périple d'Hannon*, BAR Supp. Ser. 3, 1976, pp. 108–9. On the general issue of the speed of ancient ships, see Lionel Casson, *Ships and Seamanship in the Ancient World*, Princeton: Princeton University Press, 1971, pp. 281–96.

28 See, for example, the detailed critique by Cary and Warmington, pp. 115–17; also Alan B. Lloyd, "Were Necho's Triremes Phoenician?" *JHS* 95, 1975, 45–61, a study of Necho's seapower.

29 B. H. Warmington, *Carthage*, revised edition, New York: Praeger, 1969, p. 68.

30 Herodotos 3.136–8.

31 Juba (*FGrHist* #275), fr. 35 = Pliny, *Natural History* 6.175.

32 Herodotos 4.196. The unsuccessful attempt by Sataspes (supra, pp. 20–1) may also have added to the confusion: Herodotos' slippage from Phoenicians to Carthaginians (4.42–3) may be significant.

33 Pliny, *Natural History* 2.169.

34 Confusion of Phoenicians and Carthaginians was a common problem among the Greeks. At Herodotos 2.32, his description of the coast of north Africa, "Phoenician" is used where "Carthaginian" is meant. See also Euripides, *Troades* 221, where the Phoenicians are described as opposite Sicily. On this problem in early Greek literature, see Guy Bunnens, *L'expansion phénicienne en Méditerranée, Études de philologie, d'archéologie et d'histoire ancienne* 17, Brussels 1979, pp. 109–44.

theorists to be dismissive of all circumnavigations, even contemporary ones. There is no further evidence of Phoenician interest in the idea of circumnavigation of Africa, and exploration outside the Pillars soon became a Carthaginian priority. Around 500BC, Himilco and Hanno, both certainly of the Magonid family and perhaps even brothers, simultaneously expanded knowledge of the Atlantic to the north and south. Himilco may have reached the British Isles; Hanno went as far, perhaps, as Cameroon. These represent the greatest era of Carthaginian maritime exploration. Although the voyages can be seen together as a parallel demonstration of the widest reach of Carthaginian geographical knowledge, that of Himilco is barely known whereas a portion of Hanno's actual report has survived, the earliest extant *periplous*.[35]

Himilco's journey is not documented in extant literature before Roman times. The earliest reference is by Pliny, who recorded that at the same time as Hanno, Himilco was sent to learn what was beyond the extremities of Europe ("ad extera Europae noscenda missus"),[36] cited in a summary of African coastal exploration that lists, in addition to the two Carthaginians, Eudoxos of Kyzikos, Seleukid explorers, and Gaius Caesar.[37] The other extant record of Himilco's journey is in the *Ora maritima* of Avienus. Although Himilco is not in the list of sources for the poem,[38] Avienus stated that he learned about the Carthaginian from ancient Punic records.[39] The explorer is named three times,[40] but the information is remarkably sparse given the extent of his voyage. His date depends on that of Hanno, which is itself uncertain, but was perhaps shortly after 500BC.[41] The locale of Himilco's exploration was beyond the known limits of Europe, presumably in the context of his own day, not the wider view of the sources of the Roman period. By his time Phokaians and Massalians had gone at least as far as Ophioussa, and probably beyond to the northwest corner of Brittany. Whether Himilco knew about these travels is debatable given the Greek reticence about their own explorations.

The tone of the three citations of Himilco is similar: an emphasis on the hazards of the journey. In the first entry,[42] the reader is told that there are no winds for sailors and that the ocean is sluggish (*pigri*). There is such a large amount of seaweed that it stops ships, and moreover the ocean is shallow with numerous sea monsters. The second entry[43] repeats the lack of wind and the shallows, and adds that there is always fog and that the ocean is infinite and with a boundless swell. The final entry[44] again tells of the wide extent of the ocean, its swell, the seaweed, and the monsters. Some of these

---

35 Infra, pp. 129–32.

36 Pliny, *Natural History* 2.169.

37 Pliny, *Natural History* 1.5.

38 Avienus, *Ora maritima* 42–50.

39 Avienus, *Ora maritima* 414–15.

40 Avienus, *Ora maritima* 117, 383, 412.

41 A certain Euktemon of Athens is the source for comments in the *Ora maritima* (364–5) about the shallowness and thickness of the sea that are similar in diction to Himilco's description of the same phenomena. If Euktemon is the mathematician of the fifth century BC, and if his comments show awareness of Himilco, the Carthaginian was known to the Greeks by that time.

42 Avienus, *Ora maritima* 117–29.

43 Avienus, *Ora maritima* 375–89.

44 Avienus, *Ora maritima* 402–13.

comments are remindful of the difficulties faced elsewhere by Euthymenes and the explorers recorded by Pseudo-Skylax, and may be propaganda designed to frighten Greeks away from areas that the Carthaginians considered their own. It is unlikely that Himilco encountered the Sargasso Sea, as some have assumed, for it is in the western Atlantic, beyond the Azores and far from any point he is likely to have reached.[45] It is more probable that he came to the area four days beyond the Pillars of Herakles used by the fishermen of Gades, a place thick with seaweed that appeared when the tide was low – hence a coastal location – and where tuna of unusual size were caught and sent to Carthage.[46]

The substantive points in the *Ora maritima* about Himilco's journey are few. Only the first of the three citations provides any information beyond the fact of the publication of his report and the perils of the areas that he reached. Here the comments about Himilco are connected to an intrusive digression that describes the Sacred Island (Sacra Insula), two days away from the Oistrymnides.[47] The Sacred Island is inhabited by the Hierni: nearby is another island where the Albiones live, who may have been known to the Tartessians, but only through trade. Himilco, according to his report, investigated the Sacred Island but found the going difficult for the reasons already cited: rather than a two-day journey, it was in fact one of four months. This is such an exaggeration that it has long been suspect as Carthaginian misdirection, but it may also be a vestige of the total length of Himilco's cruise, perhaps showing that he went elsewhere, such as the Atlantic islands.[48] After these sparse comments about the problems of reaching the Sacred Island, Avienus' description of Himilco's explorations abruptly breaks off without any further information, and the text returns to the Oistrymnides.

Assuming the distance of two days is correct – perhaps information from a Phokaian or Massalian source – and that the Oistrymnides are part of Brittany, it seems obvious that Himilco crossed over to the British Isles. In fact the Greek for Sacred Island – ἱερὰ νῆσος, or without the initial aspirate in the Ionic of Massalia – seems close to the Greek name for Ireland – Ἰέρνη – and thus Himilco may have reached that island.[49] Wherever the Sacred Island was, its single characteristic recorded in the *Ora maritima* is the richness of its sod (*caespes*), typical of Ireland from ancient to modern times.[50] Attribution is extremely hypothetical and the lack of supporting information is not helpful, but it may be that Himilco was the first

---

45 Nevertheless, when Columbus discovered the sea in 1493, it was presumed that he had reached the region described by Himilco: see Cary and Warmington, p. 46. See also Walter Woodburn Hyde, *Ancient Greek Mariners*, New York: Oxford University Press, 1947, pp. 123–4.

46 [Aristotle], *On Marvellous Things Heard* 136.

47 Avienus, *Ora maritima* 108–29. On the Oistrymnides, or Oistrymnic Bay, see supra, pp.10–11.

48 Carpenter, *Beyond*, p. 214. Pliny's citation of Himilco in a catalogue of African explorers and his use of his report in his African book seems to indicate that the Carthaginian also went south (*Natural History* 2.169, 1.5).

49 Philip Freeman, *Ireland and the Classical World*, Austin: University of Texas Press, 2001, pp. 28–32. On ancient names for Ireland, see Pomponius Mela, *Chorographie*, ed. A. Silberman, Paris: Les Belles Lettres, 1988, p. 285.

50 See Pomponius Mela 3.53.

from the Mediterranean to reach Ireland and to document its name. Whatever Greek source his report passed into would have been the earliest in ancient literature to have the name, although confused. It is not cited again in extant texts until the first century BC.[51] Avienus also seems to have obtained the ethnym Albiones from the synthesis of Himilco's report. The related toponym was considered the ancient name for Britain.[52] The Albiones were known to the Tartessians, which may have led the Carthaginians to investigate the district, but in such a way as to discourage others from following.

Nevertheless, it seems that around 500BC Himilco was sent to investigate the extreme northwestern reaches of Europe and to go beyond the continent insofar as possible. He may have been searching for sources of tin,[53] although there is no indication of this in the scanty extant material. But the Carthaginians were reacting to reports obtained at Tartessos – and perhaps the Greek cities – about lands beyond Europe that were wealthy and thus worthy of exploration. Himilco followed the established route to the Oistrymnides and then made the two-day jump to the land of the Hierni – in Greek this became the Sacred Island – missing the extremity of Cornwall.[54] He learned about, but perhaps did not visit, the nearby lands of the Albiones: here there was no toponym but only the ethnym, and no specific detail. Yet it is possible that returning from Ireland he touched the Welsh coast, some 130 miles away, or Cornwall. He does not seem to have gone up the English Channel, if Avienus' comments about the deserted coast beyond the Oistrymnides refer to him.[55] But any particular benefit that the voyage had for the Carthaginians is no longer known, although there are hints of colonization.[56]

There are also suggestions of a southern journey, since Pliny's knowledge of the explorer was only in an African context. Yet the Carthaginian desire to discourage Greek followers meant that his travels were expressed in negative, almost impossible terms, and these details came to override the actual discoveries that Himilco had made. Only the barest outline of the voyage became available to the Greeks: it may have been Ephoros who first disseminated it, and his account influenced Pytheas in his epic journey to the far north.[57]

The culmination of Carthaginian exploration, and indeed the best documented and most-studied voyage made by that state, is the West African journey of Hanno.

---

51 Caesar, *Bellum gallicum* 5.13, as Hibernia. Diodoros (5.32.3) has Iris.

52 Pliny, *Natural History* 4.102.

53 Hennig. vol. 1, pp. 96–107; Warmington (supra n. 29), p. 76.

54 From Ushant at the northwest corner of Brittany to the closest point of Ireland (Old Head of Kinsale, southwest of Cork), is about 250 miles, possible in two days of hard sailing.

55 Avienus, *Ora maritima* 130–3: the text is so convoluted that it is virtually impossible to determine whether the source is Himilco or the Greek *periplous* that makes up the bulk of the *Ora maritima*: a Greek mythological reference (*Lycaonis aethra*) may suggest the latter. See Cary and Warmington, p. 46; C. F. C. Hawkes, *Pytheas: Europe and the Greek Explorers*, n. p., n. d., p. 22.

56 Avienus, *Ora maritima* 114–15.

57 Hawkes (supra n. 55), p. 25; on Pytheas, see infra, chapter 4.

Not only does an actual text survive, in Greek translation,[58] but his explorations were probably known to Greeks from the time of Herodotos.[59] The author of the Pseudo-Skylax *Periplous* also knew about the results of Hanno's explorations,[60] as did a certain Palaiphatos, perhaps also of the fourth century BC.[61] The first in extant literature to cite Hanno by name, other than his actual report, was the author of the Aristotelian *On Marvellous Things Heard*.[62] Eratosthenes was probably familiar with Hanno's travels,[63] and Polybios may have used Hanno's account in his own explorations.[64] Knowledge of the explorer then seems to have languished until the Roman period, when a variety of sources show familiarity with him, perhaps because of the interest in West Africa due to an expanded Roman presence and the researches of Juba II of Mauretania, who wrote a treatise during the Augustan period titled *The Wanderings of Hanno*.[65] Strabo, quoting Eratosthenes, did not name the Carthaginian explorer but knew about him,[66] and he was well known to Pomponius Mela, who summarized his report.[67] Pliny emphasized Hanno's importance as a source for West Africa.[68] Arrian

---

58 *GGM*, vol. 1, pp. 1–14. Much of the extensive modern literature on Hanno discusses specific topographic details. More generally, see Hennig, vol. 1, pp. 86–96; Thomson, pp. 73–6; Cary and Warmington, pp. 63–8; Carpenter, *Beyond*, pp. 81–100; Ramin (supra n. 27); Desanges, *Recherches*, pp. 39–85; Jehan Desanges, "Le point sur le Périple d'Hannon: controverses et publications récentes," in *Enquêtes et documents* 6: *Nantes–Afrique–Amerique*, Nantes 1981, pp. 13–29; J.-G. Demerliac and J. Meirat, *Hannon et l'empire punique*, Paris: Les Belles Lettres, 1983, pp. 63–183. A summary of previous scholarship and a detailed bibliography appears in Alfredo Mederos Martín and Gabriel Escribano Cobo, "El periplo norteafricano de Hannón y la rivalidad gaditano-cartaginesa de los siglos IV-III a. C," *Gerión* 18, 2000, 77–107. Material on Hanno from this chapter has appeared as the present author's "The West African Voyage of Hanno the Carthaginian," *AncW* 24, 2004.

59 Herodotos 4.196.

60 Pseudo-Skylax 112. Whether Hekataios knew about Hanno is not proven, although the toponym "Lizas" (Hekataios [*FGrHist* #1], fr. 355), a river, is remindful of Hanno's Lixos river, and Hekataios' "Melissa," said to be a Libyan city (fr. 357), is identical to Hanno's "Melitta," since Hanno's Greek text is in Attic. There is also the city of Thrinke, "near the Pillars" (fr. 356). Yet Euthymenes, not Hanno, may have been Hekataios' source, and any correlation between the toponyms is highly speculative.

61 Palaiphatos, *On Unbelievable Tales* 31. On his date, see the edition of Jacob Stern, Wauconda, Ill.: Bolchazy-Carducci, 1996, pp. 1–4. He did not mention Hanno by name but referred to the "Annon" river in west Africa and has other data seemingly drawn from the report.

62 [Aristotle], *On Marvellous Things Heard* 37. Ephoros may also have used the report (*FGrHist* #70, fr. 53); see Jerker Blomqvist, *The Date and Origin of The Greek Version of Hanno's Periplus*, Lund: CWK Gleerup, 1979, p. 54.

63 Strabo 1.3.2.

64 Pliny, *Natural History* 6.199; infra, pp. 99–104.

65 On this work, and Juba's role in making Hanno better known, see Roller, *Juba*, pp. 177, 189.

66 Strabo 1.3.2.

67 Pomponius Mela 3.90–95. On his knowledge of the African coast, see Jehan Desanges, "La face cachée de l'Afrique selon Pomponius Mela," *GeoAnt* 3–4, 1994–5, 79–89.

68 Pliny, *Natural History* 2.169; 5.8, 6.200–1. On Pliny's knowledge of Hanno, see Pliny, Book 5 (ed. Desanges), pp. 103–6. Xenophon of Lampsakos, who wrote a *periplous* sometime in the century after the fall of Carthage, may also have known about the explorer (Pliny, *Natural History* 6.200). See Olimpio Musso, "Il Periplo di Annone ovvero estratti bizantini da Senofonte di Lampsaco," in *Mediterraneo medievale: scritti in onoro di Franceso Giunta*, n. p., 1989, pp. 955–63.

also made a brief reference to the journey.[69] The occasional later citations add nothing beyond what is extant from the first century AC.[70]

Hanno's report, one of the most striking documents of ancient exploration, is remarkable in its detail yet brevity. This is the earliest extant description of Mediterranean peoples going far beyond the areas previously known to them. Needless to say it has excited much comment since ancient times. Despite its significance, the report is difficult to understand: the text is unclear and corrupt in numerous places, and ambiguity is strengthened by the fact that it is a translation which uses Greek terminology that might not have accurately reflected the Punic original. When and by whom the translation was made is still a matter of controversy. There is evidence that several versions of the text were known in antiquity.[71] And, obviously, the geographical context of the report has generated the most comment: Hanno's toponyms have been located at practically every point on the West African coast from Morocco to Cameroon.

The expedition can be dated to before the fourth century BC, when various Greek sources cite it; Herodotos also seems to show awareness of it. It most likely took place in the fifth century BC, the probable date of the existing Greek text.[72] Yet there were later independent versions of the text and commentaries on the journey, such as that by Juba II. The explorer himself must have been from the prominent Magonid family and probably lived in the early fifth century BC, but his exact identity is uncertain. Although called "king" of Carthage in the extant text, this is of little help. Most modern commentators avoid speculation as to who Hanno was.[73]

In addition to the difficulties of determining the date of Hanno's cruise and when Greeks became aware of it, the very existence of the voyage itself has repeatedly been called into question. Most of the arguments against its veracity have been based on conditions of the winds – especially on the return – and

---

69 Arrian, *Indika* 43.11–12.

70 Ptolemy, *Geography* 4.6.9, 16; Martianus Capella 7.621.

71 On some of the problems with the text, see Ramin (supra n. 27), pp. 64–6.

72 Blomqvist (supra n. 62), pp. 18–52. A mid-fourth century BC date was suggested by José A. Martin García, "El periplo a África de Hannón," *AMal* 15, 1992, 55–84; 350–300BC was the opinion of G. Marcy, "Notes linguistiques autour de Périple d'Hannon," *Hésperis* 20, 1935, 21–72; and 348–264BC that of Mederos Martín and Escribano Cobo (supra n. 58), pp. 77–107. The Classical style of the text has been suggested, rather implausibly, to be an imitation from later times (Gabriel Germain, "Qu'est-ce que le *Périple* d'Hannon? Document, amplification littéraire ou faux intégral?" *Hespéris* 44, 1957, 205–48).

73 Stéphane Gsell suggested that Hanno and the explorer Himilco were the sons of Himilcar, who died in 480BC at the battle of Himera (*Histoire ancienne de l'Afrique du Nord*, Paris: Hachette, 1914–1928, vol. 1, pp. 517–18). Those who venture to identify the explorers usually sustain this view: for example, see R. C. C. Law, "North Africa in the Period of Phoenician and Greek Colonization, *c.* 800 to 323 BC," *CHA* 2, 1978, 121–2; Warmington (supra n. 29), p. 60.

speculations on the abilities of contemporary seamen,[74] the lack of physical evidence from West Africa,[75] and the rather weak suggestion that certain passages are formulaic,[76] something easily explained by the convoluted history of the text. Yet arguments based on the limitations of ancient seamanship are dangerous and often eventually turn out to be fallacious: the astonishing voyages of both the Vikings and Polynesians were dismissed until archaeological and other cultural evidence demonstrated their existence. There is no doubt that, for Hanno, the winds would have been especially adverse on the return[77] – as late as the eighteenth century it was easiest to travel from tropical west Africa back to Europe via the northern South American coast – but it is somewhat convoluted to argue that a journey could not have taken place because of sailing conditions that would not have been encountered until long after the voyage was underway. Moreover, it was possible for ancient sailors to tack, although inefficiently – no closer than seven points to the wind.[78] Nevertheless, it remains obvious that a seaman far from home would have used any possible means to return, however arduous.

The early date of the Greek translation rules out a Hellenistic or Roman forgery, the era in which fabricated tales of fantastic voyages to mythical places flourished. The text serves no purpose except to recount a voyage, and does so rather dryly. Its very obscurity and matter-of-fact tone argue against a literary creation of late times.[79] This is not to dismiss the complexities of understanding the text, which is preserved in a ninth-century manuscript far removed from the actual voyage nearly a millennium and a half earlier.[80] How the Greek text relates to its Punic original is unclear: there was Hanno's report, which presumably was filed in the Carthaginian state library, as well as another

---

74 The foremost proponent of the falsity of Hanno's account is Raymond Mauny, put forth in his "La navigation sur les côtes du Sahara pendant l'antiquité," *RÉA* 57, 1955, 92–101 and repeated in numerous other articles over the following 25 years (see bibliography); see also his "Trans-Saharan Contacts and the Iron Age in West Africa," *CHA* 2, 1978, 297–9, which includes some literary objections to the text. See also P. Salama, "The Sahara in Classical Antiquity," *General History of Africa* 2, ed. G. Mokhtar, Paris 1981, pp. 513–19; Raoul Lonis, "Les conditions de la navigation sur la côte atlantique de l'Afrique dans l'antiquité: le problème du 'retour'," in *Afrique noire et monde méditerranéen dans l'antiquité*, Dakar 1978, pp. 147–162; and Germain (supra n. 72), who seems to have little feeling for the existing text as translated summary (p. 229). Solid refutations of Mauny's thesis are provided by Michael F. Doran, "The Maritime Provenience of Iron Technology in West Africa," *TI* 9, 1977, 97–8 and Gilbert-Charles Picard, "Le Périple d'Hannon n'est pas un faux," *Archeologia* (Paris) 40, May_June 1971, 54–9. Arguments for and against the voyage are discussed by Serge Lancel, *Carthage: A History*, tr. Antonia Nevill, London: Blackwell, 1995, pp. 106–9.

75 For a summary of the few and questionable archaeological finds, see Raymond Mauny, "Les contacts terrestres entre Méditerranée et Afrique tropicale occidentale pendant l'antiquité," in *Afrique noire et monde méditerranéen dans l'antiquité*, Dakar 1978, pp. 131–2, but this negative evidence should not be overvalued.

76 N. H. H. Sitwell, *The World the Romans Knew*, London: Hamish Hamilton, 1984, pp. 61–3.

77 See the map in Mauny (*RÉA*, supra n. 74), p. 95.

78 Casson (supra n. 27), pp. 273–4, citing numerous ancient sources. Tacking is first discussed in extant ancient literature in the Aristotelian *Mechanika* (7 [851b]).

79 Blomqvist (supra n. 62), pp. 10–13.

80 Infra, p. 129.

Punic version deposited – or set up on an inscription – in the Carthaginian Temple of "Kronos,"[81] probably a summary of the report in the library. This public inscription may have been translated into Greek within a couple of generations of its placement. The report itself was probably not known to the Greek world until the fall of Carthage in 146BC and the dispersal of its library, which was in part translated (into Latin) and then given to the Numidian kings.[82] A century later, with the end of the Numidian kingdom, it was removed to Rome by C. Sallustius Crispus when he was governor of Africa, and used by him in his historical researches.[83] Juba II may have been the first to consider Hanno's actual report, in creating his published commentary as well as portions of his later treatise, *Libyka*.[84] Thus there were at least two distinct versions of Hanno's material, the inscription in Carthage – in all probability the source of the extant Greek text – and Juba's commentary, used by (at least) Pomponius Mela, Pliny, and Arrian, all of whom supplied information about Hanno not in the extant text.[85] This may also explain why Hanno seems so little known in the Hellenistic period, before Juba published. And Pliny's phrase: "fuere … Hannonis … commentarii," even hints at a third version, since both the existing Greek text and Juba's commentary were extant in his day.

In addition to these issues of the transmission of the text, interpretation is made difficult by its fragmentary form. There appear to be three gaps.[86] The first is near the beginning, where the account of preparation for the voyage jumps to the expedition passing the Pillars of Herakles, yet with no description of the voyage from Carthage to that point – arguably not relevant to the report and perhaps omitted by the Greek translator– no mention of Gades, and a shift from the third person to first, from Hanno's orders to the narrative itself. The second gap seems to be after leaving the territory of the Lixitai where there is at least one toponym missing: Hanno sailed from the Lixitai for two days and then sailed on "from there" (ἐκεῖθεν). And the final sentence of the text, about returning home because of the lack of provisions, is abruptly tacked on to the end of the narrative, almost giving the impression that the Greek translator grew tired of his work. Different texts were known in Roman times. According to Pliny, the expedition visited Gades and was supposed to circumnavigate the continent. Arrian reported that one segment of the journey, the eastward part, lasted 35 days, longer than the 31½ days of the entire existing text. Pomponius Mela

---

81 The use of καὶ ἀνέθηκεν implies that the Greek was derived from an inscription, although setting up a public inscription about a voyage contrasts with the secretiveness usual for such reports (Carpenter, *Beyond*, p. 82). The epigraphic origin of the text may be alluded to by Aristeides (48 [356 Dindorf]). On the Punic original, see Stansilav Segert, "Phoenician Background of Hanno's Periplus," *MélBeyrouth* 45, 1969, 501–18.

82 Pliny, *Natural History* 18.22–3.

83 Sallust, *Jugurtha* 17–19.

84 Roller, *Juba*, p. 189.

85 Pomponius Mela 3.90–5; Pliny, *Natural History* 1.5, 2.169, 5.8; 6.200–1; Arrian, *Indika* 43.11–12. Martianus Capella's juxtaposition of Mauretania, Hanno, and the circuit of Africa (7.621) may also indicate reliance on Juba.

86 On these gaps, see René Rebuffat, "Recherches sur le Bassin du Sebou II: Le Périple d'Hannon," *BAMaroc* 16, 1985–6, pp. 259–60.

remarked that Hanno described the countryside as devoid of human activity ("commeatu deficisse"), a sharp contrast to the conditions of the text.

According to the extant report, the expedition set forth with 60 pentekonters and 30,000 people.[87] The first place reached after the Pillars was Thymiaterion,[88] where the first city was founded. The name is only known elsewhere (as Thymiateria) in the Pseudo-Skylax *Periplous* and the *Ethnika* of Stephanos of Byzantion.[89] Its location cannot easily be determined. Hanno reported that it was two days beyond the Pillars, but at the same time implied that the Pillars were at the edge of the External Sea, which is not the case. The first lacuna in the text is at the beginning of this sentence, so the sense may not be clear. Pliny's statement that Hanno sailed from Gades[90] may resolve some of this confusion, but not with certainty.

It is impossible to determine where two days' sailing from the Pillars would lead, especially for this large cumbersome expedition near the beginning of its journey: the adverse currents through the Straits of Gibraltar may have meant slow going. Suggestions for Thymiaterion have ranged from Tingis[91] (modern Tangier) to any one of a number of points on the Atlantic coast as far south as the mouth of the Oued Sebou (ancient Sububus) near modern Kenitra.[92] Tingis fits the description well, but it had long existed in Hanno's day,[93] whereas Thymiaterion was said to have been founded by the expedition. The advantage of the Oued Sebou location is the later existence in the region of a similar toponym, Tamousiga or Tamousida,[94] but whose remains, at modern Sidi Ali ben Ahmed, seem no earlier than the second century BC.[95] Yet to place Thymiaterion in this area requires a substantial reworking of the extant text, because it is cited before the territory of the Lixitai, which, it seems, could only be in the area of Lixos, north of the Oued Sebou. Moreover, the next toponym after Thymiaterion is Soloeis, which is often identified with modern Cape Spartel at the northwest corner of Africa. Thus it seems that Thymiaterion could be Tingis, the first settlement after the Pillars. The only alternative is to restructure the text and place the

---

87 On these improbable numbers, see Demerliac and Meirat (supra n. 58), pp. 64–7; Gloria Vivenza, "Altri considerazioni sul *Periplo* di Annone," in *Economia e storia* 2. ser. 1.1, 1980, 101–10. Hanno's fleet is discussed by René Rebuffat, "Le pentécontores d'Hannon," *Karthago* 23, 1995, 20–30, and his seamanship by Carlo De Negri, "Considerazioni nautiche sul 'Periplo' di Annone," *MSE* 3, 1978, 35–65.

88 Unlike many of the toponyms in Hanno's text, this is a purely Greek word ("censer," Herodotos 4.162) and so may be descriptive, or the use of a Greek word for a similar-sounding foreign toponym.

89 Pseudo-Skylax 112; Stephanos of Byzantion, "Thymiateria."

90 Pliny, *Natural History* 2.169.

91 See, for example, Enrique Gozalbes Cravioto, "Algunas observaciones acerca del Periplo de Hannon," *HispAnt* 17, 1993, 7–20; Lancel (supra n. 74), pp. 102–3.

92 The views were summarized by Ramin (supra n. 58), pp. 78–9. See also (for the Oued Sebou) Demerliac and Meirat (supra n. 27), pp. 68–74. In the Pseudo-Skylax *Periplous* (112), Thymiaterion is far down the coast, after Lixos.

93 Tingis was mentioned by Hekataios (*FGrHist* #1, fr. 354), probably earlier than Hanno. The site seems to have remains from the eighth century BC: see Michel Ponsich, "Tangier antique," *ANRW* 2.10.2, 1982, 798–800.

94 Ptolemy, *Geography* 4.1.4, 13.

95 M. Euzannat, "Thamusida," *PECS*, 902.

site later, after Soloeis, or to assume that Soloeis and the Lixitae territory, the two best-known names in the *periplous*, are not at the places that have regularly been associated with those names from the fourth century BC to modern times.[96]

If Thymiaterion is Tingis, one can speculate why Hanno said that the city was founded by the expedition when Tingis clearly was not. Foundations are often renamings or rebuildings, or additions to existing populations, not totally new cities. It may be that Hanno wanted to give the expedition a dramatic start by an early "foundation" – ἐκτίσαμεν,[97] the word used in his instructions – or that it represented a formal claiming by Carthage of a site that had been established in Phoenician days, or the conversion of a small trading post into a proper city.

The next toponym is Soloeis. It was a heavily wooded promontory west of Thymiaterion, which the expedition rounded. This seems to conform to the wooded bluffs of the extreme northwest corner of Africa, modern Cape Spartel, where the coast turns sharply from almost due west to slightly west of south (Figure 9). At this point the expedition dedicated a shrine to "Poseidon." Then it sailed east for half a day. Yet one cannot turn east of south after entering the Atlantic until just north of Safi, nearly 300 miles beyond the Pillars of Herakles, at modern Cape Beddouza, which is another possibility for Hanno's Soloeis.[98] The fact that yet another toponym can easily be located in two widely separated places is, unfortunately, typical, and indicative of the almost insurmountable problems in detailed topographic interpretation of the text.[99]

After Soloeis, the expedition sailed easterly to a lake, notable for its reeds and elephants,[100] and then established a number of towns. Unlike Thymiaterion, where the word ἐκτίσαμεν was used, these cities were described by κατῳκήσαμεν, which refers more to a settlement rather than a city foundation:[101] the impression is of small outposts, perhaps to investigate the commercial potential of a specific area. The next point reached was the large Lixos river, the first major stream cited, in the territory of

---

96 Demerliac and Meirat (supra n. 58), pp. 74–9, 87–90.

97 This word is normally used of city foundations: see Herodotos 1.167, etc.

98 Ramin (supra n. 27), pp. 80–1.

99 The extensive bibliography on Hanno's toponyms begins with Gsell (supra n. 73), vol. 1, pp. 479–519. Others include W. Aly, "Die Entdeckung des Westens," *Hermes* 62, 1927, 317–30; Marcy (supra n. 72), pp. 21–72; Thomson, pp. 73–6; Cary and Warmington, pp. 63–8; Ramin (supra n. 27), pp. 77–92; Desanges, *Recherches* pp. 39–85; Gilbert-Charles Picard, "Le périple de Hannon," in *Phönizer im Westen*, ed. Hans Georg Niemeyer, *Madrider Beiträger* 8, 1982, 177–80. Still others are more specific to individual toponyms and are cited in the bibliographies to the works above or in the text. It is of little profit to repeat all the arguments and controversies, and of little relevance to understanding Hanno, since most of the toponyms occur on the earlier – and perhaps less interesting – part of the voyage, off modern Morocco. Nevertheless, all topographical reconstructions remain hypothetical.

100 This may be one of the earliest citations of elephants in Greek, if the Greek translation is in fact from the fifth century BC. Only Herodotos (3.97 etc.) may be earlier. It certainly is the first documentation of them in northwest Africa. They were known to have roamed wild in the High Atlas from early times (Juba, fr. 50 = Philostratos, *Life of Apollonios* 2.13).

101 For example, Herodotos 1.96 (settling the Medes in villages) or 2.102 (those settled on the Erythraian Sea).

Figure 9 Cape Spartel, the northwest corner of Africa. View north.
Photograph by Duane W. Roller.

the pastoral Lixitai, where the expedition stayed for a while, becoming friends, and eventually taking some Lixitai on board as interpreters. A number of exploratory journeys may have been made from here.[102] Lixos and the Lixitai should be one of the easier topographical points in Hanno's narrative, since the name has survived (as Leukos) into modern times as the major river of northwest Morocco. High above the mouth of the Leukos river is the Hellenistic and Roman site of Lixos, the most impor- tant city in the region (Figure 6).[103] But the topographical difficulties of equating this with Hanno's site are, once again, immense. The historic city of Lixos is less than 50 miles down the Atlantic coast from the mouth of the Straits of Gibraltar, and the context of the narrative presumes a point much farther south, and only after the coast has turned easterly. Yet the existence of interpreters at Lixos, who, by necessity, spoke Punic, implies a location not far down the coast.[104] Once again there seems to be an impossible confusion of toponyms.[105]

---

102 John W. Taylor, "A Nigerian Tin Trade in Antiquity," *OJA* 1, 1982, 319.

103 On the site of Lixos, see Michel Gras, "Le mémoire de Lixus," in *Lixus*, *CÉFR* 166, 1992, 27–44; on the literary evidence, Jehan Desanges, "Lixos dans les sources littéraires grecques et latines," *Lixus*, *CÉFR* 166, 1992, 1–6.

104 On the role of the interpreters with regard to the toponyms, see René Rebuffat, "Les nomades de Lixus," *BAC* 18b, 1988, 78–80.

105 Toponyms do move, and a term applied to a region can localize when settlement has taken place, or a local term may be applied to an entire region.

Beyond Lixos it was desert, and the coast began to turn toward the east. The expedition found a small island where they stopped for an extended period of time, naming it Kerne.[106] Again the location is uncertain, because in addition to the usual problems, there is a gap in the text between the Lixos and Kerne. Hanno's calculations placed Kerne at the same distance from the Pillars of Herakles as was Carthage, but given the meanderings of the coast it is difficult for a modern critic to use this statement to determine the location of Kerne. The straight-line distance from Carthage to the Pillars, about 800 miles, brings one to the desolate coast of the Western Sahara, where, to be sure, there is today a toponym of "Herne" and a bay, the estuary of the Río de Oro, at modern Dakhla (formerly Villa Cisneros), much as Hanno described.[107] Over 200 miles to the south is the Bay of Arguin with the island of Arguin in it, another possible location.[108] One argument in its favor is that, unlike Herne, Arguin island is visible to a sailor coming from the north, whereas Herne lies nearly 35 miles up its bay. Arguin was more suitable for settlement and had a fishing establishment and fort in early modern times,[109] but Herne seems to have been mostly uninhabited since the prehistoric period, except for occasional fishermen's camps.[110] Arguin island, despite the toponym Herne, seems the better choice.[111] Others have argued for an island in the Senegal delta,[112] or as far north as Essaouira or Mogador on the Moroccan coast (Figure 8), which had a similar topography in antiquity and was a location of early Carthaginian settlement,[113] or even on the lower Oued Sebou.[114] Wherever Kerne was, it was significant enough to be known to the author of the Pseudo-Skylax *Periplous* in the fourth century BC,[115] so it remained an important Carthaginian outpost for some time.

106 Ramin (supra n. 27), pp. 85–92. This may be a Phoenician descriptive word: see Segert (supra n. 81), p. 517.

107 Raymond Mauny, "Cerné l'île de Herné (Río del Oro) et la question des navigations antiques sur la côte ouest-africaine," in *Conferencia internacional de africanistas occidentales* 2, Madrid 1954, pp. 73–80. But the toponym may be a recent name with no continuity with antiquity (Lancel [supra n. 74], p. 107). A detailed discussion of the site, with many plans and photographs, is by Théodore Monod, "À propos de l'île Herné (baie de Dakhla, Sahara occidental)," *BIFAN* 41b, 1979, 1–34.

108 Ramin (supra n. 27), p. 90.

109 *Africa Pilot*, eleventh edition, London: Hydrographic Office, 1953, vol. 1, p. 222.

110 Archaeological investigations on Herne have revealed nothing that would identify it as Kerne, but this negative evidence is by no means definitive. See J. M. J. Gran Aymerich, "Prospections archéologiques au Sahara atlantique (Rio de Oro et Sequiet et Hamra)," *AntAfr* 13, 1979, 7–21.

111 See the map, Demerliac and Meirat (supra n. 58), p. 97; Jacques Ramin, "Ultima Cerne," in *Littérature gréco-romaine et géographie historique, Mélanges offerts à Roger Dion, Caesarodunum* 9bis, 1974, 439–49.

112 D. B. Harden, "The Phoenicians on the West Coast of Africa," *Antiquity* 22, 1948, 143–5.

113 On Mogador as the location of Kerne, see M. Euzennat, "Le Périple d'Hannon," *CRAI* 1994, 559–79; see also Cary and Warmington, pp. 64–6.

114 René Rebuffat, "Voyage du Carthaginois Hannon, du Lixos à Cerné," *BAC* 18b, 1982 (1988), 198–201, and Rebuffat (supra n. 86), pp. 257–70, where much of the expedition is placed along the Sebou.

115 Pseudo-Skylax 112. Ephoros, writing no later than the 330s BC, may also have mentioned the site (fr. 172 = Pliny, *Natural History* 6.198).

After Kerne the description becomes more interesting, as the expedition reached remote and mysterious country. In fact, the character of the voyage has changed.[116] No more cities or settlements were established. The local inhabitants became hostile almost everywhere, and the Lixitai interpreters were only occasionally useful.[117] Fires and strange noises were seen and heard on the shore at night, perhaps not unusual but unnerving nonetheless.[118] There is an emphasis on the strange flora and fauna: sweet-smelling trees, crocodiles, and hippopotami. Great rivers were numerous. Active volcanic phenomena came to be frequently observed: fire flowing into the ocean, odoriferous air, and beaches too hot to walk on. It is not difficult to assume that the expedition has passed the desert and entered the tropics with its great rivers, beginning with the Senegal, eventually reaching the volcanic region of Cameroon and the Bight of Biafra. Only four toponyms and one ethnym are cited beyond Kerne, although most of the expedition – 26 of the 31½ days recorded in the text – was after this point. This is strong proof of the validity of the journey, because explorers in remote areas without useful interpreters would have little access to toponyms, whereas a fictional author could not resist the tendency to make them up.

The first of the four toponyms is a large river, the Chretes or Chremetes,[119] followed almost immediately by another river with crocodiles and hippopotami. One of these may be the Senegal,[120] the farthest point reached by Euthymenes, perhaps a few years earlier.[121] Two of the toponyms are Horns (κέρας), the first of the West, the second of the South. Both are described as bays, a standing topographic meaning for the word since early times.[122] The two horns are described similarly: a bay with an island in it that itself had a lake on it, with another island in the lake. The wording is slightly different, however, in the two places, yet the possibility of duplication is high, at least

116 This sudden change in the nature of the text has led to the suggestion that it may be an amalgamation of two or more reports, which is possible but perhaps unnecessary: see M. Euzennat, "Pour une lecture marocaine du Périple d'Hannon," *BAC* 12–14b, 1976–8 (1980), 243–6.

117 This may mean that the expedition has passed the Senegal, a traditional language frontier: see Ramin (supra n. 27), p. 69, and the maps in Francis Lacroix, "Les langues," in *Histoire générale de l'Afrique noire* 1, ed. Hubert Deschamps, Paris 1970, pp. 76–7. At the very least it is proof of venturing far south. On the varying usefulness of the interpreters, see Jehan Desanges, "Des interprètes chez les 'Gorilles': Réflexions sur un artifice dans le 'Périple d'Hannon'," in *Atti del i Congresso Internazionale di Studi Fenice e Punici* 1, Rome 1983, pp. 267–70.

118 Fires were commonly encountered by explorers to West Africa, from Hanno to Suetonius Paulinus (in the 40s AC: Pliny, *Natural History* 5.7) and Mungo Park in 1795–9 (Mungo Park, *Travels in the Interior Districts of Africa*, ed. Kate Ferguson Masters, Durham: Duke University Press, 2000, p. 238).

119 The exact form is uncertain: see Gsell (supra n. 73), vol. 1, p. 489.

120 Cary and Warmington, p. 66.

121 The dates of Euthymenes and Hanno are so close that it is impossible to tell who was responding to whom, or if either knew about the other. Euthymenes seems slightly earlier, but such precision is highly speculative. But see Desanges, *Recherches*, pp. 49–50.

122 Hesiod, *Theogony* 789; Jehan Desanges, "Le sens du term 'Corne' dans le vocabulaire géographique des grecques et des romains: À propos du 'Périple d'Hannon'," *BAC* 20–21b, 1984–5 (1989), 29–34.

Figure 10 Carthage Harbor. The "kothon." The interior island is on the right.
Photograph by Duane W. Roller.

in detail.[123] The word κέρας can also mean the spur of a mountain,[124] which suggests that a prominent peninsula marked the location of a sheltered bay. An example of such terrain is the Bay of Gorée, just below Cap Vert, the westernmost point of Africa, where modern Dakar is located – the largest seaport between Casablanca and Lagos, which owes its location to the fine qualities of its topography. In the bay, today considered the safest anchorage on the west coast of Africa,[125] is the volcanic Île de Gorée, perhaps the island mentioned by Hanno. This is the most suitable place for his Horn of the West.[126]

Eventually Hanno reached the Bight of Biafra, where the African coast turns south.[127] There are numerous offshore islands here that lie in a line running from

123 Such topography, however, may have been of special interest to the Carthaginians. Sheltered islands were most suitable for settlement, and the strange repetition of an island with a lake on it and another island in the lake is remindful of the unique Carthaginian style of harbor, the *kothon* (Figure 10), so named for its resemblance to a type of Greek pottery, and constructed not only at Carthage but at a number of outposts (Strabo 17.3.5; Jerker Blomqvist, "Reflections of Carthaginian Commercial Activity in *Hanno's Periplus*," OrSue 33–34, 1984–6, 56–7).

124 Xenophon, *Anabasis* 5.6.7; see also *LSJ*.

125 *Africa Pilot* (supra n. 109), vol. 1, p. 234.

126 There is some merit to the suggestion that these repeated patterns of islands and lakes refer to the lagoons along the Ivory Coast (Carpenter, *Beyond*, p. 99). The Horn of the West has also been placed as far as the Niger delta (Demerliac and Meirat [supra n. 58], pp. 133–5).

127 See the maps, Demerliac and Meirat (supra n. 58), pp. 137, 144.

Figure 11 Mt Cameroon, the Chariot of the Gods.

Photograph by Susan Weinger.

Fernando Poó (Bioka), the largest and nearest the coast, to Annobon, 400 miles to the southwest. These islands align with Mt Cameroon (Fako) on the mainland – at 4100m, the highest point on the West African coast. All these features are part of a volcanic chain. There is little doubt that Mt Cameroon, the only active volcano on the African coast, which can be seen from over a hundred miles away, is Hanno's next toponym, the Chariot (or Support) of the Gods (θεῶν ὄχημα),[128] described as a huge mountain that spewed forth fire at night (Figure 11).[129] Three days beyond the volcano, Hanno reached his last toponym, the Horn of the South. It is most likely Cape Lopez, the southern edge of the Bight of Biafra and the westernmost point on

128 The basic meaning of ὄχημα is "support" (Euripides, *Troades* 884), but it is more commonly used to mean a chariot or even an animal being ridden (*LSJ*). Except for the repetitions noted below, there is no other evidence of ὄχημα being used topographically, but this is a toponym far beyond the Greco-Roman world, and one which, moreover, comes from the local language of the region as translated first into Punic and then Greek. Pliny cited it twice, one (*Natural History* 5.10) in the context of Polybios' African expeditions, and the other (2.238) as the largest volcano in Ethiopia, used here in its generic meaning of sub-Saharan Africa. The toponym is also cited by Ptolemy (*Geography* 4.6.9, 16). See also Hennig, vol. 1, pp. 93–5; P. Schmitt, "À la recherche du Char des Dieux," in *Littérature gréco-romaine et géographie historique, Mélanges offerts à Roger Dion, Caesarodunum* 9bis, 1974, 473–9. The first to connect Mt Cameroon with Hanno seems to have been the explorer Richard Burton (1821–90), who climbed the mountain in 1862. See his *Abeokuta and the Camaroons Mountains: An Exploration*, London: Tinsley Brothers, 1863, vol. 2, pp. 27–30.
129 The description is somewhat reminiscent of Herodotos 4.184, on Mt Atlas. A local name for Mt Cameroon is Mongo ma Loba, or Mountain of Heaven (Harden [supra n. 112], p. 146). The Lixitai interpreters were still occasionally useful, so Hanno may have learned the local name.

the southern African coast. Here the expedition had an unfortunate encounter with the wild group called the Gorillai, who had hairy bodies.[130] Three females were caught and their skins brought back to Carthage.[131] But then the expedition, rather suddenly, turned back. Allegedly it was because of the shortage of provisions, but the increasingly hostile locals, the volcanic phenomena, the lessening reliability of the interpreters, and a general fear of being far from home would all have played a role. Moreover, they were at the point where the African coast, after running east–west for over a thousand miles, had turned sharply south, and it would no longer have been possible to argue that they were two-thirds of the way around a triangular continent: if the Carthaginians believed, as did the Greeks, that Africa was long and narrow, with its major extent east–west, any hint that the coast ran far south from the Horn of the South would have been defeating.[132] Yet there may have been more to the expedition, as the last sentence of the extant text – about not sailing farther for lack of provisions – is abrupt and seems tacked on to the end of the existing narrative. Arrian knew of a longer journey and Pliny believed that Hanno had been commissioned to encircle the continent. But the return would have been difficult, because of the opposing trade winds – this is the most common reason advanced by modern scholars for the impossibility of the voyage – and it is often suggested that Hanno would have had to stand far out to sea, perhaps even encountering the Cape Verdes or Canaries.[133]

Nevertheless Hanno went far, and there seems little doubt that he penetrated deep into the West African tropics, going beyond Euthymenes, who only touched them at the Senegal River. Although the actual purpose of the expedition remains uncertain,[134] the report states that it was to found cities. This, however, cannot have been the sole reason, and most of the foundations were in the first few days.[135] Like Himilco's explorations, the search for metals may have played a role.[136] Precious metals have long been

---

130 The name appears as a Greek toponym, Gorgades, home of the Gorgons, in the *Natural History* (6.200) of Pliny. This may reflect the linguistic interest of Juba II, who wrote on the Greek derivation of the Latin language (see Roller, *Juba*, pp. 170–3) and may have applied the same technique to Punic. Nevertheless the term "Gorillai" was the origin of the modern name of the ape, although whether this is what Hanno saw is debatable. In 1847 Thomas S. Savage (1804–80), a Protestant Episcopal missionary, used Hanno's text to name a large ape that he found on the Gabon river, well south of any point that Hanno seems to have reached. See Thomas S. Savage, "Notice of the External Characters and Habits of *Troglodytes gorilla*, a New Species of Orang From the Gabon River," *Boston Journal of Natural History* 5, 1847, 417–26.

131 Although the Gorillai are presented in the *periplous* as human, the Carthaginians had a particular interest in apes (Blomqvist [supra n. 123], pp. 59–60), which even became a subject of Greek and Roman comedy by the third century BC (Plautus, *Poenulus* 1072–5, from a Greek play of unknown authorship titled the *Karchedonios* [line 53]).

132 This is reinforced by Arrian (*Indika* 43.11–12), who reported that Hanno's difficulties began when he turned south, after sailing east 35 days.

133 Demerliac and Meirat (supra n. 58), pp. 153–83. On early Mediterranean knowledge of the Cape Verdes and Canaries, see infra, pp 47–9.

134 On this, see Ramin (supra n. 27), pp. 93–7.

135 The inordinate number of trade items mentioned in the brief report is indicative of a commercial purpose (Blomqvist [supra n. 123], pp. 57–60).

136 Warmington (supra n. 29), pp. 69–70.

a common product of West Africa, with tin coming from Nigeria. Although there is no certain evidence of ancient exploitation of this tin,[137] anecdotal information about its existence might have come to the Mediterranean, thus explaining the parallel and contemporary voyages of Hanno and Himilco as having the same goal, a search for tin.[138]

Regardless of the purpose of the journey, Kerne became the major Carthaginian trading post in West Africa and to some extent replaced the Pillars of Herakles as the end of the inhabited earth.[139] Somewhat over a century after Hanno, the author of the Pseudo-Skylax *Periplous*[140] visited the outpost – or received an account from someone who had – and reported on a flourishing trade with the locals, although the need at that time to pitch tents when the traders arrived at Kerne may indicate that the permanent post did not last. Animal products such as skins and ivory, as well as local wine and perhaps gold,[141] were traded by the locals for precious goods such as aromatics. Even Attic pottery was imported, and this may have been the means by which iron technology came to West Africa, an unexpected by-product of Hanno's voyage.[142] The post remained viable until at least the fall of Carthage – Polybios may have visited it at that time[143] – and "Kerne" continued as an important West African toponym well into the Roman period, even if its location was confused and it became a formula for remoteness.[144]

Yet the effect of Hanno's voyage on Greco-Roman knowledge of the Atlantic was minimal. Carthaginian secretiveness and the failure of the full text to be translated

137 R. D. Penhallurick, *Tin in Antiquity*, London: Institute of Metals, 1986, pp. 10–12.

138 Except for Mogador, which was occupied from the seventh century BC, and has been suggested to be a possible location of Kerne, physical evidence of an early Carthaginian presence on the further coast of West Africa is uncertain. Carthaginian pottery has been discovered at Cap Rhir (where the Atlas reaches the ocean), but only from the latter third century BC. A single piece of contemporary Iberian pottery was also found. This implies an outpost, but no direct association with the time of Hanno. See René Rebuffat, "Vestiges antiques sur la côte occidentale de l'Afrique au sud de Rabat," *AntAfr* 8, 1984, 39–40.

139 Gabriella Amiotti, "Cerne, 'ultima terra'," in *Il confine nel mondo classico*, ed. Marta Sordi, *CISA* 13, Milan 1987, pp. 43–9.

140 Pseudo-Skylax 112.

141 Herodotos 4.196 and Palaiphatos, *On Unbelievable Tales* 31, may allude to this. But see Lucan 9.424–5, about the resources of Africa: "non aere neque auro excoquitur." Whether gold was a trade product has long been disputed: see R. C. C. Law, "The Garamantes and Trans-Saharan Enterprise in Classical Times," *JAH* 8, 1967, 188–9, which supports the idea of a gold trade, but see also the more detailed refutation by Timothy F. Garrard, "Myth and Metrology: The Early Trans-Saharan Gold Trade," *JAH* 23, 1982, 443–61, who has made a strong case that the gold trade from West Africa to the Mediterranean did not exist until the late third century AC.

142 Iron-smelting appeared in the Nok culture of West Africa around 500 BC (Doran [supra n. 74], pp. 89–98). Excavations at the site of Taruga produced evidence for smelting with an earliest radio-carbon date of 440 ± 140 BC, which is thought to have been introduced rather than indigenous. The Nok people may have supplied tin to the Carthaginians, although the evidence is far from certain (Taylor [supra n. 102], pp. 321–2).

143 Pliny, *Natural History* 6.199.

144 Ptolemy, *Geography* 4.6.33; Amiotti (supra n. 139), pp. 43–9.

into Greek at an early date meant that many details of the voyage emerged only hundreds of years later, although the report of Hanno remained the most detailed account of the West African coastline until the Portuguese explorations of early modern times. The Massalians had some hints of the extensive Carthaginian explorations, but their own secret ways meant that even their voyages – those of Euthymenes and Pytheas – were little known to others. When Carthage fell, Scipio Aemilianus and his cultural advisor, Polybios, were astonished to learn of the extent of Carthaginian exploration, and Polybios himself was sent down the West African coast to investigate.[145] Yet the data obtained at Carthage, Massalia, and on the African coast, was itself contradictory and obscure, and thus did not enter mainstream Hellenistic geographical scholarship. In fact, it was easily dismissed, starting with Strabo,[146] if not earlier, a skepticism that has lasted into modern times and which unfortunately has diminished the achievement of the Carthaginian expedition under Hanno.

145 Infra, pp. 99–104.
146 Strabo 1.3.2.

3

THE ATLANTIC
ISLANDS AND BEYOND

Since the earliest days of Greek culture, there have been tales about islands beyond the Pillars of Herakles that had a special, magical quality. Such mythical places had long been associated with the far west. The earliest reference in Greek literature is Homer's description of the Elysian Fields, where Menelaos was fated to end his days, a place at the limits of the earth where the Ocean always provides fair breezes and there is no winter.[1] According to Hesiod, the home of heroes was on the shores of the Ocean, a fertile paradise called the Islands of the Blessed, or Islands of the Dead (μακάρων νῆσοι).[2] Pindar cited specific heroes who lived there, such as Kadmos, Peleus, and Achilles.[3] Others residing in this mythical world included the Hesperides, the daughters of the Night.[4] As the guardians of the golden apples that were the key to divine immortality,[5] they too were associated with a world beyond death. Place and aspect were thus intertwined: the world beyond death was the world beyond the Pillars of Herakles, and, eventually, beyond the Ocean. Localization is futile, in part because the concept is largely dependent on pre-Greek myths.[6] There are even hints that the Blessed Islands were originally within the Mediterranean.[7] Yet as knowledge moved west, so did the islands, and even as late as the first century BC they remained a powerful cultural force, somewhere out in the Atlantic, the refuge from the troublesome world of the collapse of the Roman Republic. They continued as a significant part of cultural geography after antiquity.[8]

1 Homer, *Odyssey* 4.561–9; see also 15.403–14.
2 Hesiod, *Works and Days* 166–73.
3 Pindar, *Olympian* 2.68–80.
4 Hesiod, *Theogony* 274–5, 517–18; Euripides, *Hippolytos* 742–51.
5 Hesiod, *Theogony* 215–16.
6 It may be Egyptian or even Sumerian, perhaps connected with the setting sun: see Paul T. Keyser, "From Myth to Map: The Blessed Isles in the First Century BC," *AncW* 24, 1993, 149.
7 Cretan connections occur in many of the early citations; see also Pliny, *Natural History* 4.58. Homer's Ogygia has a looseness of place, both in and beyond the Mediterranean, and even Plato's Atlantis fits into this context. See also Diodoros 5.82; Strabo 3.2.11, and Dimitri Nakassis, "Gemination at the Horizons: East and West in the Mythical Geography of Archaic Greek Epic," *TAPA* 134, 2004, 215–31.
8 Vincent H. Cassidy, "Other Fortunate Islands and Some That Were Lost," *TI* 1, 1969, 35–9; Keyser (supra n. 6), pp. 162–7. On islands as a cultural paradigm, see Emilio Gabba, "True History and False History in Classical Antiquity," *JRS* 71, 1981, 55–60. Ancient literary references to the islands have been collected by Valerio Manfredi, *Le Isole Fortunate: Topografia di un mito*, Rome: "L'Erma" di Bretschneider, 1996.

However meaningless it may be to locate the Blessed Islands, efforts to discover them or presumptions that they had been found became increasingly common as Greeks explored the Atlantic and perhaps heard rumors both of the riches of the west and the Carthaginian discoveries beyond the Pillars. The tales of the Kassiterides, possible contacts with the British Isles, and awareness of numerous small islands off the northwest coast of France all contributed to a feeling that discovery of the Blessed Islands was imminent, or already had been made. Any island in the Ocean became, for a time, a candidate for the Blessed Islands.

Within the Atlantic there are four groups that might have served as their possible location.[9] From north to south, these are the Azores, Madeira, the Canaries, and the Cape Verdes. Some were certainly known from early times; others may not have been reached in classical antiquity. The Azores (Açores) lie 830 miles west of Cape Roca on the Portuguese coast. They are an archipelago stretching northwest for 400 miles, virtually in the middle of the Atlantic, almost equidistant from Europe, Africa, and North America. There are ten major islands and a number of smaller ones, all volcanic in origin. The largest is São Miguel, 80km across, and the highest point in the group is the summit of Pico at an elevation of 2150m. The name is Portuguese, from *açor*, "hawk," a conspicuous feature of the islands. To the southeast 480 miles lie the Madeira group, 360 miles from the African coast at Mogador and 425 miles from the southwest corner of Spain beyond Gades. They are also volcanic, consisting of several rocks and two main islands, Madeira itself and, about 30 miles to the northeast, Porto Santo; Madeira is 50km across and reaches a height of 1800m. The name seems to come from the madera tree, or, more generically, may mean "wooded." Further to the southeast are the islets known as the Salvages, of which the largest is Great Piton, 160 miles from Madeira and 8km^2 in size, considered part of the Madeiras. Another hundred miles beyond are the Canaries, or Canarias, the only Atlantic group to preserve an ancient name,[10] visible 60 miles off the African coast. They are an archipelago extending over 250 miles with seven major islands. Tenerife, an active volcano, rises to 3600m. The final group is the Cape Verdes (Ilhas do Capo Verde), lying off the west coast of Africa 300 miles west of their eponymous cape. These are ten islands extending over 200 miles, divided into two clusters about 50 miles apart, with the highest point, at 2700m, on Fogo. They too are volcanic and, like all the groups except the Spanish Canaries, have been Portuguese since the fifteenth century. All these are possible locales for the Islands of the Blessed, although it must again be emphasized that mythical places may be constantly sought but need not ever be found.

By about 300BC Greeks became aware of a Carthaginian story of exploration to a large island several days off the coast of Africa.[11] It was noted for its fertility, navigable rivers, and thick wooded mountains. The Phoenicians had originally

---

9 Discussion of ancient knowledge of Iceland is reserved for infra, pp. 78–87.

10 Pliny, *Natural History* 6.205.

11 Timaios (*FGrHist* #566), fr. 164 = Diodoros 5.19–20; see also the Aristotelian *On Marvellous Things Heard* 84. Etruscan interest in these islands also implies knowledge at an early date.

discovered it when a storm drove their ships far out to sea. The Carthaginians then learned of the island, and attempted to hide its location by killing all the inhabitants. They considered it a possible refuge in case of disaster, and it became inhabited by the wealthy. There is much in this tale that is formulaic and folkloric, and it seems to reflect existing Greek thought about both the Islands of the Blessed and the nature of the Carthaginians. Yet there is little reason to doubt the essence of the tale: that Phoenicians, or, more probably, Carthaginians, perhaps on a fishing expedition,[12] accidentally happened upon an island far out in the Atlantic. The discovery may belong to the time of Hanno and Himilco,[13] perhaps even part of the elusive southern voyage of Himilco,[14] or Hanno's return from West Africa.[15] Some of the description cannot be true and has become myth: no Atlantic island has navigable rivers. The island is unlikely to be part of the Canaries, which are visible from the mainland. But the emphasis on woodlands is strongly remindful of Madeira, and the mention of a single island conforms best to that island, whose sole companion might have been missed.[16]

It is only in the late fourth century BC that a report of this discovery appears in extant Greek literature, which does not record the location of the island.[17] Although Hellenistic geographical and historical sources do not seem to comment further on it, seamen retained awareness of the place. In the early first century BC, the Carthaginians' wooded island became better known, due to the activities of the Roman adventurer Q. Sertorius. Around 81 BC he encountered some sailors on the southwest coast of Spain who recently had been to two Atlantic islands, which they identified as the Islands of the Blessed.[18] These had a moderate climate and were rich in fertility. Sertorius was strongly tempted to retire there. Half a century later Horace reiterated the theme and again described the islands as a refuge from the continuing civil war.[19] It is possible that the Azores are meant, but the insistence on two islands that are southwest from Gades is a perfect description of the Madeiras. Although the tale has evolved from one to two islands, there seems little

12 R. C. C. Law, "North Africa in the Period of Phoenician and Greek Colonization, *c.* 800 to 323BC," *CHA* 2, 1978, 134.
13 Keyser (supra n. 6), pp. 155–6.
14 For a possible itinerary of Himilco's southern voyage, see Carpenter, *Beyond*, p. 214.
15 On this, see supra, p. 41.
16 Cary and Warmington, pp. 69–71; Stéphane Gsell, *Histoire ancienne de l'Afrique du nord*, Paris: Hachette, 1914–1928, vol. 1, pp. 519–23.
17 Other occasional and uncertain references to Atlantic islands are too vague to be equated with it: for example, Strabo 2.3.5; Pliny, *Natural History* 6.199; Avienus, *Ora maritima* 164–5.
18 The source for the tale is Sallust's *Histories*, as preserved by Plutarch (*Sertorius* 8–9; Sallust, *Histories*, book 1, fr. 100–2 McGushin). On the islands and their importance to Sertorius, see C. F. Konrad, *Plutarch's Sertorius: A Historical Commentary*, Chapel Hill: University of North Carolina Press, 1994, pp. 106–11. Philip O. Spann (*Quintus Sertorius and the Legacy of Sulla*, Fayetteville: University of Arkansas Press, 1987, p. 50) believed that the Canaries were meant, but this does not conf0rm to Plutarch's precise description.
19 Horace, *Epode* 16.21–2; see also Cicero, *de finibus* 5.53.

doubt that the single Carthaginian island and those reported to Sertorius are the same.[20]

Knowledge of the Madeiras, then, seems to have existed at the vague fringes of Carthaginian, Greek, and Roman thought from perhaps the latter sixth century BC. Yet their distance from the coast meant that there was no regular contact or trade, and the tales of rich houses and luxuriant gardens are more fantasy than reality. The islands hardly entered the mainstream of ancient geographical knowledge, remaining more the mythical Islands of the Blessed rather than any specific place.[21] No actual ancient toponym is known with certainty, although it may have been Aprositos – "Inaccessible."[22] In early modern times, the Portuguese were impressed by their wooded nature, as the Carthaginians and Greeks had been, and called them the "Wooded Islands," but this cannot be any toponymic survival from antiquity.

The Canaries by contrast became well known to ancient geographical writers. Lying only 60 miles west of Africa, they would have been hard to miss. There is no explicit evidence of their early discovery,[23] but Euthymenes and Hanno would have passed by, as probably did Sataspes, the anonymous author of the African *periplous* in Pseudo-Skylax's account, and others.[24] Evidence of abandoned habitation was seen on two islands in the latter first century BC[25] but exactly what this represented in terms of early settlement is not known. They entered geographical knowledge due to the

---

20 Keyser (supra n. 6), pp. 158–60. They were said to be 10,000 stadia (ca. 1000 miles or more) away, too far, but distances at sea were often overestimated (Strabo 2.5.24), and Sertorius was exactly where the Madeiras are closest to the European mainland. The Madeiras were also known to the obscure geographer of the first century AC, Statius Sebosus, who called them the Fortunate Islands and provided accurate sailing directions from the Canaries (Pliny, *Natural History* 6.202); his information may have come from Juba II.

21 On the Madeiras as the Islands of the Blessed, see Gabriella Amiotti, "Le Isole Fortunate: mito, utopia, realtà geografica," in *Geografia e storiografia nel mondo classico*, ed. Marta Sordi, CISA 14, 1988, pp. 166–77.

22 The name Aprositos appears only in Ptolemy's *Geography* (4.6.34), where it is one of the Canary Islands (to Ptolemy, the Islands of the Blessed). His list, however, differs from that of Pliny (*Natural History* 6.202, derived from Juba II [*FGrHist* #275, fr. 44]). Ptolemy's six islands have only two in common with Pliny's seven, and one, Herasnesos (Pliny's Junonia), is cited a second time elsewhere. Another one of Ptolemy's names, Kentouria, is derived from Latin (*centurio*), but not from Pliny. Ptolemy's tantalizing name Aprositos has a sense of remoteness, and its position at the beginning of his list suggests a northern location more appropriate to Madeira. The word does not seem to have been otherwise used toponymically, but is used topographically, especially of mountains (Polybios 3.49.7, regarding Hannibal in the Alps; Strabo 1.3.18, on Methone).

23 Rodrigo de Balbín Behrmann *et al*, "Datos sobre la colonizacíon púnica de las Islas Canarias," *Eres (Arqueología)* 6, 1995, 7–28.

24 Herodotos' description of Mt Atlas (4.184), a complete circle so high that its summits are always in cloud, may refer to Tenerife in the Canaries (Walter Woodburn Hyde, *Ancient Greek Mariners*, New York: Oxford University Press, 1947, pp. 117–18). It certainly does not conform to the physical aspect of Mt Atlas, but if this is an early reference to the Canaries, it has become isolated from its proper geographic context, as Herodotos' account is of a mountain in the desert of North Africa. His alternate name for Mt Atlas, the Pillars of the Sky (or Ouranos), is remindful of Hanno's Support (or Chariot) of the Gods.

25 Pliny, *Natural History* 6.204–5.

explorations of Juba II of Mauretania. Shortly after 25BC he commissioned an expedition to discover the Islands of the Blessed.[26] As king of Mauretania and a proven scholar – who had written on Hanno's expedition – he was naturally interested in the history, geography, and culture of his kingdom. Moreover, it was believed that he was a descendant of Herakles,[27] and this led him to curiosity about the Garden of the Hesperides, site of the hero's last labor, and by association the Islands of the Blessed.[28] It is not known how Juba's explorers found the Canaries, but his knowledge of Hanno's account in a fuller version than has survived may have been of assistance. Juba's report on the islands, originally part of his *Libyka*, was summarized by Pliny the Elder.[29] Pliny's material is confused, with impossible and inconsistent sailing directions that may also have incorporated knowledge about the Madeiras.[30]

According to Pliny, Juba visited several of the Canaries and gave them descriptive names, perhaps learned from local fishermen. Only one of these has survived in Juba's Greek, Ombrios, the first island visited by the expedition. Pliny or an intermediary translated Juba's names into Latin but Ombrios survived in Pliny's text along with its Latin equivalent, Pluvialia. The other islands were (in Latin) Junonia,[31] Capraria, Ninguaria, Canaria, Invallis, and Planasia.[32] Canaria was so named because of the many dogs found on it, two of which were brought back to Juba. On Canaria there were ruined buildings and on Junonia the remnants of a temple, which probably was the reason for that island's name. Juba's expedition recorded with care the characteristics of the islands that they landed on, such as the trees of Ombrios, the lizards of Capraria, and the rich flora of Canaria. Also noted were carcasses on the beach and the snowy heights of Ninguaria. Strangly the islands were never settled in antiquity and, despite the detail with which they were described, like Kerne they simply became remote toponyms. In the fourteenth century, when they were rediscovered by Spanish sailors, Pliny's names were resurrected, although all except Canaria – which became the name for the entire group – were eventually forgotten. Juba's report on the Canaries is a rare example of an ancient geographical reconnaissance that did not lead to exploitation or settlement. Although the Canaries were reported to be abundant in

26 Roller, *Juba*, pp. 196–8.

27 Plutarch, *Sertorius* 9.

28 Juba, fr. 6 = Athenaios 3.83c.

29 Pliny, *Natural History* 6.201–5 = Juba, fr. 43, 44. The account mixes information from Juba and Statius Sebosos, whose exact role in the transmission is not clear.

30 According to Pliny, the islands were 675 miles southwest of Juba's Purple Islands, and the course to them was northwest 250 miles, and then east 375 miles, an absurdity that actually creates a circuit returning almost to the starting point, probably the triangle of the Purple Islands, Canaries, and Madeira. Also mixed in are sailing directions derived from Statius Sebosus which distinguish between the Canaries, 750 miles from Gades, and the Fortunate Islands 250 miles west of northwest, a perfectly reasonable location for Madeira.

31 The double citation of this island by Ptolemy (*Geography* 4.6.34) may be a reflection of Pliny's confused sailing directions.

32 For modern identifications and the probable original Greek names, see Duane W. Roller, *Scholarly Kings: the Fragments of Juba II of Mauretania, Archelaos of Kappadokia, Herod the Great and the Emperor Claudius*, Chicago: Ares Publishers, 2004, p. 57.

flora and fauna of every type, with specific mention of date palms, honey, papyrus, and fish, there is no evidence of any further interest. Juba believed that they were the Islands of the Blessed, and perhaps this meant that settlement would not have been appropriate.

Greco-Roman contact with the other two island groups in the Atlantic is problematic. The Cape Verdes and Azores are far from both the coast and any regular sailing routes. Neither is mentioned definitively in ancient literature, and the surviving vague hints offer little. If Hanno went far out to sea on his return, he might have encountered the Cape Verdes. Himilco's possible four-month journey,[33] which by necessity would have been south of the Pillars, may also have touched those islands. One of them might also be an island seen by Eudoxos of Kyzikos around 100BC,[34] yet all this is the vaguest grasping, and there is no physical evidence on the Cape Verdes to support that they were visited in antiquity.

Evidence of ancient contact with the Azores is also questionable.[35] Strabo's Kassiterides were ten in number, the same as the Azores, but this is probably coincidence.[36] The island that Sertorius learned about was 10,000 stadia off the coast, and although its characteristics apply better to the Madeiras, the distance favors the Azores. Thus it is possible that vague knowledge of those islands was mixed into what Sertorius heard, or Sallust's and Plutarch's recension of it.[37] Himilco's four months would have provided ample time to visit the Azores, and indeed Carthaginian coins have allegedly been found on the island of Corvo. As with so many such discoveries, however, the circumstances are dubious and the evidence has been lost. Moreover, Corvo is the most remote of the Azores, actually the closest to North America: it and its companion Flores lie over 100 miles west of the rest of the archipelago.

In 1778 J. Podolijn published in the *Göteborgske Wetenskap og Samlingar* an account of the discovery of a number of Carthaginian coins on the beach of Corvo.[38] They had been found in November 1749 in a pottery vessel after a major storm. Nine of the coins were sent to Lisbon and then to Madrid; the ultimate disposition of these (as well as the remainder) is unknown. Seven were identified as "Carthaginian" and two as "Kyrenaikan." Drawings appear in the article, and despite the poor quality of the renderings there is no doubt that Carthaginian horse coins are depicted.[39] The

33 Avienus, *Ora maritima* 117.
34 Strabo 2.3.5.
35 Cary and Warmington, pp. 70–1.
36 Strabo 3.5.11. There are also ten Cape Verdes.
37 Plutarch's fantasy about the Island of Kronos (*Concerning the Face That Appears on the Globe of the Moon* 26, about which, see infra, p. 53) refers to islands far to the west of Britain, perhaps also a hint of the Azores.
38 The article is reprinted (in part) and translated into German in Hennig, vol. 1, pp. 138–147; a French translation appears in Thèodore Monod, "Les monnaies nord-africaines anciennes de Corvo (Açores)," *BIFAN* 35b, 1973, 231–8. Podolijn's name appears as "Podolyn". See also Willy Schwabacher, "Die Azoren und die Seefahrt der Alten," *SchwMbll* 12, 1962–3, 22–6; and B. S. J. Isserlin, "Did Carthaginian Mariners Reach the Island of Corvo (Azores)? Report On the Results of Joint Field Investigations Undertaken On Corvo in June 1983," *RStFen* 12, 1984, 31–46.
39 Barclay V. Head, *Historia Numorum: A Manual of Greek Numismatics*, new and enlarged edition, Oxford: Clarendon Press, 1911, pp. 877–91.

latest seem to date from the late third century BC.[40] Although the authenticity of this find, and what it means for the early history of the Azores, has been argued since the eighteenth century,[41] the fact remains that a few late coins are hardly proof of settlement or even awareness of the islands. The existence of nine coins in almost a complete vacuum is not encouraging. Coins travel easily, even long after they have ceased to be valid currency, and it is more probable that they arrived on Corvo through a shipwreck, even in medieval or modern times, or that they were in the possession of a modern settler and were washed on the beach as a result of the storm.

A brief archaeological survey on Corvo in 1983 was inconclusive.[42] The project focused on a hillock just west of the modern village of Corvo, and, although pottery fragments perhaps of the fourth and third centuries BC were found, the material was ambiguous. This region is certainly worthy of further study, but at present these questionable finds, even if they arrived on Corvo in antiquity, are not sufficient to prove Carthaginian knowledge of the Azores.[43] In summation, then, only the Canaries were well known by Roman times. There was some information about the Madeiras, but not enough to bring them into the mainstream of geographical knowledge. There is a possibility that ancient mariners encountered the Cape Verdes and Azores, but these were probably single accidental discoveries that were soon almost forgotten.

Any study of ancient penetration into the Atlantic raises the question of whether any Greek or Roman managed to cross the ocean in its entirety. This has been argued since the earliest days of modern exploration, and hints in numerous ancient texts have been interpreted, even finagled, to prove ancient knowledge of the Americas.[44] One cannot deny that these suggestions throughout ancient literature inspired explorers such as Columbus, and that errors in ancient geography were also of assistance to those seeking westward routes to the east, but this does not address the actual issue of Greco-Roman crossing of the Atlantic.

The idea of a world beyond the Atlantic appears in Greek thought by at least the fourth century BC.[45] Plato's Atlantis may be part of the emergence of such an idea, and the controversies about Atlantis that erupted by Hellenistic times allowed the tale to be used as proof of a western continent.[46] But Atlantis is a distraction, and it is only

40 Monod (supra n. 38), p. 233.
41 Hennig, vol. 1, pp. 142–6; Monod (supra n. 38), pp. 231–8, with bibliography.
42 Isserlin (supra n. 38), pp. 31–46.
43 Equally questionable are sixteenth-century reports of bronze sculpture fragments on Corvo: see Hennig, vol. 1, p. 151; Isserlin (supra n. 38), pp. 33–6.
44 On the pervasive early modern theme of Carthaginians in America, see Enrico Acquaro, "Karthager in Amerika," in *Karthago* (ed. Werner Huss, *Wege der Forschung* 654, Darmstadt 1992), pp. 394–400. See also Anton Elter, "Das Altertum und die Entdeckung Amerikas," *RhM* n. s. 75, 1926, pp. 241–65.
45 On ancient views of the shape of the earth and how this affected ideas about the Atlantic, see Vincent H. Cassidy, *The Sea Around Them*, Baton Rouge: Louisiana State University Press, 1968, pp. 15–24; W. G. L. Randles, "Classical Models of World Geography and Their Transformation Following the Discovery of America," in *The Classical Tradition and the Americas* 1.1, ed. Wolfgang Haase and Meyer Reinhold, Berlin 1994, pp. 7–18. For geographical theory generally see Thomson, especially pp. 152–68.
46 Poseidonios (*FGrHist* #87), fr. 28 = Strabo 2.3.6.

with the era of Aristotle that hints emerged about the far west of the world.[47] The first phase of this theorization concerns the possibility of crossing from the Pillars of Herakles to India, the feasibility of which was probably first put forth by Aristotle.[48] Although his argument is part of a theoretical discussion of the extremities of the earth, it may have created a conceptual linkage between the Pillars and India that encouraged explorers such as Eudoxos of Kyzikos. Aristotle even suggested that the two regions could be joined by land, arguing that the presence of elephants in both northwest Africa and India was evidence of a physical connection.[49] Eratosthenes also raised the question of sailing from Spain to India across the Atlantic,[50] although he believed that the size of the Ocean would make this impossible: Poseidonios felt that it would be a journey of 70,000 stadia.[51]

By the second century BC, another focus of geographical theory is apparent: the idea that the inhabited world is only a small part of the earth's surface. Strabo derivatively set forth this idea, asking whether the part of the world outside what was known could be inhabited,[52] and suggesting that if this were so, those who lived there would be significantly different, living in "another world" (ἄλλην οἰκουμένην). This may have had its basis in the theories of Epikouros,[53] but Strabo more directly reflected the ideas of Krates of Mallos, the ambassador to Rome of Attalos II of Pergamon. Krates had constructed a globe, allegedly the first, showing the inhabited parts of the earth, and had theorized that there were other continents.[54] He was primarily a Homeric scholar and used certain verses in the *Odyssey* to develop his ideas.[55] This belief, that there were other land masses beyond what was known, became pervasive, and new geographical discoveries were often suggested to be part of a new continent.[56]

In the Roman period, with its expanding geographical horizon, the theory that much of the world was as yet unknown became intertwined with political thought. To Cicero, Roman power was, in a global sense, quite limited, and there were those who lived near the setting sun who would never know about Rome.[57] In fact, some lived directly opposite to Rome ("partim etiam adversos stare vobis") which may mean as far south of the equator as Rome was north. Vergil could make this idea politically

---

47 Pythagoras of Kroton conceived of the *antipodes*, the "opposite feet," based on the idea that everything had its opposite, including the land mass of the earth (Diogenes Laertios 8.26). Plato was also said to have made use of the concept (Diogenes Laertios 3.24). But this is mathematical theory, not geography, although it influenced later thought. See Anna-Dorothee von den Brincken, "Antipodes," *TTEMA*, 27–9.

48 Aristotle, *Meteorologika* 2.5.

49 Aristotle, *On the Heavens* 2.14.

50 Strabo 1.4.6.

51 Poseidonios (*FGrHist* #87), fr. 28 = Strabo 2.3.6.

52 Strabo 2.5.13.

53 Epikouros, *Letter to Herodotos* 74; see also Lucretius 2.1074–6.

54 Strabo 1.2.24; 2.5.10.

55 For example, Homer, *Odyssey* 1.22–5, about the far Ethiopians.

56 See, for example, Polybios 3.38; Hipparchos, fr. 5 Dicks (= Pomponius Mela 3.70), on Taprobane; Dio 39.50.3, on Britain.

57 Cicero, *Republic* 6.20–2.

correct, writing of a world beyond the heavens that Augustus would eventually include within the Roman state.[58] Yet Pliny raised the question as to why people on the opposite side of the world do not fall off, adding that they would think the same about the ones on his side.[59] In addition he wrote that the Ocean divided the earth into two parts and that half the world was inaccessible.[60] Pliny's tone is somewhat disbelieving and a little derisive, but he also attached a catalogue of far-flung exploration.[61] Included are references to the circumnavigation of Africa, including Hanno and Eudoxos, and the curious incident of Indians who had recently ended up on the north European coast.

Such reports, although of uncertain veracity, helped to establish the idea that there was much of the world that was unknown and that the Ocean was not the limit of the inhabited earth. Almost contemporary is Seneca's famous prophecy that an era will come when the Ocean will no longer be the limit of knowledge, and new worlds will be revealed.[62] Seneca also echoed the theories of Aristotle and Eratosthenes in believing that one could sail west from the Pillars to India, but unlike his predecessors, he felt that it could be accomplished in a few days.[63] But his younger contemporary Quintilian felt that whether there was land beyond the Ocean was debatable.[64]

A parallel development to the geographical, astronomical, and political theorizing about the extremities of the world was the fantasy allegory, which was generally used as a basis for social and political criticism.[65] Plato's Atlantis was the first, followed by Theopompos' description of a continent beyond the Ocean that supported unusually large animals and people.[66] Other early examples of the genre include the writings of Hekataios of Abdera, from the fourth century BC, whose *On the Hyperboreans* was set in the far north,[67] Euhemeros of Messene, active around 300BC, whose fantasy world was in the Indian Ocean,[68] and probably Antiphanes of Berga, who wrote about the frozen north.[69] These are perhaps less relevant to concepts of the Atlantic but show the

58 Vergil, *Aeneid* 6.792–800.

59 Pliny, *Natural History* 2.161–2. His source may have been, in part, Dikaiarchos of Messana.

60 Pliny, *Natural History* 2.171–5.

61 Pliny, *Natural History* 2.167–70.

62 Seneca, *Medea* 375–9. On the significance of this passage to early modern exploration, see James S. Romm, "New World and '*novos orbos*': Seneca in the Renaissance Debate Over Ancient Knowledge of the Americas," in *The Classical Tradition and the Americas* 1.1, ed. Wolfgang Haase and Meyer Reinhold, Berlin 1994, pp. 77–116. Similar thoughts appear in the Aristotelian treatise *On the Cosmos* (3), roughly contemporary to Seneca: there are inhabited places across the Atlantic, some of which may even be larger than the known world.

63 Seneca, *Naturales quaestiones* 1, Pref. 13.

64 Quintilian 7.2.5.

65 Klaus Geus, "Utopie und Geographie. Zum Weltbild der Griechen in frühhellenistischer Zeit," *OT* 6, 2000, 55–84; Federica Cordano, *La geografia degli antichi*, Rome: Laterza: 1992, pp. 87–96.

66 Theopompos (*FGrHist* #115), fr. 75c = Aelian, *Diverse History* 3.18.

67 *FGrHist* #264, fr. 7–14.

68 *FGrHist* #63, fr. 1–11, especially fr. 2, 3 (= Diodoros 6.1, 5.41–46).

69 Plutarch, *How One Might Become Aware of His Progress in Virtue* 6 (79a).

wide reach of the genre.[70] More germane is Plutarch's famous account of an island 5,000 stadia off Britain where Kronos was imprisoned.[71] It was located beyond Ogygia, which Homer had placed far out to sea – five days, according to Plutarch. The island of Kronos was difficult to reach because of the muddiness, sluggishness and even congealed nature of the ocean. Moreover, there was extensive land beyond it, where the sun rarely set. Great expeditions travelled between these areas, and a stranger eventually came from this region to Carthage and revealed all.

Because Plutarch's tale lacks any fantastic or magical qualities beyond its geographical remoteness, it excited wide interest from early modern times, considered by many as a reference to America. It seems obvious, however, that it is nothing more than another allegory, based to some extent on what was known about the Atlantic islands. The difficulty of sea travel points to Himilco; the congealing of the sea and the long daylight to Pytheas.[72] The connections with Carthage and Kronos suggest Hanno, as do the great provision-laded expeditions, which are also reminiscent of Eudoxos. Thus, although the story is knowledgable about geographical exploration and scholarship of Plutarch's era, it does not contain any specific information about the far side of the Atlantic.[73]

More fantastic in character is a story by Lukianos of Samosata, written in the second century AC.[74] The author, after candidly revealing that his account consists of falsehoods (ψεύσματα), described a journey beyond the Pillars of Herakles. In a common beginning to such tales, a great storm blew him far from land, in this case for 80 days, which brought him to an island where an inscription revealed that both Herakles and Dionysos had preceded him. The land was a paradise where the rivers flowed with wine and grapevine women attempted to seduce Lukianos' companions. Although the storm connects with Kolaios (and Odysseus), and there is a faint relationship to the general popular image of exploration beyond the Pillars, it is firmly grounded in a fantasy world, lacking even the credible specifics of Plutarch's tale.

In addition, there is the report of a certain Euphemos of Karia, who also lived in the second century AC. His tale was preserved by Pausanias, who said he had talked to Euphemos.[75] Euphemos related that he was blown out into the unexplored external

---

70 A certain Antonius Diogenes, of uncertain date, wrote *The Unbelievable Things Beyond Thoule*, obviously influenced by Pytheas. See Susan A. Stephens and John J. Winker, *Ancient Greek Novels: The Fragments*, Princeton: Princeton University Press, 1985, pp. 101–72; J. R. Morgan, "Lucian's *True Histories* and the *Wonders Beyond Thule* of Antonius Diogenes," *CQ* n. s. 35, 1985, 475–90.

71 Plutarch, *Concerning the Face That Appears on the Globe of the Moon* 26. On this work see Paul Coones, "The Geographical Significance of Plutarch's Dialogue *Concerning the Face Which Appears In the Orb of the Moon*," *TIBG* n. s. 8, 1983, 361–72.

72 On Pytheas, see infra, chapter 4. His influence on geographical fantasies is discussed by Stefano Magnani, "Una geografia fantastica? Pitea di Massalia e l'immaginario greco," *RivStorAnt* 22–3, 1992–3, 25–42.

73 On the allegory, see Plutarch, *Moralia* 12, ed. Harold Cherniss and William C. Helmbold, Cambridge, Mass.: Harvard University Press, 1957, pp. 20–3.

74 Lukianos, *True Narratives* 1.

75 Pausanias 1.23.5–6.

sea and encountered the Islands of the Satyrs, inhabited by promiscuous wild red-haired men with tails. They attacked the women on Euphemos' ship, eventually obtaining one as a prize, whom they abused totally. Pausanias presented the tale uncritically and as true, but there are several difficulties beyond the obvious of its setting in a fantasy world. Most notably, the term "external sea" and the assertion that sailors do not sail on it are anachronisms reflecting an early state of knowledge long before Pausanias' day. The story is reminiscent of Kolaios and certain elements of Hanno's report, with some knowledge of the Atlantic islands. The fantastic nature of the inhabitants and the lateness of the account, as well as the total obscurity of Euphemos, make it unlikely that it is anything other than a fantasy, most likely the plot of a satyr-play.[76]

None of these alleged reports of visiting the western Atlantic stands up to critical examination. They have their origins in consistent ideas about geographical symmetry, and the realization – apparent after Hellenistic determination of the earth's size – that the known world could only be a small portion of its surface. Often they are a melange of existing material about exploration. They served certain literary and cultural needs, especially in the Roman period,[77] and as exploration went farther, the fantasies incorporated new discoveries, not always consistently. Although there was indeed another continent, and more, waiting to be discovered, and although explorers from the fifteenth century onward seized upon every piece of supposed literary evidence to support – and help finance – their own voyages, there is no evidence in ancient literature that anyone from the Mediterranean went beyond the Atlantic islands.[78]

It remains, however, to be seen if there is any physical evidence to counter this lack of literary support for early voyages to America. There are numerous anecdotal tales about Greco-Roman artifacts being discovered in the New World, but upon examination none of them can be sustained. For example, in the 1830s there was allegedly discovered (by a laborer) in Montevideo, Uruguay, an inscription (now lost) which read: "In the reign of Alexander, son of Philip, king of Makedonia, in the sixty-fifth Olympiad, Ptolemaios … "[79] One cannot have much faith in an inscription that places Alexander in the late fifth century BC, although perhaps it was badly copied.[80] The three famous names seem to have been used for dramatic effect, and it is remarkably convenient that all traces of both the explanatory part of the text and the monument that supported the inscription were lost. Unfortunately this is the nature

---

76 There have been some attempts to see the red-haired men as inhabitants of the West Indies, but this hardly deserves comment (Cary and Warmington, pp. 71–2).

77 Romm, *Edges*, pp. 156–71.

78 This is not to say that Greeks and Romans were not in the New World in spirit during the colonization of the Americas, especially the Spanish portions: see the interesting study by David A. Lupher, *Romans in a New World: Classical Models in Sixteenth-Century Spanish America*, Ann Arbor: University of Michigan Press, 2003.

79 Paul Gaffarel, *Histoire de la découverte de l'Amerique* vol. 1, Paris: Arthur Rousseau, 1892, pp. 163–4.

80 It need hardly be added that dating by Olympiads did not exist until well after the time of Alexander: see E. J. Bickerman, *Chronology of the Ancient World*, second edition, Ithaca: Cornell University Press 1980, pp. 75–6.

of Greco-Roman "finds" in America: suspiciously informative and inevitably lost, and rarely handled by those qualified to interpret them.[81]

Alleged coin finds are frequent in the New World. There are reports of a hoard from the time of Alexander the Great – a remarkably common period of New World finds – Roman coins from the third or fourth century AC from Panama, or coins of Augustus found in an unspecified mine.[82] Many of these finds are legitimate in the sense that they report the discovery of actual Greek or Roman coins in an American context, although some may be forgeries.[83] But there is no likelihood that they were brought to their ultimate findspot in antiquity. They may have been in the possession of early European settlers, or even have arrived accidentally in ship's ballast, later dispersed and eventually rediscovered.[84]

Thus there is no evidence that any Greek or Roman came to the New World.[85] Both literary and archaeological accounts that seem to support such early contact are spurious. This does not mean, however, that the crossing was not made, accidentally, at some time, but it had no impact on either the New World or the Mediterranean. Most likely, any Greco-Roman seaman who reached the New World did not live to return.[86] Shortly after 100BC, Eudoxos of Kyzikos set forth from Gades, attempting to go to India and planning to spend the winter on an island that he had discovered.[87] He was never heard from again. Almost 1,600 years later, Pedro Álvarez Cabral (b. 1467?) attempted exactly the same journey.[88] On 29 August 1499, Vasco da Gama returned from reopening the route to India that Eudoxos had discovered, and on 8 March 1500 Cabral was sent by King Manuel of Portugal to replicate and build on da Gama's journey. Cabral's expedition soon passed the Canaries and the Cape Verdes (22 March). What happened next is uncertain, but on 21 April signs of land were sighted, and the next day they saw the

81 As an example of a remote but legitimate find, one only has to consider the discovery of Roman coins from the late third century AC in Iceland (infra, p. 83).

82 Gaffarel (supra n. 79), pp. 163–6, summarizes these; see also Hennig, vol. 1, pp. 145–54. One may also add the vague discovery of an Augustan coin in the "Spanish Indies" early in the colonial period: see João de Barros and Diogo do Couto, *The History of Ceylon, From the Earliest Times to 1600 A. D.*, translated and edited by Donald Ferguson, *JRAS-C* 20, no. 60, 1908, 84.

83 Cary and Warmington, p. 72.

84 An interesting find comes from the Porcupine Bank, some 130 miles west of Ireland. There a trawler dredged at 150 fathoms a Roman *olla* of no later than the second century AC, probably from the cargo of a wrecked ship. It is of no significance regarding transatlantic travel but demonstrates the easy portability of objects, and is certainly one of the most remote finds from antiquity. It is now in the Welsh National Museum. R. G. Collingwood and M. V. Taylor, "Roman Britain in 1933," *JRS* 24, 1934, 220–1; Séan P. Ó Ríordáin, "Roman Material In Ireland," *Proceedings of the Royal Irish Academy* 51c3, 65–6.

85 On this see Hyde (supra n. 24), pp. 159–64.

86 For an interesting account of the hypothetical possibility of ancient transatlantic travel, see Vincent H. Cassidy, "New Worlds and Everyman: Some Thoughts on the Logic and Logistics of Pre-Columbian Discovery," *TI* 10, 1978, 7–13.

87 On Eudoxos, see further, infra, pp. 107–11.

88 The journey is summarized in William Brooks Greenlee (tr. and ed.), *The Voyage of Pedro Álvarez Cabral to Brazil and India*, London: Hakluyt Society, 1938, pp. xvii-xx; the reports to King Manuel from Brazil, written by members of Cabral's staff, are on pp. 5–40. Other documents relating to this discovery are also in this volume.

Brazilian coast. Soon they took possession of the territory for Portugal at the safe harbor they named Porto Seguro. In fact, Cabral had been blown so far that he was well south of the closest point of Brazil to Africa. He was nonetheless able to send a ship back to Lisbon and to continue on to India himself. His journey across the Atlantic has a familiar combination of weather, currents, and a hint of premeditation,[89] like that of Kolaios, and strangely seems to complete the journey on which Eudoxos was lost. It is thus possible that Cabral was not the first to be blown across the narrows of the South Atlantic, only the first to live to report on it. Any ancient settlement in the Americas probably would have met the same fate as that established around AD1000 by the Vikings at L'Anse aux Meadows in Newfoundland, self-destructing after a year or two, due to lack of supply lines and an inability to gain any superiority over the indigenous population in a pre-gunpowder world.[90]

89 A combination of these factors is usually advanced as the reason for the detour: see Greenlee (supra n. 88) xlvi–lx. The Portuguese were acquainted with the tale of Eudoxos (J. H. Thiel, *Eudoxus of Cyzicus*, Groningen: J. B. Wolters, n. d., pp. 56–7).
90 Helga Ingstad and Anne Stine Ingstad, *The Viking Discovery of America*, St John's: Breakwater, 2000, p. 180.

4

PYTHEAS OF MASSALIA

It has long been assumed that the scantness of Greek activity beyond the Pillars of Herakles between 500BC and late Hellenistic times was due to Carthaginian hindrance.[1] Evidence of such interference is circumstantial rather than explicit, based on limited Greek exploration of the Atlantic after this date in contrast to its earlier frequency, the poor knowledge of the Atlantic in Classical geographical sources, and a sudden insistence in the fifth century BC that sailing beyond the Pillars was neither possible nor desirable. Some of this must come from the long-standing Greek uncertainty about the External Sea, but nevertheless there is a new emphasis on the danger of movement beyond the Pillars and the inability of obtaining accurate information about what lay beyond.[2] There is also an astonishing ignorance about the Atlantic. Herodotos' knowledge is amazingly sparse: "I have never seen, nor, despite my efforts, been able to learn from anyone whether there is an ocean beyond Europe."[3] Given the already extensive Greek exploration, this is strange, and seems to indicate that by the time of Herodotos earlier voyages had been forgotten and there was little contemporary Greek knowledge of the Atlantic.

Perhaps indicative of the political situation is a treaty between the Romans and the Carthaginians. Dated to the first year of the Roman Republic, traditionally 509BC, it excludes the Romans from bringing their ships into certain areas.[4] Although the treaty refers to the territory around Carthage and the Libyan coast, it demonstrates that the

---

1 Cary and Warmington, pp. 47–8, 62; Carpenter, *Beyond*, p. 146; Rhys Carpenter, *The Greeks in Spain*, New York: Longman, Green, 1925, pp. 33–6. The alleged Carthaginian interference is disputed by A. Trevor Hodge, *Ancient Greek France*, Philadelphia: University of Pennsylvania Press, 1999, pp. 28–30; see also Paul Fabre, "Les grecs à la découverte de l'Atlantique," *RÉA* 94, 1992, 12–13.

2 The Carthaginians were said to drown anyone who attempted to find the Pillars (Strabo 17.1.19, from Eratosthenes). See also Pindar, *Olympian* 3.44–5; *Nemean* 3.20–1; 4.69; Euripides, *Hippolytos* 743–7; [Aristotle], *On Marvellous Things Heard* 84. Some of the emphasis on the dangers of sea travel in Avienus' *Ora maritima* (380–9, 406–13) is from a Carthaginian source (Himilco) and may reflect their propaganda: see Vincent H. Cassidy, *The Sea Around Them*, Baton Rouge: Louisiana State University Press, 1968, p. 5.

3 Herodotos 3.115.

4 Polybios 3.22. On the date, see F. W. Walbank, *A Historical Commentary on Polybius*, Oxford: Clarendon Press, 1959–79, vol. 1, pp. 339–40; on its significance, see R. L. Beaumont, "The Date of the First Treaty Between Rome and Carthage," *JRS* 29, 1939, 74–86.

Carthaginians did attempt to control the shipping of other states within territory that they considered their own, which would have included areas outside the Pillars. This far western region is not named in the treaty because it was nowhere near the Roman sphere of interest, but it would have been an area of conflict between Carthage and the western Greek states, especially Massalia. Thus the Carthaginians may have attempted by treaty to exclude Greeks from sailing through the Pillars of Herakles, although it is debatable how successful this policy was: the Massalians, at least, seem to have been able to ignore it on occasion. Indeed, Massalia repeatedly emphasized and publicized its defeats of those who disputed their sea power, including the Carthaginians.[5]

Nevertheless, the promising Greek exploration beyond the Pillars of Herakles came temporarily to an end early in the fifth century BC. The reasons are obscure: active Carthaginian hindrance or even passive discouragement, or perhaps merely the end of the expansionism of the Greek states that had begun in the eighth century BC. The Massalians had established outposts along the French and Spanish coasts in the sixth century BC, but archaeological evidence shows that Greek trade with Tartessos ended by around 500BC,[6] indicative of a retrenchment and perhaps a cessation of seaborne movements through the Pillars. Whether the Carthaginians had anything to do with this is debatable, but they may have encouraged the belief that there was nothing of interest to the Greeks in these regions. The general changes in the balance of power may also have played a role. The defeat of the Carthaginians at Himera in 480BC[7] diverted their interests away from Europe and toward Africa and beyond the Pillars, making Greek involvement there far more difficult.

For over a century after Euthymenes, there is no record of Greek travel on the Atlantic. Changes only began to take place in the second half of the fourth century BC: the anonymous traveller to Kerne cited in Pseudo-Skylax's text may be the first indication.[8] Sometime in the decade of the 320s BC, another traveller embarked on one of the most significant voyages of exploration of any era. He was Pytheas who set forth from Massalia: within a century his voyage was equated with that of the Argonauts, one who "explored the entire northerly part of Europe as far as the limit of the cosmos."[9]

Early in 334BC, Alexander the Great, who had been king of Makedonia since his father's assassination a year and a half previously, moved east from the Greek mainland into Asia Minor. Two years later he was at Tyre. The long and complex siege of that ancient Phoenician city is a well-known part of his career.[10] As it began, the Tyrians unsuccessfully requested Carthaginian assistance[11] and eventually may have

---

5 Strabo 4.1.5; Pausanias 10.8.6, 10.18.7 (dedications at Delphi); Thoukydides 1.13 – actually referring to a Phokaian defeat of the Carthaginians in connection with the foundation of Massalia.

6 John Boardman, *The Greeks Overseas: Their Colonies and Trade*, fourth edition, London: Thames and Hudson, 1999, pp. 214–24.

7 Herodotos 7.166.

8 Pseudo-Skylax 112; supra, p. 19.

9 Polybios 34.5.9 = Strabo 2.4.2.

10 The ancient sources are Arrian, *Anabasis* 2.15.6–24.6; Diodoros 17.40–7; Quintus Curtius 4.2–4; Plutarch, *Alexander* 24–5.

11 Diodoros 17.40.3; Quintus Curtius 4.3.19.

sent some of their women, children, and old men there.[12] Moreover, there were actually some Carthaginians in Tyre at the time, on a religious pilgrimage, who were spared by Alexander when the city fell.[13] These events demonstrate both the extremely close relations that the Carthaginians maintained with their mother city hundreds of years after Carthage had been founded, and that they were well informed about Alexander's activities and were likely to feel threatened by them.[14] They must have worried about his intentions after Tyre fell, and quite reasonably, for Alexander either made a declaration of war against Carthage at that time,[15] or at the very least there were rumors that a western expedition was being planned, perhaps by circumnavigating Africa.[16]

Another city that would have been concerned about Alexander's plans was Massalia,[17] who hardly needed him in their vicinity, even if he were to attack their rival Carthage. If the subsequent report that Alexander was on the Caspian Sea[18] came to be known in Massalia, this might have been seen as a prelude to an attack, since the prevailing opinion of the period was that the Caspian Sea was part of the external Ocean.[19] Alexander's presence in that region would further raise fears in the west: a journey across the northern coast of Asia and Europe would seem as possible as circumnavigating Africa.[20] This western nervousness reached its culmination in Babylon a few months before Alexander's death when numerous embassies came to the king, perhaps not coincidentally at the same time that Alexander had ordered ships

---

12 Diodoros 17.41.1–2, 46.4; Quintus Curtius 4.3.20.

13 Arrian, *Anabasis* 2.24.5; Quintus Curtius 4.4.18; whether these are the same who came for the refugees is not clear. On these Carthaginians, and the varying accounts of them, see A. B. Bosworth, *A Historical Commentary on Arrian's History of Alexander*, Oxford: Clarendon Press, 1980– , vol. 1, pp. 254–5.

14 The threat to Carthage by Alexander is outlined in brief by C. F. C. Hawkes, *Pytheas: Europe and the Greek Explorers*, n. p., n. d., pp. 42–4.

15 Quintus Curtius 4.4.18.

16 At the time of Alexander's death a decade later, plans for such an expedition were found among his papers, including building hundreds of ships to attack Carthage (Diodoros 18.4.4; Arrian, *Anabasis* 7.1; Quintus Curtius 10.1.17–18; Plutarch, *Alexander* 68.1). On these papers see E. Badian, "A King's Notebooks," *HSCP* 76, 1968, 183–204.

17 Hawkes (supra n. 14), pp. 42–4.

18 Diodoros 17.75; Plutarch, *Alexander* 44; Arrian, *Anabasis* 7.16.

19 This is a rare example of a regression in geographical knowledge. Herodotos (1.203) knew that the Caspian was an enclosed sea, a view supported by Aristotle (*Meteorologika* 2.1). Alexander, however, believed – or wanted to believe – that it was connected to the Ocean, although there is a certain amount of confusion in the sources because of the late date of the Alexander historians. Quintus Curtius' account (6.6.18–19) is unclear but implies a connection; Arrian mentioned the matter twice (5.26.2, 7.16); both citations are somewhat ambivalent as to whether Alexander's desires or actual geographical knowledge is being expressed. That the Caspian Sea was enclosed was not determined again until the thirteenth century, but still not accepted for many years (Thomson, p. 390).

20 Alexander was obsessed with the Ocean. In addition to his ideas about circumnavigating Africa and accessing its northern part through the Caspian Sea, he felt that in India he was close to the eastern Ocean and that he might even be able to circumnavigate the entire inhabited world (Arrian, *Anabasis* 5.26.1–2; see also 7.1). His obsession entered popular imagination: see Seneca the Elder, *Suasoria* 1; Quintilian 3.8.16.

to be built for a Caspian expedition.[21] The embassies were said to have come from almost the entire world, but of particular interest is the emphasis on those from the west, some from places allegedly previously unknown to the Greeks. In addition to the Carthaginians, these included Kelts, Iberians, Bruttians, Lucanians, and Etruscans as well as Libyphoenicians and Gauls. Also mentioned is an embassy from Rome, yet in such anachronistic terms that it was doubted by the later sources on Alexander, although recorded, seemingly, soon after the fact by Kleitarchos.[22] The details that made the extant source, Arrian, dubious – Alexander made a prophecy about Rome's future greatness – need not to have been part of the original report.

Nevertheless the list of envoys in Babylon early in 323 BC – whether or not it included Rome – demonstrates a peculiar interest in the activities of Alexander by the peoples of the western Mediterranean. Although the tone in the sources is more of honor to Alexander than concern, one can be certain that nervousness and curiosity about his intentions in the west was a major issue. No Greek city is mentioned by name among the embassies, but Diodoros cited "the Greek cities of Europe" immediately after the "Libyphoenicians and all those living on the coast as far as the Pillars of Herakles." These Greek cities can be none other than the Massalians and their dependencies. Morever, if the Romans were indeed involved, the Massalians were also, indirectly, since the two cities had had formal relations for nearly a century.[23]

Thus it is reasonable to assume that Alexander's activities and the rumors of his future plans significantly changed the attitudes and aspirations of the inhabitants of the western Mediterranean. The embassies represent the culmination of several years of concern that began nearly a decade previously when there were the first glimmerings of Alexander's interest in the west. The western cities would have made plans of their own to react to the assumed invasion by Alexander. They could not have known that Alexander would never come close to their territory, or indeed that he would die only a few months after the embassies and that his successors would immediately abandon the western plans.[24]

It is in this context of chaos and uncertainty that Pytheas made his epic journey into the far north. How much it reflects a Massalian reaction to Alexander cannot be known.[25] The Massalians would have made attempts to prepare themselves for Alexander's expected arrival, perhaps by learning if it were at all possible for him to reach the western Mediterranean from the Caspian Sea, but the leisurely quality of Pytheas' journey presumes a lack of urgency. Many scholars have concerned themselves with whether some specific

---

21 Arrian, *Anabasis* 7.15–16; Diodoros 17.113.

22 Kleitarchos (*FGrHist* #137), fr. 31 (= Pliny, *Natural History* 3.57).

23 Diodoros 14.93.3–4; Appian, *Italika* 8.1. The Roman dedication at Delphi after the fall of Veii in 396BC was placed in the Massalian treasury (Appian called it the "Treasury of Rome and Massalia"), which presumes an existing close relationship.

24 Diodoros 18.4.6.

25 According to Arrian (*Anabasis* 7.1.4), Alexander may have contemplated an expedition to Britain. This raises the question of whether he had heard something about Pytheas. No source but Arrian mentions such a project, yet he described it in terms indicating Britain was a formula for the remotest areas of the earth, diction of Alexander's time, not Arrian's.

arrangement was made with Carthage to allow a Massalian expedition out through the Pillars, but this seems unimportant: Carthage may have been distracted by its own preparations for Alexander, and, more importantly, as will be demonstrated, Pytheas probably did not even go through the Pillars. It is also unlikely that his journey had any official status, but at the very least the voyage demonstrates that the political realities of the era stimulated, in some Massalian circles, intense curiosity about the far north.

The earliest source to mention Pytheas is Dikaiarchos of Messana.[26] As a student of Aristotle's he would have begun to be active no later than the 320s BC.[27] There is no previous extant mention of Pytheas, significantly neither by Aristotle or Ephoros, both of whom would have taken serious interest in what Pytheas published. It is difficult to imagine that Aristotle would not have used his extensive astronomical and geographical data. Ephoros, whose history ended with the siege of Perinthos in 340BC and which was probably published within a few years,[28] would also have found the researches of Pytheas of particular note. Ephoros' wide-ranging historical work included a major section on world geography. He divided the world into four parts, the Indian, Ethiopian, Skythian, and Keltic,[29] and described, perhaps for the first time in such detail, the northern expanse of the earth.[30] This geographical reach of Ephoros' history is extensive: mention of Gades and the Spanish coast[31] is followed by a detailed description of the Keltic territory, and a discussion of the Kimmerians,[32] who lived beyond the Kelts and ever since the time of Homer had been a paradigm for the farthest ethnic group, always living in darkness.[33] Ephoros' circuit then reached the mouth of the Ister and Skythian territory.[34] It is probable that no one had previously discussed the region in such detail: earlier Greek literature has only hints of the far north.[35] Moreover, Ephoros was concerned about the effect of the tides, something also of interest to Pytheas.[36]

---

26 Strabo 2.4.2 = Dikaiarchos, fr. 124 Mirhady.

27 Dikaiarchos, fr. 4 Mirhady.

28 Diodoros 16.76.5. Ephoros also mentioned the archonship of Euainetos, five years later (*FGrHist* #70, fr. 223), perhaps the year of publication.

29 Ephoros, fr. 30a = Strabo 1.2.28. On this passage see Strabo, *Géographie* 1, ed. Germaine Aujac and François Lasserre, Paris: Les Belles Lettres: 1969, p. 196.

30 Ephoros, fr. 42 = Strabo 7.3.9. His source was probably Hekataios (see G. L. Barber, *The Historian Ephorus*, Cambridge: Cambridge University Press, 1935, pp. 118–19), supplemented by more contemporary trade information. Ephoros may also have been aware of the explorations of Himilco (supra, pp. 27–31).

31 Ephoros, fr. 129a = Pliny, *Natural History* 4.120; fr. 130 = Strabo 3.1.4. Ephoros may be the source of some of the material that ended up in the *Ora maritima* of Avienus (Hawkes [supra n. 14] p. 23), although Ephoros is not mentioned in the poem. His discussion of Gades – and to some extent the Kelts – was also probably used by the author of the *Periplous Dedicated to King Nikomedes* (150–95): he was cited by name elsewhere in the poem (472, 546 = Ephoros, fr. 144, 145).

32 Ephoros, fr. 131, 134 = Strabo 4.4.6, 5.4.5.

33 Homer, *Odyssey* 11.13–19.

34 Ephoros, fr. 157 = Strabo 7.3.15.

35 The Kelts were first mentioned by Hekataios of Miletos (*FGrHist* #1, fr. 54–6), unless one of the sources buried in the *Ora maritima* of Avienus is earlier. Herodotos placed the Kelts at the source of the Ister or beyond the Pillars of Herakles (2.33, 4.49) – not so much a contradiction as evidence of two routes to their territory – and believed that they were the second most westerly ethnic group. He also mentioned the Kimmerians a number of times (1.6 etc.), although generally in terms of their impact on Asia Minor and Skythia.

36 Ephoros, fr. 132 = Strabo 7.2.1.

Ephoros' histories appeared at about the same time Alexander was beginning to raise concern among the western Greeks about a possible attack via the Caspian Sea. Within a few years Pytheas' expedition replicated the northern literary circuit of the historian. This seems more than coincidence, and whether Pytheas went forth as an official envoy of Massalia or not, his journey was connected to the issues of the era. Ephoros' failure to mention a traveller who visited many of the places that he discussed is indirect proof that Pytheas' journey was a response to the historian, and not available to him as data.

Few facts can be determined about Pytheas.[37] There is a single statement about the man himself, from Polybios, that he was a private individual and poor.[38] Even this became controversial, because Polybios, who enjoyed the subsidy of Scipio Aemilianus for his own explorations,[39] knew that field research was expensive,[40] and used Pytheas' poverty as a way of discrediting his travels. Yet the statement – which Polybios did not dispute – suggests that Pytheas set forth on his inquiries without state support. Polybios' dislike of merchants and his indirect mention of Pytheas in such a context[41] has led to the assumption that the latter was indeed a trader or merchant, but the evidence is circumstantial.[42] An anonymous epigram in the *Greek Anthology* honors a certain Pytheas, famed for his outstanding learning, who has now gone to the Blessed Isles.[43] The subject of this epigram will never be known, but it is interesting

---

37 The bibliography on Pytheas is enormous, and he has excited the interest not only of students of geography and astronomy but Arctic explorers such as Fridtjof Nansen (*In Northern Mists*, tr. Arthur G. Chater, New York: Frederick A. Stokes, 1911, vol. 1, pp. 43–73) and Vilhjalmur Stefansson (*Ultima Thule*, New York: MacMillan, 1940, pp. 1–107). There are numerous editions of the fragments of Pytheas, most notably those of Mette (1952), Stichtenoth (1959), Roseman (1994), and Bianchetti (1998, with thorough previous bibliography). Among the detailed studies of the past century one may cite Cary and Warmington, pp. 47–56; Gaston-E. Broche, *Pythéas le Massaliote*, Paris: Société Française d'Imprimerie et de Librairie, 1935, but see the comments on this work by D. R. Dicks, *The Geographical Fragments of Hipparchus*, London: Athlone Press, 1960, pp. 181–2; Hennig, vol. 1, pp. 155–82; Thomson, pp. 143–51; W. Aly, *Strabon von Amaseia* 4, Bonn: Rudolf Habelt, 1957, pp. 461–75; F. Gisinger, "Pytheas" (#1), *RE* 24, 1963, 314–66; Carpenter, *Beyond*, pp. 143–98; Federica Cordano, *La geografia degli antichi*, Rome: Laterza, 1992, pp. 104–9; Hawkes (supra n. 14), with many imaginative suggestions and route maps; the recent semi-popular study by Barry Cunliffe, *The Extraordinary Voyage of Pytheas the Greek*, London: Allen Lane, 2001; Serena Bianchetti, "Eutimene e Pitea di Massalia: geografia e storiografia," in *Storici greci d'Occidente*, ed. Riccardo Vattuone, Bologna, 2002, pp. 447–85; Stefano Magnani, *Il viaggio di Pitea sull'Oceano*, Bologna: Pàtron, 2003; and H.-G. Nesselrath, "Pytheas," *RGA* 23, 2003, 617–20. On his scientific reputation, see Walter Mohr, "Des Pytheas von Massalia Schrift 'Über den Ozean'," *Hermes* 77, 1942, 28–45; Karlhaus Abel, "Zone" (#1), *RE Supp.* 14, 1974, 1028–33; and Aubrey Diller, "Pytheas of Massalia," *DSB* 11, 1975, 225–6. On Strabo's use of Pytheas' data, see Germaine Aujac, *Strabo et la science de son temps*, Paris: Les Belles Lettres, 1966, pp. 40–8. Numerous articles cited in the following pages concern particular topics. There is often a distinct national bias concerning the location of Pytheas' more remote toponyms.

38 Polybios 34.5.7 = Strabo 2.4.2: ἰδιώτῃ ἀνθρώπῳ καὶ πένητι; on this, see Broche (supra n. 37) 20–2.

39 Pliny, *Natural History* 5.9; see also infra, pp. 91–103.

40 Polybios 12.27.6.

41 Polybios 4.39.11 (disdain of merchants' information); 34.10.6 = Strabo 4.2.1; see also Polybios 4.42.7, revealing a dislike of sailors' tales.

42 See F. W. Walbank, "The Geography of Polybius," *ClMed* 9, 1947, 161.

43 *Greek Anthology* 7.690.

that the name Pytheas should be coupled with intellectual activity and the paradigm of far-flung travel.[44]

The second known fact is the title of Pytheas' work, On the Ocean (Περὶ τοῦ ᾽Ὠκεανοῦ),[45] which is cited only by two obscure sources, the astronomer Geminos of Rhodes,[46] probably of the Julio-Claudian period, and the Byzantine scholar Kosmas Indikopleustes.[47] The fact that a writer on astronomy should quote the title of Pytheas' treatise is itself significant, for it demonstrates the third and last fact known about him: that he was an educated man. Unlike most other ancient explorers, whose reports were essentially limited to seamanship, toponymic geography, ethnography, and trade issues, Pytheas made significant contributions to geography as an intellectual discipline and to astronomy. He was called philosophos[48] and doctissimus.[49] Even Strabo, who quoted Pytheas only to criticize him, grudgingly called his efforts historia, or research.[50] The breadth of his title – showing virtually no geographical limitations – indicates the wide range of Pytheas' research.[51] Thus even on such skimpy information he can be set apart from the other travellers and explorers of antiquity: a scientist who travelled probably not as an instrument of state policy but, like Herodotos, for reasons of pure research, taking several years, and becoming the first to see the entire Ocean as his area of endeavor.[52]

That he does not seem to have been an envoy of the Massalian government raises questions about the very nature of his journey, and why he was driven to embark upon it, an issue related to Pytheas himself, in particular his education, and where he might have received it. This was the era of Aristotle, who had founded his school, the Lykeion – generally known today as the Lyceum – perhaps in part because of a dispute over the management of Plato's Academy[53] in 335–334 BC.[54] Aristotle was head of the

---

44 See Roger Dion, "La renommée de Pythéas dans l'Antiquité," RÉL 43, 1965, 456–9.

45 This is a rare title, only used again, as far as is known, by Poseidonios (FGrHist #87, fr. 28 = Strabo 2.2.1), probably in direct imitation (K. Zimmermann, "Review of Bianchetti: Pitea," CR n. s. 50, 2000, p. 30; J. J. Tierney, "The Celtic Ethnography of Posidonius," ProcRIA 60c, 1960, 196), and perhaps by Athenodoros of Tarsos (on the rationale for this, see Germaine Aujac, "Les traités 'Sur l'Océan' et les zones terrestres," RÉA 74, 1972, 74–5). A more generic title, Journey Around the Earth (Περίοδος γῆς), was cited by the scholiast to Apollonios of Rhodes (4.761–5a). Some have seen this as a separate treatise (e. g. Hodge [supra n. 1], pp. 130–1).

46 Geminos, Introduction to Phenomena 6.9.

47 Kosmas, Christian Topography 2.80.6; for Kosmas' life and career see Wanda Wolska-Conus, "Cosmas Indikopleustes," TTEMA, 129–31.

48 Kleomedes, Meteora 1.4.208–10.

49 Martianus Capella 6.609. On Martianus, see Cassidy (supra n. 2), pp. 54–5.

50 Strabo 7.3.1.

51 On this see Pytheas, ed. Roseman, p. 1.

52 It has been suggested that the overt or official reason for his travels (if one were needed) was either carto-graphic – obtaining latitudes of far northern points (O. A. W. Dilke, Greek and Roman Maps, Ithaca: Cornell University Press, 1985, pp. 29–30) – or a Massalian interest in the tin and amber-producing areas (Hennig, vol. 1, pp. 155–82). No single reason covers the diversity of his interests and the range of his travels, and the fact remains that his scholarly conclusions survived while political and mercantile concerns – if they existed at all – were forgotten.

53 Diogenes Laertios 5.2: the founding is discussed by John Patrick Lynch, Aristotle's School: A Study of a Greek Educational Institution, Berkeley: University of California Press, 1972, pp. 68–75.

54 Diogenes Laertios 5.10 (second year of Ol. 111).

school for 13 years before withdrawing to Chalkis during the convulsions in Athens after the death of Alexander, a few months before Aristotle's own death.[55] Yet during those years he managed to attract a wide range of students. Although the list preserved in the anonymous Latin *Life of Aristotle*[56] names only six – Theophrastos of Eresos, Phanios of Eresos, Eudemos of Rhodes, Klytos of Miletos, Aristoxenos of Taras, and Dikaiarchos of Messana – it is of great interest that they came from throughout the Greek world. One expects that these students might have been of assistance to Aristotle in his own researches. Klytos, for example, wrote on the history and culture of Miletos,[57] and thus could have provided his teacher data on his own native city for inclusion in Aristotle's work on its constitution, part of his collection on the political organization of 158 Greek states. Such a wide-ranging work would require contacts throughout the world, whether or not they came to the Lyceum.

One place Aristotle needed a contact was Massalia, not only to write his *Constitution of Massalia*,[58] but for the general information on that region of the Greek world that is revealed in his writings.[59] It will never be known who his Massalian informant was, but a likely candidate is Pytheas. There were close relations between Athens and Massalia in the mid-fourth century BC:[60] Demosthenes' uncle Demon had been sued by a Massalian, Zenothemis, as part of a complex scheme involving another Massalian, the shipowner Hegestratos, who – according to Demosthenes – conspired to borrow funds from Demon against a non-existent cargo and then to sink his ship, and thus the alleged collateral for the loan, which would cancel repayment.[61] The speech demonstrates that Massalia and Athens were in regular commercial contact at the time of Pytheas, and it is not unreasonable that Pytheas himself might have come to Athens,[62] as his language reflects that of Aristotle (and even Plato) in a number of places.[63] Aristotle, however, in his discussion of the phenomena of the Arctic,[64] seems to have had no knowledge of Pytheas' research, indicating that any association would have been before Pytheas' voyage.

The most that can be said with certainty is that Pytheas' journey and the research performed during it, which resulted in the treatise *On the Ocean*, occurred probably in the 320s BC or very shortly thereafter,[65] since it was unknown to (yet based on) Aristotle, and

55 Diogenes Laertios 5.5–6.
56 *Life of Aristotle* 46–7.
57 FGrHist #490; Athenaios 12.540, 14.655.
58 Athenaios 13.576. Comments on the government of Massalia also appear in the *Politics* (5.5.2, 6.4.5).
59 See, for example, Strabo 4.1.7. In addition, the Aristotelian *On Marvellous Things Heard* (87, 89) describes some unusual features of the region of Massalia.
60 Lionel Casson, "Traders and Trading: Classical Athens," *Expedition* 21.4, 1979, 30.
61 Demosthenes 32.
62 Pytheas, ed. Roseman, p. 148.
63 Pytheas, ed. Roseman, pp. 127–9. The most famous example is Pytheas' description of the "sea lung" (Polybios 34.5.3–5 [= Strabo 2.4.1]), a term found in Aristotle's *History of Animals* (5.15) and his *Parts of Animals* (4.5; see also Plato, *Philebos* 10; Pytheas, ed. Mette, p. 7; and infra, p. 85).
64 Aristotle, *Meteorologika* 2.5; see also *On the Heavens* 2.14.
65 It has been suggested that the obscurity of Pytheas' treatise was because its publication occurred just at the time of the death of Alexander, and the resulting chaos meant either few copies or a narrow dissemination (Hawkes [supra n. 14], p. 45).

first quoted by Aristotle's student Dikaiarchos. This date of around the time of Alexander has been upheld by most scholars.[66] Those who suggest other dates seem to have substantial flaws in their argumentation. Paul Fabre has proposed 380–360 BC,[67] based on a dubious passage of Servius[68] which attributed mention of Thoule, Pytheas' most famous toponym, to a certain Ktesias and a Diogenes. Who this Ktesias was is not certain, but if it is the best-known person of that name, the physician at the court of Artaxerxes II, this puts citation of Thoule as early as the beginning of the fourth century BC.[69] But the thread is extremely thin: in addition to the uncertain identification of Ktesias one must contend with the remoteness and uniqueness of Servius' comment and the general irrelevance of Thoule to Ktesias's area of interest. The Diogenes is probably Antonius Diogenes, author of the fantasy *Incredible Things Beyond Thoule*, universally considered to be from the Roman period, but Fabre dated his work earlier to give his theory support.[70] This all seems weak, and inconsistent with other data about Pytheas.

Christina Roseman has suggested that the journey was around 350BC with publication 30 years later, although her reasons are vague and would sever any direct association between the voyage and the world of Aristotle.[71] Some have dated Pytheas to after the era of Alexander: Cary and Warmington suggested 310–306BC,[72] based on an assumption that Pytheas had to go through the Pillars at a time when the Carthaginians were diverted, in this case by their defense against Syracuse. Although dangerously precise speculation, this date is plausible if one believes that Pytheas went through the Pillars, which seems unlikely. Rhys Carpenter[73] has the latest suggested date, 240–238BC, but this requires arguing away citations by Dikaiarchos and Timaios and again places far too much emphasis on when Pytheas could have passed through the Pillars. Many scholars use this issue as the primary criterion for dating the explorer, which seems such a distraction.[74] They also ignore the fact that *two* journeys through the Pillars, several years apart, would in theory have been necessary: if Pytheas seized a moment of Carthaginian diversion to dash through on his outward journey, how could he have hoped that the way would be free for his eventual return? The fact remains that all arguments that attempt to remove Pytheas from the era of Aristotle and Alexander are weaker than those that put him in that

---

66 A precise chronology of the voyage for given years in the later 320s BC has been calculated by Roch Knapowski, *Zagadnienia chronlogii i zasięgu podróży odkrywczych Piteasa z Marsylii, Prace Komisji Historycznej* 18, 1958, an intriguing exercise, perhaps more inventive than accurate, based on a journey through the Pillars and lasting a single year, neither of which is certain.

67 Paul Fabre, "Étude sur Pythéas le Massiliote et l'époque de ses travaux," *EtCl* 43, 1975, 25–44 (with summary of other suggested dates), and Fabre (supra n. 1), p. 16.

68 Servius, on *Georgics* 1.30.

69 *FGrHist* #688, fr. 64.

70 Paul Fabre, "Les Massaliotes et l'Atlantique," in *Océan Atlantique et Peninsule Armoricaine: études archéologiques*, Paris 1985, p. 31.

71 Pytheas, ed. Roseman, p. 155.

72 Cary and Warmington, pp. 47–8.

73 Carpenter, *Beyond*, pp. 145–50.

74 See Magnani (supra n. 37), pp. 78–89.

period.[75] Pytheas' journey may have found one of its catalysts in the publication of Ephoros' history in the 330s BC, with its extensive material on the far north; another may have been the concern in the western Mediterranean about Alexander's intentions. Whether Pytheas was at the Lyceum, or even visited Athens, cannot be proven. Yet as an educated man he had access to the latest research of his era, through study in Athens or Massalia, and this included recent developments in astronomy that he would exploit.

The earliest extant author to quote Pytheas is Hipparchos of Nikaia in the early second century BC.[76] But most of the existing references are from the *Geography* of Strabo and the *Natural History* of Pliny.[77] Other authors of the first century AC, such as Kleomedes, Geminos, and Aetios, also cited him, but briefly.[78] Yet Strabo and Pliny revealed a wide range of Hellenistic authors who knew about Pytheas: Dikaiarchos,[79] Timaios,[80] Eratosthenes,[81] Polybios,[82] Artemidoros,[83] and Xenophon of Lampsakos.[84] Whether Hekataios of Abdera can be added to this list is uncertain, but his *On the Hyperboreans*, even if a geographical fantasy, may have drawn from Pytheas' account. As a contemporary of Dikaiarchos, he would then be one of the earliest to be aware of the Massalian's explorations.[85]

The tradition about Pytheas, as collected mostly by Strabo, is almost universally hostile:[86] Strabo called him a constant liar, a creator of fables, and a fabricator.[87]

---

75 For other discussions of his date, with summaries of previous scholarship, see Gisinger (supra n. 37), pp. 314–16, Serena Bianchetti, "Per la datazione del Περὶ ὠκεανοῦ di Pitea di Massalia," *Sileno* 23, 1997, 73–84, and, most recently, the thorough analysis by Magnani (supra n. 37), pp. 15–31. But all these conclude that the 330s–320s BC is the most plausible period.

76 Hipparchos, *Commentary on the Phenomena of Aratos and Eudoxos* 1.4.1.

77 On Pliny's contradictory data regarding Pytheas, see Christina Horst Roseman, "Hour Tables and Thule in Pliny's *Natural History*," *Centaurus* 30, 1987, pp. 93–105.

78 Kleomedes, *Meteora* 1.4; Geminos, *Introduction to Phenomena* 6.8–9; Aetios 3.17.3.

79 Strabo 2.4.1–2.

80 Pliny, *Natural History* 37.35–6.

81 Strabo 1.4.2–5, 2.4.1–2, 3.2.11; Serena Bianchetti, "Pitea di Massalia e l'estremo occidente," *Hespería* 10, 2000, 129–37.

82 Strabo 2.4.1–2, 4.2.1.

83 Strabo 3.2.11.

84 Pliny, *Natural History* 4.95.

85 The fragments of Hekataios' work (*FGrHist* #264, fr. 7–14) nowhere mention Pytheas by name. Yet they include some remarkable details, such as the great circular temple of Apollo that is remindful of a megalithic stone circle (fr. 7 = Diodoros 2.47), raising the question as to whether Pytheas saw such monuments, perhaps in northwestern France. Strangely, Hekataios was more respected in antiquity than Pytheas, but modern opinion tends toward seeing *On the Hyperboreans* as a geographical and mythological fantasy (see, for example, Hawkes [supra n. 14], pp. 38–9), yet including actual data from Pytheas' report. The Hyperboreans were known to Greek literature from earliest times (*Homeric Hymn to Dionysos* 29), and although Hekataios' work may contain some contemporary geographical material, its focus is more on myth. On the Hyperboreans, see Romm, *Edges*, pp. 60–7.

86 Even Dio (39.50), hundreds of years later, was rather snappish (without naming names) about those who wrote about Britain but knew nothing about it, only indulging in academic guesswork: this can only be a reference to Pytheas.

87 Strabo 1.4.3–5. As I. G. Kidd wrote, "Pytheas. . .was one of his pet hates." (Poseidonios, *Posidonius 2: The Commentary*, ed. I. G. Kidd, Cambridge: Cambridge University Press, 1988, p. 21). See also Aujac (supra n. 37), pp. 45–8, suggesting that perhaps Strabo saw Pytheas as a rival (or even correction) to his favorite, Homer.

Sometimes the resentment is a little more personal: Polybios saw Pytheas as a rival to his own reputation as an explorer.[88] Yet much of the opposition is due to the evolution of geography as a discipline in late Hellenistic times[89] as well as the universal and often wise tendency to doubt reports of strange phenomena in the remote areas of the earth. Moreover, writers of geographical fantasies and romances often incorporated data from Pytheas, which did not help his reputation.[90] If Pytheas reported on the mild climate of the north, the reason for which – the Gulf Stream – was unknown in antiquity,[91] this would also have been further reason to discredit him.

Modern opinion, more knowledgeable about the Arctic, is more charitable. Pytheas' journey remains one of the most significant of ancient exploration. As Pytheas himself may have written, he "went along the entire coast of Europe from Gades to Tanais,"[92] travelling on occasion by foot. Since Gades is listed as the effective starting point, he may have gone overland from Massalia, an arduous journey that would have avoided any contact with the Carthaginians around the Pillars. Whether "Tanais" refers to the river of that name, the modern Don, or the city at its mouth, at the northeast corner of the Black Sea, is disputable.[93] Although going from the north of Europe to the Black Sea is quite possible, this may represent a conflation of two journeys, a later substitution of "Tanais" for another toponym to provide an eastern remote counterpart to Gades,[94] or even the assumption that one of the rivers emptying into the Baltic was in fact the Tanais, much as Euthymenes had found the "Nile" in West Africa.

Because the references to Pytheas' journey are so scattered, it is difficult to work out details of his itinerary, something that has been a problem since antiquity. Few actual

---

88 Polybios 34.5; see also 3.59.7; F. W. Walbank, "Polemic in Polybius," *JRS* 52, 1962, pp. 10–11.

89 On Pytheas' changing reputation, see Dion (supra n. 44), p. 443–66.

90 The connection between Pytheas and geographical fantasy is apparent by the time of Pliny (*Natural History* 4.95), where a report from Xenophon of Lampsakos cited Pytheas and then the Hippopodes ("The Horse Feet People") and the Panota islands, where the ears of the inhabitants covered their entire bodies. See also Pomponius Mela 3.56, and Susan A. Stephens and John J. Winkler (eds.), *Ancient Greek Novels: The Fragments*, Princeton: Princeton University Press, 1995, pp. 105–7.

91 G. W. Clarke, "Ancient Knowledge of the Gulf Stream," *CP* 62, 1967, 25–31.

92 Polybios 34.5.6 (= Strabo 2.4.1). As the text reads, the implication is that this is a second journey, after Pytheas' return from the north. This is possible, but it may be a confusion, a substitution of a more familiar – and thus more plausible to Strabo – journey along the Mediterranean coast for Pytheas' actual one in the far north. Nevertheless it has been argued that the explorations of Pytheas fall into two separate trips, one into the Atlantic and Arctic, and a second into the Baltic and along the routes to the Black Sea, and that the two extant titles are a vestige of this (see Dilke [supra n. 52], pp. 136–7).

93 On Pytheas and Tanais, see Roger Dion, "Où Pythéas voulait-il aller?" in *Mélanges d'archéologie et d'histoire offerts à André Piganiol*, ed. Raymond Chevallier, Paris 1966, pp. 1315–36.

94 The statement "Gades to Tanais" may be purely formulaic to indicate the entire navigable world (Cary and Warmington, p. 53), or all Europe, as the Tanais was the boundary between Europe and Asia (Strabo 11.1.5, 11.7.4). On this see Roger Dion, "Pythéas explorateur," *RPhil* 3. ser. 40, 1966, 201. It has also been suggested (Carpenter, *Beyond*, p. 189) that Tanais is a substitution for one of two British toponyms, Tanatis (modern Thanet in Kent) or Tamesa/Tamesis (the Thames). For these, see A. L. F. Rivit and Colin Smith, *The Place-Names of Roman Britain*, Princeton: Princeton University Press, 1979, pp. 466, 468–9.

direct quotations from the text have been identified.[95] Moreover, the ancient tradition regarding Pytheas is so negative that even when the explorer may have been quoted it was usually to be derisive, so the exact context of his words may be questionable.[96] Hidden fragments probably also exist, where Pytheas was quoted but not acknowledged.[97]

Before his departure from Massalia, Pytheas, as he was to do throughout his journey, determined the latitude,[98] which, he believed, turned out to be the same as that of Byzantion.[99] He then set forth. There is some indication that the first portion was on foot,[100] although the text of Strabo is especially confused and corrupt at this point. Travelling by foot – as it is known Pytheas did on occasion[101] – would avoid any Carthaginian blockade at the Pillars, but it is possible that Strabo was merely outlining the Massalian trade routes to the interior.[102] These had existed from at least the fifth century BC, when Massalian products and those from Greece proper penetrated the interior of France: Massalian imports began the French wine industry.[103] The easiest way across to the Atlantic would have been to go inland from Narbo (the Naro of Avienus)[104] up the gentle valley of the Alax (modern Aude), crossing over to the upper Garumna (modern Garonne), descending past the site of Toulouse to the Atlantic at

---

95 Roseman could only find nine (Pytheas [ed. Roseman], pp. 117–47), and some of these are quite dubious as representing Pytheas' actual words.

96 See, for example, Strabo 1.4.5.

97 Examples include Polybios 3.57.3 (see Walbank [supra n. 4], vol. 3, p. 394) and Diodoros 5.22. On the problem of hidden or lost fragments see Pytheas, ed. Stichtenoth, pp. 20–7, who would include long portions of the *Ora maritima* of Avienus (especially 80–145, on the Ostrymnides), and even some of the *Argonautika* of Apollonios of Rhodes (particularly 4.507–684, on the return of the Argonauts). Avienus mentioned Thoule in his *Descriptio orbis terrae* (760), although his late date makes his source uncertain.

98 On his method of measurement (using a gnomon) see Thomson, p. 153; see also Aujac (supra n. 37), pp. 165–8, who provided a summary table of his calculations. Pytheas was an important source of data for the later efforts of Eratosthenes, Hipparchos, and Poseidonios that determined the size of the earth: see Aubrey Diller, "Geographical Latitudes in Eratosthenes, Hipparchus, and Posidonius," *Klio* 27, 1934, pp. 258–69.

99 Hipparchos, *Geography*, fr. 53–5 = Strabo 1.4.4, 2.1.12, 2.5.8; Dicks (supra n. 37), 187–83; Árpád Szabó, "Strabon und Pytheas – die geographische Breite von Marseille," *Historia scientiarum* 29, 1985, 3–15. Massalia is in fact 2° north of Byzantion, and the error may not be due to Pytheas, but the sources. Other comments about Massalia preserved by Timaios (*FrGrHist* #566, fr. 70 = Strabo 4.1.8) may have derived from Pytheas (Truesdell S. Brown, *Timaeus of Tauromenium, University of California Publications in History* 55, 1958, pp 28–9).

100 Strabo 3.2.11.

101 Polybios 34.5.7 = Strabo 2.4.2.

102 Yet travelling by these known routes would also eliminate one of the most difficult sea passages of the journey, an issue ignored by most commentators (see Seán McGrail, "Celtic Seafaring and Transport," in *The Celtic World*, ed. Miranda J. Green, London 1995, pp. 275–6).

103 Boardman (supra n. 6), pp. 219–23.

104 Avienus, *Ora maritima* 587. Polybios' peculiar statement (3.38.1–2), that nothing is known about the north between Narbo and Tanais, may be a hidden slap at Pytheas that nonetheless reflects his use of the Narbo route. On this passage see Roger Dion, "Géographie historique de la France," *ACF* 65, 1965, 463–4.

the site of Bordeaux, a well-travelled itinerary from ancient to modern times.[105] This may be the way Pytheas reached the Ocean, but it would not have taken him past Gades, a place consistently associated with his journey, although in a somewhat confused fashion. Strabo seems to have connected Gades with another presumed voyage of Pytheas' that might have seemed more believable. Eratosthenes reported distances that Pytheas had allegedly recorded from Gades along the Iberian coast,[106] but even this does not mean that Pytheas actually travelled from Gades: these distances had been known for some time. A close reading of Strabo's text demonstrates that Eratosthenes' interest in Pytheas was not for the distances but for another significant statement, that northern Iberia (i.e. southern France) provided an easier means of access to the Keltic territory than the older all-Ocean route. Thus association of Pytheas' itinerary with Gades – a place that he did write about[107] – may either have been because he was there at another time, or due to the prevailing assumption that voyages on the Ocean began at Gades. Timaios gave Pytheas' voyage a mythic context by equating it with that of the Argonauts, who had sailed up the Tanais, hauled the Argo overland, and then sailed down to the Ocean and along the coast to Gades, a correspondence to Pytheas' own journey.[108] Pytheas probably was in Gades sometime during his career, but it may not have been part of his northern travels. The existence of an easier trade route, possible objections by the Carthaginians to use of the sea route, and the statement that Pytheas travelled by foot, all point to the first stage of his journey being overland to northwest France.[109]

After arrival in the northwest corner of France, Pytheas recorded a number of islands, whose names were not cited by the extant source, Strabo.[110] In addition, there was an ethnic group called the Ostimioi, mentioned in slightly varying forms here and in several other citations of Pytheas.[111] Strabo placed them near a place called Ouexisame, and recorded that they lived on a promontory which reached far out into the Ocean, in a district that was well north of Iberia and was Keltic in ethnicity. Ouexisame is consistently identified as Ushant,[112] the island off the northwest coast of Brittany that in modern times has been the navigational marker for ships leaving the English Channel in a southerly direction. When Pytheas reached Ouexisame – clearly the end of a peninsula in his day – he was still in territory

---

105 The route is outlined by Cunliffe (supra n. 37), pp. 56–62; see also his *Facing the Ocean*, Oxford: Oxford University Press, 2001, p. 332. An alternative would have been to cross from the Rhone to the Loire or Seine, a route used (in reverse) by the tin trade (Diodoros 5.23; see also Hennig, vol. 1, pp. 162–5).

106 Strabo 3.2.11.

107 Strabo 3.2.11, quoting Eratosthenes. Timaios hinted that Pytheas returned by ship to Gades (fr. 75a = Pliny, *Natural History* 4.94).

108 Timaios, fr. 85 = Diodoros 4.56.3–6. See also Brown (supra n. 99), p. 32.

109 On this portion of Pytheas' itinerary, see Stefano Magnani, "Le isole occidentali e l'itinerario piteano," *Sileno* 21, 1995, 83–102. But see Zimmermann (supra n. 45), pp. 29–30.

110 Strabo 1.4.5, quoting Eratosthenes.

111 Strabo 1.4.3, 5; 4.4.1; Stephanos of Byzantion, "Ostiones."

112 Pytheas, ed. Roseman, p. 38.

perfectly familiar to the Massalians: the Ostimioi are probably connected with the Ostrymnides of Avienus.[113]

Up to this point Pytheas had been following established trade routes.[114] But from here he entered an essentially unknown world, although some data about the lands beyond the northwest corner of Europe had long been available, perhaps even in Phokaian days.[115]

From the Ouexisame region he seems to have gone to Kantion, several days distant and opposite the mouth of the Rhenos: the two were said to be visible from one another. Presumably Kantion is the southern coast of Britain (Kent): relating it to the mouth of the Rhine may reflect not Pytheas, but Strabo, who was better informed about the river.[116] Kantion was part of the large island called Prettanike,[117] 40,000 stadia around, throughout which Pytheas travelled by foot.[118] This is one of the more remarkable statements about his career, and further evidence of extensive private exploration.[119] Several versions of Pytheas' measurements of Prettanike seem to survive, most notably that of Diodoros,[120] presenting a triangular Britain, whose European side, from Kantion – here defined as the point nearest Europe and thus the South Foreland of Kent, just northeast of Dover – to Belerion (presumably Land's End),[121] is 7500 stadia.[122] The east side from Kantion to the north end at Orka – one

113 Avienus, *Ora maritima* 90–102. On these toponyms, see François Lasserre, "Ostiéens et Ostimniens chez Pythéas," *MusHelv* 20, 1963, 107–13. Of interest, perhaps, is a gold stater of Kyrene, dated to 322–315BC, found near Lampaul-Ploudamézeus in the department of Finistère (Pierre-Roland Giot et al., *Protohistoire de la Bretagne*, Rennes: Editions Ouest-France, 1995, pp. 215–7), speculatively an artifact from Pytheas' journey.

114 Barry Cunliffe, *The Ancient Celts*, Oxford: Oxford University Press, 1997, p. 150. The trade routes are discussed by M. Cary, "The Greeks and Ancient Trade With the Atlantic," *JHS* 44, 1924, 172–7. The Iron Age site of Le Yandet, at the mouth of the Lèguer and close to the line of one of Pytheas' latitude calculations, has been suggested by Cunliffe (supra n. 37), pp. 64–9, as the type of place Pytheas might have visited.

115 Supra, pp. 91–4.

116 Strabo 1.4.3. The mouth of the Rhine is far east of, and in no way visible from, the Kentish coast, as it is understood today, but this may be unnecessarily precise. But see Joaquin Herrmann (ed.), *Griechische und lateinische Quellen zur Frühgeschichte Mitteleuropas*, Berlin: Akademie-Verlag, 1988–92, vol. 1, p. 503.

117 This seems to be the proper form, used by Strabo in several places in his 2.5 (also 4.2.1), perhaps indicating Pytheas' original spelling, since part of this section (especially 2.5.8) seem heavily dependent on him. The more common form, Brittanike, may be a Roman-period confusion with Brittany (Pytheas, ed. Roseman, p. 45). Some manuscripts of Diodoros (5.32.3) also have the form "Prettanoi." Editors and translators have often been careless about preserving the "P" form, even changing the text without comment.

118 Polybios 34.5.2 = Strabo 2.4.1. For how this might have been accomplished see Pytheas, ed. Roseman, 126. Suggestions that Pytheas went north up the west side of Britain and returned down the east side after his visit to Thoule and the Baltic (for example, Dion [supra n. 94], p. 207) raise unanswered questions as to how he would have correlated his data.

119 Another coin seems to be of particular interest: a silver one of Alexander, dated to after 326BC, from Holne Chase in Devon (Aileen Fox, *South West England*, New York: Praeger, 1964, p. 116).

120 Diodoros 5.21–2; on others, see Walbank (supra n. 4), vol. 3, p. 589.

121 On the toponym and its location, see Rivit and Smith (supra n. 94), pp. 266–7.

122 Nansen (supra n. 37), vol. 1, p. 51, has pointed out that these round figures may be translated from a formula of 1000 stadia to one day's sail.

of the northern points of Scotland, Dunnet Head or Duncansby Head – is 15,000 stadia: the name Orka is preserved in the nearby Orkneys. The west side, back to Belerion, is 20,000 stadia, a total of 42,500 stadia, very close to the round figure of 40,000 stadia of Polybios.[123]

Diodoros' measurements are followed by a description of the locals living a life of hardy simplicity, much like that of the Greeks at the time of the Trojan War. This seems anachronistic for Diodoros' own day, and a promise to discuss the ethnography of Britain in detail when he examined Caesar's campaigns – a promise never fulfilled and seemingly beyond the known limits of Diodoros' work – sets this earlier brief ethnography apart from his own era.[124] Regrettably, despite Pytheas' stated familiarity with all of Britain, any further detailed comments, if they survived, are so deeply buried in later sources that they cannot be identified. Polybios, after the fall of Carthage, went as far as the Liger (Loire), and could learn nothing about either Prettanike or Pytheas,[125] perhaps a further indication of the private nature of the Massalian's trip, something ultimately not conducive to the survival of his data.

Few facts can be gleaned from Pytheas' stated intimacy with the British Isles. He seems to have made several calculations of latitude, as he had done at Massalia, determining the maximum midwinter solar elevation at six and four *peches* – the length from the elbow to the tip of the fingers.[126] These latitudes have been calculated at 54°17' – just north of York – and 58°17' – very close to the northern end of Scotland and perhaps a sighting at that point. Strabo also provided distances from Massalia, which were probably originally derived from latitudes. These are 6,300 and 9,100 stadia, which may be at 52°12' and 56°12' – about the latitudes of Cambridge and Dundee. Needless to say these calculations are fraught with immense variables and difficulty of astronomical, geographical, and textual sorts.[127] Nevertheless they seem to give a spread across Great Britain from the latitude of Cambridge to that of the northern tip of Scotland. The midwinter sightings at widely separated places also suggest that Pytheas was in the field for several years, giving further credence to his claim to have travelled throughout Britain.[128] He may have been the first from the

---

123 How these measurements conform to modern distances is of little point since the length of a given stadion is not known with certainty, and the type of calculation Pytheas was attempting along a rugged and severely indented coast – which has changed since antiquity – has too many variables and would be exceedingly difficult. Pliny (*Natural History* 4.102), quoting Pytheas, provided a distance of 4875 miles, about 7200 km.

124 Caesar himself seems to have been familiar with some of Pytheas' data about Britain, probably through a Hellenistic geographical source (*Bellum Gallicum* 5.13). See further, infra, pp. 116–17.

125 Polybios 34.10.6 = Strabo 4.2.1; infra, p. 100.

126 Strabo 2.5.8, perhaps from Hipparchos although the transmission is not clear; see also Hipparchos, *Geography*, fr. 61 = Strabo 2.1.18. Pytheas' latitudes were also quoted by Pliny (*Natural History* 6.219), but with no attribution, although the data as well as mention of Thoule make the source apparent.

127 On the calculations see Dicks (supra n. 37), pp. 185–90.

128 On the length of his trip, see Dicks (supra n. 37), pp. 186–7. Broche (supra n. 37), pp. 239–41, calculated the minimum travel time as 187½ days without stopovers or seasonal needs. See also Magnani (supra n. 37), pp. 162–70.

Mediterranean to see the summer night of high latitudes, where the light of the sun shines dimly all night and moves in a reverse direction from the west to the east.[129] This unfamiliar phenomenon is explained with great care and precise vocabulary, using the rare word παραυγάζομαι ("to give the appearance of shining"), perhaps invented by Pytheas for this purpose.[130] In fact, innovative vocabulary is part of his treatise: προσάρκτιον ("toward the Bear" or "northerly") described his journey,[131] which was παρωκεανῖτις (along "the sea coast").[132] A striking phrase preserved only in Pliny's Latin, "angusto lucis ambitu," ("the narrow course of light"),[133] also suggests unusual diction. These rare and perhaps even new words show that Pytheas was going beyond linguistic boundaries even as he passed the limits of the cosmos – κόσμος, a word with epic overtones that Strabo dismissed as an exaggeration by Pytheas unworthy even of the god of travellers, Hermes.[134]

Pytheas may have visited the Cornish tin mines. Diodoros, immediately after his promise to discuss Britain in detail in the context of Caesar's campaigns, launched into a examination of the tin industry in Cornwall.[135] After noting local hospitality to strangers and foreign merchants, he described the process of mining and the export of tin ore to the island of Iktis,[136] six days away, which was connected to the mainland at low tide. After a digression on the tides, Diodoros further recorded how the tin was transported across the Channel and through France, eventually reaching the mouth of the Rhone. His source is not mentioned but as in the immediately previous passage on the ethnography of Britain and the following one on amber, the signatures of Pytheas are apparent, including the Massalian orientation of the tin route, the interest in tides, and the remark on the reception of strangers. Diodoros' immediate source may have been Timaios,[137] who knew Pytheas' work, a view reinforced by the citation of

---

129 Hipparchos, *Geography* fr. 58 = Strabo 2.1.18; see also fr. 57 = 2.5.42.

130 On this passage, see Dicks (supra n. 37), pp. 184–5.

131 Polybios 34.5.9 = Strabo 2.4.2.

132 Polybios 34.5.6 = Strabo 2.4.1.

133 Pliny, *Natural History* 2.186. This may be the *aurora borealis* (already known to the Greeks: see Aristotle, *Meterologika* 1.5) or even the limited sunlight seen at high latitude, in the north during summer and the south in winter. Narrow bands of light are common in depictions of the Arctic: see, for example, Rockwell Kent's "Resurrection Bay, Alaska (Blue and Gold)" (Bowdoin College, Maine), #80 in Constance Martin, *Distant Shores: the Odyssey of Rockwell Kent*, Berkeley: University of California Press, 2000, or Sydney Laurence's "Streak of Sky" (in the collection of Betty Balderston de Lancey), #37 in Kesler E. Woodward, *Sydney Laurence: Painter of the North*, Seattle: University of Washington Press, 1990.

134 Strabo 2.4.2

135 Diodoros 5.22. On this tin trade, see, cautiously, R. P. Penhallurick, *Tin in Antiquity*, London: Institute of Metals, 1986, pp. 139–47, whose use of ancient sources leaves something to be desired. See also Cunliffe (supra n. 37), pp. 73–92.

136 The actual form of this name is uncertain. Diodoros has the accusative Ἴκτιν. Pliny (*Natural History* 4.104) has "insulam Mictim," probably a dittographic error. There is also some disputable late evidence (for which see Gavin de Beer, "Iktin," *GJ* 126, 1960, 162). The presumed nominative, Iktis, used by most scholars, does not exist in ancient sources. See also Rivit and Smith (supra n. 94), p. 488.

137 Timaios, fr. 164.

Figure 12 St Michael's Mount (Iktis?)

Photograph by Letitia K. Roller.

Timaios, Iktis (as Mictim), and tin by Pliny,[138] where "Mictim" is tied into the context of Thoule, another Pythean reference.[139]

Little further can be discerned from Pytheas' information on Britain.[140] He may be the source for a list of various islands in the *Natural History* of Pliny: 40 Orcades, seven Acmodae (or Hacmodae), 30 Hebudes, and eight islands said to be between Britain and Ireland.[141] That this catalogue has some connection with Pytheas is clear by mention of the explorer at the beginning of the passage as well as the topics that follow, amber, Thoule, and the Scandiae, all associated with the Massalian's journey. The account has been updated to the Roman period and also makes use of the map of Marcus Agrippa – which itself might have had data derived from Pytheas – so Pytheas' exact contribution is, as usual, uncertain. The use of collective quantities of islands, in fact, seems to be from a map. The Orkneys and Hebrides seem obvious; the Acmodae,

138 Pliny, *Natural History* 4.104 (= Timaios, fr. 74).

139 The figure of six days may indicate a confusion with Thoule, which was the same distance from Britain (Strabo 1.4.2). Otherwise, it suggests the Isle of Wight (ancient Vectis), but St Michael's Mount near Penzance fits the description better (Figure 12). Another suggestion is Mount Batten, opposite Plymouth, supported by contemporary archaeological finds, which are lacking at St Michael's Mount (Barry Cunliffe, "Ictis: Is It Here?" *OJA* 2, 1983, 123–36; C. F. C. Hawkes, "Ictis Disentangled, and the British Tin Trade," *OJA* 3, 1984, 211–33). Nevertheless, the repetition of the six-day figure strengthens the Pythean context of the tin mines. All the possible sites for Iktis are discussed by I. S. Maxwell, "The Location of Ictis," *JRIC* n. s. 6, 1969–72, 293–319, who favored St Michael's Mount.

140 A possible itinerary up the west side of Britain is suggested by Cunliffe (supra n. 37), pp. 99–102.

141 Pliny, *Natural History* 4.103.

which Pomponius Mela located opposite the German coast,[142] may be some of the Scandinavian islands, although they also have been suggested to be the Shetlands.[143] The other eight individually-named islands, insofar as they can be identified, are mostly in the Irish Sea, including Mona and Monapia (Man and Anglesey), but also as far south as Vectis (the Isle of Wight) and Axanthos, a toponym in the class with Ouexisame and Ostrymnides: these names may represent data later than Pytheas that intrude into Pliny's text.

An essential part of Pytheas' journey is his scientific research, a connection to the world of Aristotle and Athens. In addition to his regular calculations of latitude and his tidal theory, Pytheas was interested in the movements of the visible stars,[144] especially noting that there was no star at the celestial pole but that it was marked by an empty tetragon.[145] This is perhaps his most important astronomical discovery: in this, Hipparchos contrasted Pytheas with the erroneous conclusion of Eudoxos of Knidos, who believed in the existence of a pole star.[146] In fact, the astronomical research of Eudoxos, which appeared perhaps a generation before Pytheas set forth, may have been another inspiration for his journey.[147] Pytheas' contemporary Autolykos of Pitane was also developing his theories of spherical astronomy;[148] whether Pytheas had access to his material is unknown but at the very least Pytheas' interest in aspects of the same topic demonstrates that he was at the leading edge of contemporary astronomical thought.[149]

After more than a year, perhaps, wandering around Prettanike, admiring the rustic simplicity of the natives, making a number of astronomical calculations, and perhaps even becoming aware of Ireland,[150] Pytheas headed north. Yet from Britain it becomes even more difficult to track him. There is an abundance of toponyms, some of which seem familiar but most of which are not. Even if these are located, the exact order in which they were visited remains obscure. Latitudes and solar measurements do not

142 Pomponius Mela 3.54; see also the Silberman edition, p. 286.

143 Pytheas, ed. Roseman, p. 90.

144 Kleomedes, *Meteora* 1.4; also Strabo 2.5.8; 4.5.5.

145 Hipparchos, *Commentary on the Phenomena of Aratos and Eudoxos* 1.4.1. A chart prepared by the Osservatorio Astrofisico in Arcetri shows the polar regions as seen from Massalia in 330BC. The celestial pole is between Ursa Minor and Draco, with the tetragon composed of β Ursae minoris, κ and λ Draconis, and the pole itself (Pytheas, ed. Bianchetti, fig. 2; see also her pp. 109–11); an alternative rectangle has α Draconis, rather than λ (Dicks [supra n. 37], p. 170). Regardless of which stars make up the tetragon, the viewer today, looking north on a summer night in the Northern Hemisphere, can easily see the large empty area to the left of the modern pole star (Ursae minoris α), where the pole was in Pytheas' day.

146 Eudoxos, fr. 11 (Lasserre); on this passage, see Eudoxos, ed. Lasserre, p. 187.

147 Diller (supra n. 37), p. 225; Pytheas, ed. Bianchetti, pp. 39–45. For Eudoxos' dates (perhaps 395–342BC), see Eudoxos, ed. Lasserre, pp. 137–9.

148 G. Aujac, "L'Île de Thulé, mythe ou réalité," *Athenaeum* n. s. 76, 1988, pp. 330–3.

149 Gisinger (supra n. 37), pp. 316–20.

150 W. W. Hyde, *Ancient Greek Mariners*, New York: Oxford University Press, 1947, p. 128; Philip Freeman, *Ireland and the Classical World*, Austin: University of Texas Press, 2001, pp. 33–4. The polemic about the inhabitants of Ireland at Diodoros 5.32 may have been told to Pytheas by British informants (Carpenter, *Beyond*, pp. 171–2). See also Serena Bianchetti, "Cannibali in Irlanda? Lettura straboniane," *AncS* 32, 2002, 215–34.

always provide precise information as to where they were taken, and thus there is the possibility of error: as transmitted, Pytheas' latitude of Massalia is equated with that of Byzantion, some 200km to the north. Pytheas had fixed the northern limit of Prettanike by recording that in midwinter the sun only rose to four *peches*: his next midwinter observation, whether a few days or a year later, was that it was less than three *peches*, or at least 61°17'. There are only three places in the north Atlantic where this latitude touches land: southern Greenland, the Faeroe Islands,[151] or the Norwegian coast north of Bergen. All are possible although Greenland is highly implausible. The Norwegian coast and the Faeroes are perhaps equally reasonable, yet it seems too much of a coincidence that Pytheas should calculate midwinter solar height at exactly the latitude of one of the Faeroes, one of the few points of land in the north Atlantic, unless that is where he was, having travelled 300 miles north of Scotland, perhaps passing through the Orkneys and with the Shetlands to the east. The journey must have been on local fishing boats.[152]

A hint of the sailing itinerary Pytheas might have used, although from a much later date, comes from the second chapter of the Icelandic *Landnámabók*, the *Book of Settlements*, written in the twelfth century and describing the populating of Iceland between AD870 and AD930:[153]

> From Hern Island, off Norway, one can sail due west to Cape Farewell [the southern tip of Greenland], passing north of Shetland close enough to see it clearly in good visibility, and south of the Faeroes half-sunk below the horizon, and a day's sail to the south of Iceland.

Long before settlement, fishermen would have been familiar with these waters, and would have been able to move back and forth between Scandinavia, the northern British Isles, the Faeroes, and Iceland, rarely being out of sight of land: the itinerary in the *Landnámabók* is probably far older than the ninth century. It is only 200 miles

---

151 The line is actually a short distance south of the southern end of the Faeroes at Akraberg on Suderoy (which lies at 61°24'); further south between 61°20' and 21' are the two islets of Flesjarnar and Sumbiarsteinur. The latter is the southernmost point of Faeroe territory. But all these points, as well at Pytheas' line, lie over a mere seven minutes of latitude.

152 For small boats, including the evidence from Britain (although somewhat later than Pytheas), see Lionel Casson, *Ships and Seamanship in the Ancient World*, Princeton: Princeton University Press, 1971, pp. 329–43; Cunliffe (supra n. 37), pp. 103–6. Of particular interest, perhaps, is the boat discovered at Hjortspring in Denmark, on the island of Als, just off the southeast coast of Jutland (Klavs Randsborg, *Hjortspring: Warfare and Sacrifice in Early Europe*, Aarhus: Aarhus University Press, 1995, especially pp. 19–37). Excavations in the 1920s revealed a 19m long wooden double-prowed boat (now in the National Museum, Copenhagen), with the pieces sewn together and the entire vessel tarred. It had a minimum crew of 19–22. Carbon–14 dates average to 345–325BC, exactly contemporary with Pytheas. Associated with the vessel are a number of wooden pyxides similar to Greek ceramics of the fourth century BC, perhaps imports from central Europe. Although the boat had a military rather than mercantile function, it is perhaps the closest known example to the type Pytheas might have used in the north.

153 See *The Vinland Sagas: The Norse Discovery of America*, tr. and intro. by Magnus Magnusson and Hermann Pálsson, London: Penguin 1965, p. 16.

Figure 13 Faeroe Islands. Kollafjørdur (Streymoy), typical of the scenery Pytheas might have encountered.

Photograph by Duane W. Roller.

from the Shetlands to the Faeroes and another 400 on to Iceland. Mirages would have assisted.

The Faeroes consist of 11 major islands and numerous small islets and rocks, all with the same basic shape of long and narrow, with the long axis oriented northwest/southeast. They are separated by parallel ocean channels rarely more than 2km wide (Figure 13). The largest island, Streymoy, is ca. 45km long and no more than 12km wide: the capital of the islands, Tórshavn, whose name reveals its antiquity, is at the southern end. The highest point of the Faeroes is on adjacent Eysturoy, 882m above sea level: the islands are extremely precipitous with no point more than 5km from the ocean. There are many harbors due to the indentations of the coast, especially at the heads of the fjords. Pytheas may have landed in the Faeroes, especially on the southern island of Suderoy, but it is difficult to imagine anything detaining him: although impressive visually they were certainly uninhabited and have none of the unique phenomena of Iceland.

Somewhere in this region Pytheas allegedly encountered tides that were 80 cubits high.[154] This is impossible, and in fact the tides in this area of the north Atlantic are quite moderate,[155] but Pytheas may have experienced a particularly violent storm, or

---

154 Pliny, *Natural History* 2.217. The cubit is Pliny's translation of the *peches*.

155 The maximum range in the Orkneys is 10.4 feet, and less in the other islands north of Scotland (National Oceanic and Atmospheric Administration, *Tide Tables 1995: Europe and the West Coast of Africa*, Washington 1994, p. 167); the highest range in the British Isles is at Newport in the Bristol Channel – which Pytheas probably saw – a maximum of 38.9 feet (p. 165).

heard about one from local tradition, an event that would have made the tides seem extreme.[156] Pytheas is in fact an early theorist about the tides. Most significant is Aetios' assertion that Pytheas attributed low and high tides to the phases of the moon,[157] a somewhat problematic statement that may mean that he was the first to relate tides in a general way to lunar activity: the exceptional tide north of Britain may have seemed to have been connected to the moon. Pytheas is also credited with reporting that the tides ended at the Sacred Promontory, five days or 1700 stadia from Gades[158] – hence on the coast of the Iberian Peninsula, perhaps modern Cape St Vincent – which is also impossibly confused, since tidal phenomena in this well-travelled region had long been known, and tides actually increase as one travels north from Gades to the English Channel.[159] Thus Pytheas' comment may actually have been about the seemingly diminishing tides of the far north.[160] The data that he collected about the tides passed down to Eratosthenes and then to the existing sources of the Roman period, perhaps via Seleukos of Seleukeia, who may have written the first treatise specifically on the tides.[161] Yet the material attached to Pytheas is so confused that his contribution cannot be isolated. Regardless of how far he carried his theory, connecting the moon and the tides may be his most important scientific achievement. He may also have been responsible for observations regarding the setting of the sun into the ocean, including its apparent increased size, although some of these comments, attributed in extant literature to Poseidonios and Artemidoros, may be older than Pytheas.[162]

---

156 Tremendous storm surges are possible around the British Isles and contribute significantly to land erosion and island formation. See Charles Thomas, *Exploration of a Drowned Landscape*, London: B. T. Batsford, 1985, pp. 48–52. Pomponius Mela (3.55) noted how tides in this region could turn one island into many. It has been suggested that Pytheas witnessed a violent storm in the Pentland Firth between Scotland and the Orkneys (Cary and Warmington, p. 50; on the phenomena of this region see Carpenter, *Beyond*, pp. 172–3). He may have travelled at a time of exceptional tides: see N. N. Zubov, *Arctic Ice and the Warming of the Arctic*, tr. E. Hope, Moscow: Northern Sea Route Directorate, 1948, p. 71.

157 Aetios 3.17.2; see also Pliny, *Natural History* 2.217. On these passages see Pytheas, ed. Roseman, pp. 81–2, 103–4; Pytheas, ed. Bianchetti, pp. 111–15. The connection with the moon is attributed to Euthymenes in *On the History of Philosophy* (88; cf. Hermann Diels, *Doxographi graeci*, Berlin: Walter de Gruyter, 1879, p. 634) in the corpus of Galen, probably an error.

158 Strabo 3.2.11; from Eratosthenes. Strabo's understanding of tides was minimal (see 1.3.11–12), so he is probably the source of many of the problems regarding Pytheas' data. Strabo realized that there was some confusion, noting that 350 stadia a day is an exceptionally low rate of travel.

159 National Oceanic and Atmospheric Administration (supra n. 155), pp. 161–2.

160 A comment by Timaios (fr. 73 = Aetios 3.17.6) about the tidal effect of rivers in Keltic territory – presumably the west coast of France – may also have been derived from Pytheas (Cary and Warmington, p. 49).

161 Poseidonios, fr. 86 (= Strabo 3.5.8–9). Seleukos of Seleukeia (or Babylon) was active in the second century BC. His material was used by Poseidonios and then Strabo, whose account of tidal phenomena here is much more straightforward than when he discussed Pytheas' reports, although still somewhat skeptical. Whether Seleukos had access to Pytheas' account is unknown, but Seleukos seems to have been the first after Pytheas to connect the moon and tides, and to develop a coherent scientific theory about the process. See further, Duane W. Roller, "Seleukos of Seleukeia," to appear in *AntCl*.

162 Poseidonios, fr. 45 (= Strabo 3.1.5); Poseidonios (supra n. 87), pp. 462–3.

Figure 14 Iceland, as Pytheas might first have seen it: the southeast coast from out to sea.
Photograph by Duane W. Roller.

Six days from Prettanike Pytheas reached Thoule, his most famous discovery (Figure 14).[163] The crossing was made from the island of Berrice – the name is preserved only in Latin – the largest island in its region but otherwise unknown,[164] perhaps Streymoy, the largest of the Faeroes, or Mainland, the largest of the Shetlands. But the context is more Scandinavian than British, so Berrice may be the mainland point Pytheas returned to from Thoule. Analysis of Thoule – the name also appears as Thyle, Tyle and, in Latin, Thule[165] – is more inscrutable than most problems in Pythean topography. In addition to the usual difficulties that surround every piece of his route, Thoule has become not

163 Strabo 1.4.2, perhaps from Eratosthenes; see also Pliny, *Natural History* 2.186–7. Whether Pytheas actually visited Thoule, or merely heard about it, has been disputed by modern scholars, perhaps unnecessarily. Strabo (2.4.1) seems to contrast Pytheas' travels throughout Britain with his merely reporting (προσιστορήσαντος) on Thoule, but to make such a distinction seems questionably precise, although it fits into existential ideas about a Thoule that "can be perceived but not approached" (Romm, *Edges*, pp. 157–8). The extensive data about Thoule is enough to assume that he had been there, and, moreover, Kleomedes (*Meteora* 1.4.208–10) wrote specifically that the tradition was that Pytheas had visited the place. On Pytheas and Thoule see Richard Hennig, *Von rätselhaften Ländern*, Munich: Delphin-Verlag, 1925, pp. 95–138; G. MacDonald, "Thule oder Thyle," *RE* 2. ser. 11, 1936, 627–30; Gisinger (supra n. 37), pp. 332–44; Pytheas, ed. Bianchetti, pp. 150–95; Ian Whitaker, "The Problem of Pytheas' Thule," *CJ* 77, 1981–2, 148–64, which concisely summarizes the data.

164 Timaios, fr. 74 = Pliny, *Natural History* 4.104.

165 Yet it remained purely a Greek toponym. For a long – and ultimately fruitless – etymological discussion of the name, see Luigi De Anna, *Thule: le fonti e le tradizione*, Rimini: Il Cerchio, 1998, pp. 9–11.

only a major geographical crux from Hellenistic to modern times[166] but a significant cultural paradigm, beginning in the Roman period.[167] It became the stock formula for remoteness, a view perhaps first expressed by Vergil,[168] with whom a famous phrase entered cultural awareness, "ultima Thule," symbolic of the wide reach of Augustus' power, yet having only the vaguest connection with the place discovered by Pytheas.[169] Seneca expanded the metaphor in his notable passage in the *Medea* that was such an inspiration to early modern exploration and which also created the phrase "New World."[170] Thoule came to be a northern counterpart to the less famous Kerne,[171] and by the time of Ammianus Marcellinus it was identified with any far-off place, with no real connection to geography.[172] In modern times, its mystical fame was strengthened by usages such as Goethe's "King of Thule."[173]

Yet parallel with these literary versions were the constant attempts to rediscover Pytheas' Thoule: by Roman times it became part of the British Isles (a view reinforced by Strabo's connection of the two places, however much in ridicule).[174] In the first century AC Vespasian was said to have conquered it,[175] and later C. Julius Agricola also went there.[176] In the sixth century AC Prokopios was anxious to visit it, but never did.[177] Obviously these "discovered" Thoules were merely places in the remote north that had little relationship to Pytheas' travels: Agricola, for example, seems to have been in the Shetlands. The search for Thoule, and the assumption that any newly-found northern landmass was it, continued beyond antiquity. In the early eighth century AC Irish monks discovered Thoule either in Iceland or Norway, and by the following century another Irish monk, Dicuil, in his *Liber de mensura orbis terrae*, described how 30 years previous to his day, or about AD795, a group of monks had lived on "Tyle" for six months: his description implies Iceland.[178]

---

166 One of Strabo's complaints about Pytheas is that no one had ever found Thoule again (1.4.3). In Strabo's day it already had moved closer to Britain, and a few years later Pomponius Mela (3.57) seemed to locate it in the Baltic (see Piergiorgio Parroni, "Surviving Sources of the Classical Geographers Through Late Antiquity and the Medieval Period," *Arctic* 37, 1984, 356).

167 On this evolving attitude toward Thoule, see Monique Mund-Dopchie, "La survie littéraire de la Thulé de Pythéas," *AntCl* 59, 1990, 79–97, who cited literary uses of the name from Vergil to Umberto Eco; see also István Borzsák, "Ultimus Thules," *AAntHung* 41, 2001, 217–24.

168 Vergil, *Georgics* 1.30.

169 On Ultima Thule and its cultural meaning, see Romm, *Edges*, pp. 121–71.

170 Seneca, *Medea* 363–379 ("novus orbis"). His thinking may have been inspired by his father, who wrote of "another world' ("alius orbis": *Suasoria* 1.1).

171 Katherine Clarke, *Between Geography and History: Hellenistic Constructions of the Roman World*, Oxford: Clarendon Press, 1999, pp. 24–5.

172 Ammianus Marcellinus 18.6.1.

173 Goethe, *Faust* 2759.

174 Strabo 1.4.3; see H. J. W. Wijsman, "Thule Applied to Britain," *Latomus* 57, 1998, 318–23.

175 Silius Italicus 3.597.

176 Tacitus, *Agricola* 10.5.

177 Prokopios, *History of the Wars* 6.15. His detailed description of the large population and its cultural life indicates that Scandinavia was probably meant.

178 Dicuil 7.7–13; see the Tierney edition, p. 115; Gunnar Karlsson, *The History of Iceland*, Minneapolis: University of Minnesota Press, 2000, pp. 9–10. On Dicuil, see Werner Bergmann, "Dicuil," *TTEMA*, 151–2.

Thoule also came to be confused with similarly-named places elsewhere, such as Tyre in Lebanon or Tylos, modern Bahrain, in the Persian Gulf; thus it lost the limited geographical coherence that it had had. By the early Renaissance, it had become an essential element of the westward movement of European explorers: Columbus was said to have visited "Tile" in 1477 and sailed 100 leagues west of it,[179] although by his time Thoule was located in so many places that any connection with the Arctic is unnecessary.[180] In 1910, Knud Rasmussen applied the name to the indigenous culture of Greenland,[181] and in 1950 Ultima Thule became the name of an American air base on that island. This continuing evolution of Thoule has little to do with Pytheas but demonstrates the difficulty a modern critic has in comprehending where the Massalian had actually gone.[182]

The remoteness of Thoule is emphasized by Strabo's comment that no one except Pytheas mentioned it, even those familiar with the other islands around Britain and Ireland.[183] To Strabo – who received some of his information on Thoule from Eratosthenes – this was cause for rejection of the existence of the place: he felt that in his day Ierne (Ireland) was the most northerly land.[184] Strabo ignored other possible interpretations: that Thoule was not mentioned elsewhere because it was not to be found in the islands around Britain and Ireland, and because Pytheas was indeed the only one ever to have reached it. In fact, Strabo had already reported Pytheas' statement that Thoule was six days north of Britain, which would hardly put it in the category of "small islands around Brettanike." Strabo, following Eratosthenes, located Thoule 11,500 stadia north of the parallel of the Borysthenes, but he felt that habitation was not possible that far north, and indeed no further than 9000 stadia north of the Borysthenes parallel. This parallel was defined as where the midsummer day was 16 hours long, which Strabo believed was the center of Britain.[185] In fact it is at 48°42' north latitude, that of Paris, so all these calculations are highly suspect. Precision is even more difficult because of the uncertain length of the stadion and because Strabo's

179 Fernando Cólon, *The Life of the Admiral Christopher Columbus*, tr. Benjamin Keen, New Brunswick, N. J: Rutgers University Press, 1959, p. 11; Stefansson (supra n. 37), pp. 109–222; De Anna (supra n. 165), pp. 31–45.

180 As early as the twelfth century, one of the locations of Thoule was directly west of the Mediterranean, more in the area of Columbus' interest than the Arctic: see Vincent H. Cassidy, "The Voyage of an Island," *Speculum* 38, 1963, p. 601. Yet Columbus' report (supra n. 179) placed "Tile" at 73° north latitude, "not 63° as some [Ptolemy] affirm," thereby replacing the latitude of Iceland with an even more northern point, essentially that of Jan Mayen Island, which has been suggested, although implausibly, as a possible location of Thoule. Jan Mayen seems totally outside ancient and even medieval knowledge; it was "discovered" in the early seventeenth century. The issue remains one of the many mysteries of Columbus' early life.

181 Knud Rasmussen, *Greenland By the Polar Sea*, tr. Asta and Rowland Kenney, London: William Heinemann, 1921.

182 On this evolution, see Cassidy (supra n. 180), pp. 595–602.

183 Strabo 1.4.3.

184 Strabo 2.1.13.

185 The calculation of the parallel is from Hipparchos, *Geography*, fr. 57 = Strabo 2.5.42; see also Strabo 1.4.4, Pliny, *Natural History* 6.219; Dicks (supra n. 37), pp. 184–5.

figure was probably reduced to stadia from other measurements. Yet 11,500 stadia (6,900,000 feet), even at a minimum foot length, could hardly be much less than 2000km. This distance from 48°42' passes through the center of Iceland, central Greenland, and the coast of Norway near Namsos. At Namsos, the coast runs northeast, as it has for many kilometers, and it is difficult to imagine that this far northeastern continental point was where Pytheas sighted land.[186] Central Greenland also seems excessively remote. Thus all indications, however questionable, point to Iceland as the location of Thoule, although certainty is far from possible.[187] Iceland is on rare occasions visible from the Faeroes,[188] so Pytheas may have received reports of additional land to the northwest. Moreover, bird migration paths may have shown the route.[189] The major arguments against Iceland are that it was deserted at this time yet Pytheas seems (but not with certainty) to have described its inhabitants,[190] and the presence of bees at Thoule, which are generally believed not to have been in Iceland before modern times.[191]

Assuming that Thoule is Iceland, Pytheas probably sighted it, as did generations of Vikings, at the Vestrahorn, the point of land closest to the Faeroes. On a coast noted for its ruggedness, the Vestrahorn (elevation 888m.) is nonetheless a prominent landmark (Figure 15). Immediately to the west is the Skarðsfjörður, where the modern port of Höfn is, one of the rare harbors on the south coast. It was perhaps here that Pytheas landed. His informants might have advised him to travel west along the southern coast to observe the mixture of volcanic and glacial phenomena that makes Iceland unique, where, today at least, glaciers come to within a few hundred meters of the coast (Figure 16) and the country is repeatedly devastated by the phenomenon known as the "jökulhlaup", a volcanic eruption that causes glacial melting, with the

186 The most articulate argument in favor of Norway, although not without national bias, is that of Nansen (supra n. 37), vol. 1, pp. 43–73, who was able to bring a unique perspective to the issue. Like Pytheas, he was a rare combination of humanist, scholar, and explorer, and like Pytheas, for a while he had the honor of being the European who had travelled farthest north. He had the utmost respect for Pytheas, writing that "no other single traveller known to history has made such far-reaching and important discoveries" (vol. 1, p. 73). See also Tadeusz Loposzko, "Ultima Thule—Północne krańce świata," *Meander* 30, 1975, 292–304.

187 The Faeroes have also been suggested, yet seem too far south (see Dilke [supra n. 52], p. 136; see also the discussion by Hennig, vol. 1, pp. 166–71). The Shetlands (proposed by Roger Dion, "L'esplorazione di Pitea nei mari del nord," in *Geografia e geografi nel mondo antico: guida storica e critica*, ed. Franceso Prontera, Rome 1983, p. 211), as well as others, are even further south. The eastern Baltic (Pytheas, ed. Stichtenoth, p. 30) is implausible. Possible locations are summarized by Serena Bianchetti, "Pitea e la scoperta di Thule," *Sileno* 19, 1993, pp. 9–24, although practically everyone who writes about Pytheas has his or her own theory. Iceland extends over slightly more than three degrees of latitude (300km), which gives some allowance for the vagueness of the calculations.

188 Pytheas, ed. Roseman, p. 107; Broche (supra n. 37), pp. 150–1. The mirages of the Arctic, which make a distant land rise up and appear to float, may also have played a role. In the summer of 2004, the present author saw the Westman Islands, 10km off the southern coast of Iceland, rise into the air and double their size.

189 Hawkes (supra n. 14), p. 34; Cunliffe (supra n. 37), pp. 119–20.

190 Strabo 4.5.5; see Nansen (supra n. 37), vol. 1, pp. 54–5.

191 Cary and Warmington, p. 52; on the weakness of this argument see Broche (supra n. 37), pp. 187–8.

Figure 15 Iceland. Vestrahorn, view from the east.
Photograph by Duane W. Roller

Figure 16 Iceland. Skaftafell National Park, where glaciers approach the coast.
Photograph by Duane W. Roller.

expected terrifying results: the most recent in this region was in September 1995. Pytheas' scientific observations and conclusions vigorously suggest that he sailed extensively along the south coast, but he probably could not stay anywhere on this totally barren land, where, as he suggested, the world was not yet formed.[192] In fact the south coast of Iceland is without harbors for hundreds of kilometers west of Höfn.[193]

East of the Vestrahorn, as the coast turns northerly, it becomes a series of fjords that mark the eastern district of Iceland. It is here, at Bragðavellir, less than 50km airline distance from the Vestrahorn, that three Roman coins were found (Figure 17).[194] Further along the coast is the Seyðisfjörður, where the modern ferry connects Iceland with the Faeroes and Europe. Clearly this is the region of Iceland that has long had the closest contact with the rest of the world. Pytheas might have explored these fjords, but they would have seemed little different from what he had already seen in Scotland and the Faeroes and thus perhaps of little interest. He was not where Iceland was to be settled over a thousand years later: that was in the north and west, a much more benign region than the south and east.[195] Yet Pytheas was exposed to the most unusual regions of coastal Iceland, and this allowed him to develop his scientific theories about the formative stages of the earth.

This difficulty of landing may have meant that Thoule became of little interest to Pytheas beyond its remoteness and unusual phenomena: there is no evidence of a lengthy stay as on Prettanike. Thoule had no nights at midsummer and no days at midwinter[196] and was at the Arctic or summer tropic.[197] Continuous daylight and night is not limited to points above the Arctic Circle, and it is clear that Pytheas was not anywhere that the sun was visible continuously in summer: the long northern twilight could be seen far to the south. There was, however, a place called the Bed of the Sun where the sun disappears for a few hours, cited in a rare direct quotation from Pytheas.[198] This sounds suspiciously like an actual toponym, a mountain range

---

192 Strabo 2.4.1.

193 The next harbor beyond Höfn is at Þorláksháfn, nearly 300km to the west; it was here that Bjarni Herjolfsson lived, who first sighted America (*Grænlendinga Saga* 2–3). This coast is so inaccessible that ferries to the Westman Islands must sail along the coast for over 60km to land at Þorláksháfn.

194 Three coins of the late third century AC were discovered. The finds were made separately over a period of 30 years and themselves fall within the narrow range of AD270–305. No other Roman antiquities have been discovered on the island. Although it is possible, as is the nature of casual and remote coin finds, that they were carried to the island in much later times, it seems more likely that at the end of the third century AC a single ship landed in the southeast, perhaps at the time of the adventurer Carausius, and the coins were deposited as a votive offering. Another possibility is that Scandinavians or Saxons originally in Roman service brought the coins. This find seems much more realistic that the convenient discoveries from the New World (supra, pp. 54–5). See Haakon Shetelig, "Roman Coins Found in Iceland," *Antiquity* 23, 1949, 161–3; F. M. Heichelheim, "Roman Coins From Iceland," *Antiquity* 26, 1952, 43–5; J. M. Alonso-Nuñez, "A Note on Roman Coins Found in Iceland,' *OJA* 5, 1986, 121–2.

195 John Haywood, *The Penguin Historical Atlas of the Vikings*, London: Penguin, 1995, p. 93.

196 Pliny, *Natural History* 4.102; also 2.187; Kleomedes, *Meteora* 1.4.208–10; Martianus Capella 6.595.

197 Strabo 2.5.8.

198 ὅπου ὁ ἥλιος κοιμᾶται (Geminos, *Introduction to Phenomena* 6.9), or ἡ ἡλίου κοίτη (Kosmas Indikopleustes, *Christian Topography* 2.80.6–9). See also Pomponius Mela 3.57.

Figure 17 Iceland. Bragðavellir Farm, where Roman coins were found.
Photograph by Duane W. Roller.

or ridge that it went behind at midsummer midnight.[199] If Pytheas saw this on Thoule, it supports Iceland as the location, where mountains rise to over 2000m: from its southern coast there would be many places that the midsummer sun could disappear, although a specific location, perhaps in the region of the Vestrahorn, is pure speculation. On the other hand, from the coast of Norway the sun would set in the ocean.

Some information about Thoule also appears in the *Geography* of Ptolemy,[200] although the exact connection with Pytheas is unclear, as Ptolemy wrote after various Romans believed that they had located Thoule. To Ptolemy, it was consistently the northernmost place, his twenty-first parallel at 63° north of the equator. It was far north of the Orkades and was a single island with dimensions 2° 40' east–west and 35' north–south, or an east–west axis five times its north–south dimension. The longest day was 20 hours. The data are mixed: the length of the day is exceedingly far south, inconsistent with the location north of the Orkades, which itself suggests the Shetlands (not, however, a single island),[201] but the shape (although not the size) is similar to Iceland.

---

199 The Irish monks on Iceland around AD795 actually saw such a place (Dicuil 7.11).
200 Ptolemy, *Geography* 1.24; 2.3.31–32; 6.16.1; 7.5.12; 8.3.3. On Ptolemy's assimilation of the contradictory data available to him, see Germaine Aujac, "L'île de Thulé, de Pythéas à Ptolémeé," in *Géographie du monde au Moyen Âge et à la Renaissance*, ed. Monique Pelletier, Paris 1989, pp. 181–90.
201 Carpenter, *Beyond*, pp. 182–3.

Thoule was also a day south of the frozen or solid sea (πεπηγυῖα θάλαττα).[202] The participle used here is from πηγνῦμι, a standard Greek word whose root meaning seems to be "to stick in"[203] but by Classical times had come to mean "to make solid" or "to freeze."[204] The phrase "frozen sea" was used by Herodotos about the Skythian territory:[205] thus there is nothing unusual in Pytheas' diction. His frozen sea could be the Arctic ice pack, icebergs, or even frozen inlets or glaciers.[206] From Herodotos, Pytheas would have known that such a phenomenon existed in the far north even he did not see it himself, and he may merely have received reports from local informants.

In contrast to the frozen sea, there was a place where the sea boils.[207] This is a difficult passage, because it is not clear whether the sea is boiling, breathing (both from ζέω), or living (from ζῶ). The idea of both a boiling and a living sea had long existed: the former is often connected with volcanic phenomena.[208] If the sea were a breathing one, the explanation becomes more metaphysical, but again it is not an unfamiliar idea and would be another connection between Pytheas and the intellectual world of Classical Athens.[209] On the other hand, a boiling sea is remindful of the volcanic activity of Iceland, which would have been impressive even to one familiar with the vulcanism of the Mediterranean, and the contrast between a frozen and boiling sea in such proximity – a unique feature of Iceland – would have been notable.

Another strange metaphysical concept associated with Thoule, and perhaps an animate ocean, was the "sea lung" (πλεύμονι θαλαττίῳ ἐοικός), which Pytheas reported that he had seen.[210] This too connects with Aristotelian ideas:[211] at Thoule the earth, sea, and air had not yet come into existence, but were a mixture like a sea lung in which all were suspended, everything bonded together, a metaphysical concept going back to the very beginnings of Greek intellectualism.[212] There have been many explanations for this enigmatic passage, from marine fauna to the rise and

202 Strabo 1.4.2; Pliny, *Natural History* 4.104 ("mare concretum"); see also 37.35; see further, Trevor Murphy, *Pliny the Elder's Natural History: The Empire in the Encyclopedia*, Oxford: Oxford University Press, 2004, pp. 179–81.

203 Cf. Homer, *Iliad* 13.442.

204 Cf. Aischylos, *Persians* 496.

205 Herodotos 4.28.

206 Nansen (supra, n. 37), vol. 1, p. 67, with some knowledge of the topic, felt that Pytheas could not have gone far enough to have seen drift ice, and he seems to have travelled at a time of reduced polar ice. On this, see Zubov (supra n. 156), p. 71.

207 Scholia to Apollonios of Rhodes, *Argonautika* 4.761–5a. The passage seems to indicate that Pytheas wrote about the Lipari islands and the forge of Hephaistos, but this is standard mythological lore and no proof of autopsy. Broche (supra n. 37), pp. 167–70, but see Pytheas, ed. Bianchetti, pp. 206–8.

208 For example, Strabo 1.3.16, regarding Thera.

209 Aristotle, *Metaphysics* 1.3; Strabo 1.3.8; Pomponius Mela 3.2. See Poseidonios (supra n. 87), pp. 793–4; Pomponius Mela, ed. Silberman, pp. 247–8.

210 Polybios 34.5.13–4 (= Strabo 2.4.1).

211 The language is also a reflection of Platonic thought: see *Phaidon* 111e–112e.

212 Romm, *Edges*, pp. 22–3. See also James J. Tierney, "Ptolemy's Map of Scotland," *JHS* 79, 1959, 134 for the suggestion that Pytheas was influenced by Herodotos' description of the Central Asian steppes (4.31).

fall of coastal ice.[213] Because it is connected with the actual formative stages of the earth, it would seem also to relate to the unusual characteristic of the northern Ocean – its ability to be both boiling and frozen – and thus represents Pytheas' attempt to construct a scientific theory to account for this, building on Aristotelian ideas of the animate ocean and formative processes of the earth.[214] His familiarity with the south coast of Iceland would allow the germination of these theories.

Strabo has preserved a brief ethnography of Thoule, based on Pytheas.[215] Domesticated plants and animals were scarce or even nonexistent, and the nourishment of the locals was basic: millet (a generic term for any wild grain),[216] herbs, fruit, and roots. There were perhaps other grains and honey, in meager quantities, and a grain-derived drink. Threshing had to be indoors because of the constant rain.[217] This economy borders on mere gathering, although there seems to have been hardly any planting. There was perhaps beekeeping but little else. The impression is one of a life barely above subsistence level, remindful of societies in Bronze Age Denmark that ate weeds.[218] Although Strabo placed this community at Thoule, it may be a generalized comment about how someone from the abundant Mediterranean viewed the poor northern economies.[219]

Today's visitor to Iceland cannot help but be aware of the uniqueness of the island, which has phenomena that collectively exist nowhere else on the earth. Unusual to the modern world traveller, the nature of Iceland would have been bizarre beyond belief to an explorer from the ancient Mediterranean. Although the active volcanic and glacial activity means that the modern form of the land is different from what it was in Pytheas' day, the basic characteristics would have been the same. Most immediately striking – whether to Pytheas or a visitor of the twenty-first century – is that Iceland is without trees: there are vistas of hundreds of square kilometers without a tree in sight. Glacial and volcanic phenomena are always impressive, but in Iceland they occur together, creating strange contrasts such as the Jökulsá (Glacier River), which runs barely 20km from the Myrdal glacier to the ocean, often carrying ice but smelling of

213 Pytheas, ed. Roseman, pp. 127–31; Pytheas, ed. Mette, pp. 7–8; Walbank (supra n. 4), vol. 3, pp. 590–1; Cary and Warmington, p. 52; Thomson, pp. 148–9; Hawkes (supra n. 14), p. 37, saw it as a sticking of the ship in freezing water, held like a jellyfish, which is another definition of the phrase (Plato, *Philebos* 10). In 1783 a submarine vent 70 miles southwest of Reykjanestá – the southwest point of Iceland – ejected pumice which covered the ocean for hundreds of square miles and hindered shipping: see Richard F. Burton, *Ultima Thule: A Summer in Iceland*, London: William P. Nimmo, 1875, p. 6.

214 Two of Pytheas' ideas may have come together in the theory of Athenodoros of Tarsos, who saw the rise and fall of the tides as a type of breathing (Strabo 3.5.7).

215 Strabo 4.5.5.

216 Andrew Dalby, *Food in the Ancient World From A to Z*, London: Routledge, 2003, pp. 218–9.

217 Interior threshing floors can still be seen in the Faeroe Islands, and there are many examples in the collections of historical farm buildings common throughout Scandinavia, such as the Skansen in Stockholm.

218 Kristian Kristiansen, "The Consumption of Wealth in Bronze Age Denmark. A Study in the Dynamics of Economic Processes in Tribal Societies," in *New Directions in Scandinavian Archaeology*, ed. Kristian Kristiansen and Carsten Paludan-Müller, Odense, n. d., p. 182; see also Cunliffe (supra n. 37), pp. 108–13.

219 Another northern ethnology, about the people to the north of the Black Sea (Strabo 7.3.18), may have been derived from Pytheas (Aujac [supra n. 37], p. 270).

sulphur. New land is created regularly in Iceland: the island of Surtsey off the south-west coast appeared in 1963, and reached a peak size of 2.7km². Plants began to grow within a year, and by 2002 there were 60 species, and ten of animals.[220] Pytheas was astutely correct when he wrote that the earth had not reached its final form at Thoule: this is a process still underway today, and the modern visitor has the feeling of being on an alien planet where nothing is familiar and the world is still being born. The very nature of Iceland is the strongest proof that Thoule can be nowhere else.

From Thoule, Pytheas began the final part of his journey, toward the Baltic.[221] Interestingly, Strabo is not the source for this last stage: he only knew that Pytheas had gone beyond the Rhine to Skythia.[222] It is probable that, since hardly anything more was known about the Baltic and Scandinavia in Strabo's day than in Pytheas', Strabo could not continue his theme of discrediting him because he had no additional data with which to refute him. Strabo did make a connection between Thoule and Skythia through a tribe called the Roxolanoi, who were supposedly the most distant of peoples.[223] But the Roxolanoi are not particularly remote – they lived on the north shore of the Black Sea – so Strabo may have included them only to reject Pytheas' statements about Thoule as the farthest place.

The major source for Pytheas' travels beyond the mouth of the Rhine is Pliny, supplemented by Pomponius Mela. Pliny's material seems to have been derived from Timaios,[224] but he combined material of several periods, including his own, so the contribution of Pytheas is not certain.[225] The list of toponyms may indicate the route: Berrice, "ex qua in Tylen navigetur," Bergos, Dumna, and Scandia. Berrice has been located in the Faeroes or Shetlands, or even on the Norwegian mainland.[226] Bergos suggests the Norwegian coast (Figure 18).[227] Dumna is believed to be Lewis and Harris in the Outer Hebrides.[228] Scandia may be on the Swedish coast: the modern town of Skanör is at the southwestern point of Sweden. Although these toponyms are specula-tively located, they all conform vaguely to a route between Iceland and the Baltic.

220 Edward Weinman, "Life Takes Root," *Iceland Review* 41, 2003, 28–33.

221 For a summary of ancient knowledge about the Baltic, see Luigi De Anna, *Conoscenza e immagine della Finlandia e del settentrione nella cultura classico-medievale*, *Turun Yliopiston Julkaisuja* ser. B, vol. 180, Turku 1988, pp. 17–86.

222 Strabo 1.4.3. "Skythia" is a generic term for the far northeast, and is not always limited to the north shore of the Black Sea.

223 Strabo 2.5.7, 7.2.4; Erich Diehl, "Roxolani," *RE Supp.* 7, 1940, 1195–7.

224 Pliny, *Natural History* 4.94, 104, 37.35–36 = Timaios, fr. 74, 75; Pomponius Mela 3.33; Serena Bianchetti, "Plinio e la descrizione dell'Oceano settentrionale in Pitea di Marsiglia," *OT* 2, 1996, 73–84.

225 On Pytheas' northern toponyms, see Silvana Boschi Banfi, "Note sulle Tule," *NumAntCl* 5, 1976, 291–5.

226 Pytheas, ed. Roseman, p. 94; Dietrich Stichtenoth, "Pytheas von Marseille, der Entdecker Mittel- und Nordeuropas," *Das Altertum* 7, 1961, 156–66.

227 Fabre (supra n. 70), p. 41. On some of the possible Norwegian toponyms, see Stefano Magnani, "Da Massalia a Thule: annotazioni etnografiche pitenae," in *Dall'Indo a Thule: i Greci, i Romani, gli altri*, ed. Antonio Aloni and Lìa de Finis, Trento 1996, p. 342.

228 Rivit and Smith (supra n. 94), p. 342. If so, this is the most anomalous of the toponyms in the list.

Figure 18 Approaching the Norwegian coast at Bergen.

Photograph by Duane W. Roller.

Pytheas' name for the Baltic may have been the Sinus Codanus, or Kodanos, described as filled with islands, of which the most important is Scatinavia.[229] As he approached this region, he came to a great estuary of the Ocean called Metuonis, which extended for 6000 stadia. Its coasts were populated by the Guiones – identified by Pliny as a Germanic people, but probably anachronistically. From the estuary it was a day's sail to the island named Abalus, which was a source of amber, used both locally as fuel and sold to neighboring peoples.[230] The island was also called Basilia ("Kingdom"), perhaps a generic term more sociological than topographical.[231] Another name, Balcia, is perhaps connected with "Baltic". Basilia was three days from the Skythian coast, near the sluggish sea (in Pliny's Latin, *mare pigrum*), which seems different from the frozen sea near Thoule, both geographically and linguistically, although it may merely be Pliny's latinization of the

229 Pliny, *Natural History* 4.96; J. Svennung, *Skandinavien bei Plinius und Ptolemaeus*, Uppsala: Almqvist and Wiksell, 1974, pp. 49–51; De Anna (supra n. 221), pp. 33–7. On the Sinus Codanus, see G. Neumann and R. Wenskus, "Codanus Sinus," *RGA* 5, 1984, 38–40.

230 Mention of an amber island named Baunonia, a day from the coast (said to be Skythian), cited by Timaios (fr. 75a = Pliny, *Natural History* 4.94), may also be from Pytheas (Brown [supra n. 99], pp. 25–6).

231 The name, however, may be a hellenized form of a local toponym; see Willy Krogman, "Die Bernsteininsel *Basileia*," in *VII Congresso Internazionale di Science Onomastiche: Atti del Congresso e Memorie della sezione toponomastica* 2, Florence 1963, pp. 205–20. Krogman's suggestion is that the local toponym was Baswaleia and that it is modern Helgoland, certainly a possibility, but not reconciled with the apparent Baltic location of the island.

term.[232] The sea would be frozen in many different and seemingly unconnected localities in the north. Pliny listed numerous other toponyms, and, as usual, the exact distribution of data among his several sources is not apparent. The Metuonis is otherwise unknown, as are the Guiones, but they may be the same as the Suiones, who lived near the *mare pigrum*.[233] If this is the case, it places Pytheas – or at least the source of his information – at the very interior reaches of the eastern Baltic, perhaps even as far as the Gulf of Finland.[234] With the usual caution about Pliny's mixing of data, nevertheless it is possible that Pytheas was the source for several comments about Scatinavia and its various ethnic groups and topography, including the unusually large Saevo Mountain.[235] Also cited is the Vistula river, which Pomponius Mela believed was joined to the Ister (Danube) and whose shores were inhabited by primitive nomads.

The context of this part of Pytheas' itinerary is the amber trade.[236] Pliny, however, had more contemporary information for the amber region, especially regarding the overland route from the Danube that had recently been explored. The topicality of this district in the Roman period thus contributed to the confusion, as has the latinizing of toponyms. But significantly Pliny's passage on Basilia is introduced with the statement that one can go from the far north to Gades by keeping the shore on one's left, which places at least some of his comments within the environment of Pytheas. Pomponius Mela's connecting of the Vistula and the Ister, Argonautic in tone, is similar. The estuary of Metuonis – over a thousand kilometers in length – cannot be any river mouth but only fits the entrance to the Baltic. The numerous Danish islands would strengthen the impression that this was a great estuary, especially if Pytheas did not sail around the north end of Denmark through the Skaggerak but followed the later Viking route through the sheltered Limfjord that separates Jutland proper from Vendyssel to its north.[237]

---

232 These multiple names may reflect differing locations for amber: it was not limited to one place and appears, or has appeared, throughout the Baltic. Pliny's sources are Hekataios (almost certainly of Abdera, [*FGrHist* #264, fr. 12]), whose information is probably derived from Pytheas, Xenophon of Lampsakos, and a certain Philemon, presumably the little-known geographer of the Julio-Claudian period (for whom, see infra, pp. 122–3).

233 Tacitus, *Germania* 44–5. The name may be reflected in modern Świnoujście at the mouth of the Oder.

234 On these issues, see Tuomo Pekkanen, *The Ethnic Origin of the* ΔΟΥΛΟΣΠΟΡΟΙ, *Arctos Supp.* 1, 1968, 33–9, 47–8.

235 Pliny, *Natural History* 4.96; Svennung (supra n. 229), pp. 42–4, who would identify this with Siggjo on the west coast of Norway, but see Nansen (supra n. 37), vol. 1, p. 85, and, most recently, H. Reichert, "Saevo," *RGA* 26, 2004, 86–8.

236 Reinhard Wenskus, "Pytheas und der Bernsteinhandel," in *Untersuchungen zu Handel und Verkehr der vor- und frühgeschichtlichen Zeit in Mittel- und Nordeuropa* 1, ed. Klaus Düwel *et al.*, *AbbGött* 143, 1985, pp. 84–108; De Anna (supra n. 221), pp. 78–81. For a study on the origin and distribution of Baltic amber, see Sven Gisle Larsson, *Baltic Amber – A Palaeobiological Study*, Klampenborg: Scandinavian Science Press, 1978, especially pp. 26–40. The best-known Baltic amber is that from the Samland peninsula northwest of Kaliningrad (p. 36), but significant deposits are found today in Jutland and southern Sweden, and there would have been others in antiquity.

237 Haywood (supra n. 195), p. 23, although it is important to remember that these coasts and waterways have changed greatly over the years. Large portions of the coast of Jutland were under water in ancient times (Karl Gripp, *Erdgeschichte von Schleswig-Holstein*, Neumünster: Karl Wachholtz, 1964, pp. 278–307), and thus the details of the Metuonis estuary may be almost impossible to locate.

Open sea would be avoided, perhaps not for 6000 stadia but for a substantial portion of that distance.[238]

Except for the Vistula, the toponyms on this last part of Pytheas' voyage cannot be located with certainty, but Abalus/Basilia may be one of the islands in the Baltic such as Gotland, or even the Scandinavian or eastern European mainland.[239] A more minimalist view places the Metuonis estuary at the Albis (Elbe) and similar-sounding Abalus at Helgoland, but this requires rejection of the 6000 stadia.[240] Citation of the Vistula–Ister trade route – whether or not Pytheas knew or made use of it – also provides an environment of the inner Baltic. It cannot be proven if Pytheas went beyond the Danish islands or the mouth of the Oder, because information might have been orally obtained. Yet he may have been responsible for the toponym "The Pillars of the North," a counterpart to those of Herakles. It appears in several sources: the earliest extant is the *Periplous Dedicated to King Nikomedes*, with later mention by Tacitus, whose awareness of it was vague.[241] Locating it is highly speculative, given the generally flat quality of the Baltic coast, but it was probably the perceived entrance to the Baltic, perhaps where the Öresund widens out south of Copenhagen.

What happened next is unknown. Pytheas may have returned along the coast to Gades, as implied by Pliny,[242] or even made the remarkable overland journey to the Black Sea, hinted at by Strabo and Pomponius Mela.[243] This would not have been as difficult as one might think: the rivers of the Baltic have their sources remarkably close to those flowing into the Black Sea. At Vitebsk, the Dvina, which empties into the Gulf of Riga, is less than 100km from the Dnieper: this route was to be perfected by Rus and Arab traders by the early ninth century.[244] Other connections exist: the sources of the Vistula are near the Dniester and Morava, and the Dvina approaches the Volga.

238 An interestingly plausible suggestion is that the 6000-stadia estuary represents a circuit of the Danish islands, from the north end of the Kattegat to the mouth of the Oder and return (Hawkes [supra n. 14], p. 9). Another possibility is that it is the distance from Skagens Odde – the north end of Denmark – to the vicinity of Kaliningrad on the Polish–Russian border, where the Baltic coast turns north (Aly [supra n. 37], pp. 473–5).

239 Pekkanen (supra n. 234), p. 39; R. Wenskus and K. Ranke, "Abalus," *RGA* 1, 1973, 5–6. Another suggestion is Vendsyssel (Hawkes [supra n. 14], pp. 9–10). See also Gisinger (supra n. 37), pp. 349–51; Svennung (supra n. 229), pp. 34–8.

240 Cary and Warmington, pp. 53–4, who also suggested that Abalus/Basilia is Bornholm.

241 *Periplous Dedicated to King Nikomedes* 188–90; Tacitus, *Germania* 34. See Pytheas, ed. Stichtenoth, pp. 94–5 – who also suggested that Avienus, *Ora maritima* 336–74, ostensibly about the Pillars of Herakles, has assimilated material about the Pillars of the North. On the passage in the *Periplous Dedicated to King Nikomedes*, which is highly corrupt (described by the editors as a "locus desperatus") see *Géographes grecs* 1, ed. Didier Marcotte, Paris: Les Belles Lettres, 2000, pp. 164–5. If Ephoros were the source (supra n. 31), the toponym was known before Pytheas, and may have inspired him.

242 Pliny, *Natural History* 4.94.

243 Strabo 2.4.1; Pomponius Mela 3.33; Joaquin Herrmann, "Volkstämme und 'nordlicher Seeweg' in der älteren Eisenzeit," *ZfA* 19, 1985, pp. 147–53.

244 Haywood (supra n. 195), pp. 106–7.

There is a suggestion of further travel after Pytheas returned home.[245] Obviously he was able to publish his findings.[246] Within a generation of his return, as the world struggled to cope with the post-Alexander realities, his ideas were being disseminated in the mainstream of Greek scientific and geographical thinking, especially as a significant source for the cartographic and astronomical researches of later Hellenistic times.[247] Indeed, his voyage came to be compared with that of the Argonauts,[248] and he was seen as a most learned man who had made the far north known to the world.[249]

245 Strabo 2.4.1.
246 The question arises as to whether there are any artifacts associated with his journey. Two coins have already been noted from Finistère and Devon (supra n. 113, 119), whose date contemporary with Pytheas and location along his route raise interest: coins are often less significant than they seem, but nevertheless these two are early and in isolated context. Perhaps more interesting is archaeological evidence from the Shetland Islands. At Clickhimin on Mainland, near Lerwick, indigenous lamps show that Massalian influences appear as early as the sixth or fifth century BC, when intrusive Iron Age settlers built a farmstead. During this period, Clickhimin seems to have existed at a cultural level similar to Pytheas' description of Thoule, including interior threshing floors. It is not difficult to see Clickhimin as the sort of place the Massalian visited, perhaps for an extended period. On the site, see J. R. C. Hamilton, *Excavations at Clickhimin, Shetland*, Edinburgh: H. M. Stationery Office, 1968, especially pp. 41, 45, 64–5, 79.
247 Dilke (supra n. 52), p. 182.
248 Scholia to Apollonios of Rhodes 4.761–5a; Timaios, fr. 85 (= Diodoros 4.56); also, by implication, Pomponius Mela 3.33. On possible influence of Pytheas on Apollonios of Rhodes, see Dag Øistein Endsjø, "Placing the Unplaceable: The Making of Apollonios' Argonautic Geography," *GRBS* 38, 1997, 381.
249 Martianus Capella 6.609.

5

HELLENISTIC EXPLORATION ON
THE COASTS OF AFRICA

After Pytheas there seems to have been little Greek exploration of the Atlantic for nearly two centuries. There are many reasons for this, not the least of which is the interest in the East generated by the activities of Alexander. In addition, the rise of Rome and its pressures on Carthage began to change the balance of power in the west: there is no record of further Carthaginian exploration beyond the Pillars of Herakles after that of Hanno and Himilco. The western Greek states also seem to have limited or even terminated their expeditions. The two Massalians, Pytheas and Euthymenes, had revealed the Atlantic from the Arctic to the tropics, and it was believed that most of the external Ocean had been explored.[1] Although there was speculation that India could be reached through the Pillars,[2] despite the activities of Alexander this was yet to be demonstrated.

Alexander's stillborn plans to circumnavigate Africa[3] resulted in some preliminary exploration of the coasts of the Indian Ocean. Nearchos and Onesikratos sailed from India to the Persian Gulf.[4] Then Alexander attempted to define the limits of the Arabian peninsula by sending forth several of those who had made the sea journey from India. Archias of Pella sailed down the west side of the Persian Gulf and discovered Tylos (modern Bahrain), but did not go any farther.[5] Androsthenes of Thasos continued beyond the mouth of the Gulf and along the Arabian coast, marvelling at the intense tropical world that was still alien to Greeks.[6] Hieron of Soloi was commissioned to go all the way around Arabia and into the Red Sea.[7] Although he went farther than anyone previous, he did not fulfill his instructions and Arrian could write anachronistically, and betraying his Hellenistic sources, that the coast of the Arabian

---

1   Strabo 1.1.8, probably quoting Eratosthenes.
2   Aristotle, *Meteorologika* 2.5; supra, p. 51.
3   Supra, pp. 59–60.
4   *FGrHist* #133, 134.
5   Arrian, *Anabasis* 7.20.7.
6   Arrian, *Anabasis* 7.20.7; Androsthenes (*FGrHist* #711), fr. 1, 2 (= Strabo 16.3.2, Athenaios 3.93); fr. 3–5 (= Theophrastos, *Plant Explanations* 2.5.5; *Research on Plants* 4.7.3, 5.4.7).
7   Arrian, *Anabasis* 7.20.7–8. As is often the case, he seems to have lost his nerve and on his return exaggerated his difficulties. But he also said that Arabia was nearly as large as India, a surprisingly accurate statement given the minimal knowledge of both peninsulas.

peninsula had never been completely explored.[8] Yet in the same passage Arrian connected these expeditions of Alexander's sea captains with that of Hanno. Although the statement is confused, since it is unlikely that Hanno was known to the explorers of Alexander's era, nevertheless it demonstrates that circumnavigation of Africa was in Alexander's mind when he sent his men out around the Arabian peninsula.

In the third century BC, Ptolemaic explorers ranged down the coast of East Africa; especially notable was Timosthenes of Rhodes, also famous as a composer, who explored for Ptolemaios II well beyond the mouth of the Red Sea.[9] As yet, however, no connection had been made between the Persian Gulf and the Red Sea, and despite the intensity of exploration in the years immediately after Alexander, by the latter third century BC knowledge of the southern coasts of the inhabited world remained separated into three discrete segments: from India to the Persian Gulf and part way around the Arabian peninsula, from Egypt down the east coast of Africa perhaps as far as or slightly beyond Ras Asin (Cape Guardafui), the easternmost point of Africa,[10] and down the west coast of Africa into the tropics. This last portion was the least known to the Greek world, because of Massalian secretiveness and the obscurity – to Greeks – of the Carthaginian reports. The early circumnavigators described by Herodotos[11] were largely ignored and even forgotten, perhaps because they were not Greek. Rumors that one could go from the Pillars of Herakles to India were rampant but untested.

For many years these remained merely rumors. Efforts turned away from actual exploration toward the collating of data and theorization. This is most apparent in the appearance of treatises specifically devoted to world geography, notably that of Eratosthenes of Kyrene.[12] Active in the last third of the third century BC,[13] he was the epitome of the Hellenistic polymath. His *Geography* was the first attempt to synthesize geographical knowledge: information acquired in the previous century made such a work possible.[14] Most of the extant fragments are in the *Geography* of Strabo, although his account tangles Eratosthenes' treatise, that of Hipparchos, who wrote *Against the "Geography" of Eratosthenes*,[15] and Strabo's own criticisms.

---

8 Arrian, *Indika* 43.9. Over a century before Arrian, Juba II (*FGrHist* #275, fr. 30–3) had described the entire coast of Arabia.

9 Strabo 9.3.10. His geographical treatise was *On Harbors*, demonstrating the practical interest of his Ptolemaic patrons. He also wrote a composition called the *Nomos Pythikos* which celebrated the contest between Apollo and the Python, with one portion musically imitating the latter's dying hissings. See also Pliny, *Natural History* 5.47, 129; 6.15, 163, 198.

10 L. A. Thompson, "Eastern Africa and the Graeco-Roman World (to A. D. 641)," in *Africa in Classical Antiquity: Nine Studies*, ed. L. A. Thompson and J. Ferguson, Ibadan 1969, pp. 29–30.

11 Supra, pp. 22–7.

12 See the valuable summary of his life by P. M. Fraser, "Eratosthenes of Cyrene," *ProcBritAc* 56, 1970, 175–207; also D. R. Dicks, "Eratosthenes," *DSB* 4, 1971, 388–93. *FGrHist* #241 includes testimonia but not his geographical fragments, which were collected by Hugo Berger, *Die geographischen Fragmente des Eratosthenes*, Leipzig, 1880.

13 Souda, "Eratosthenes."

14 Strabo 1.2.1. 2.1.1.

15 Strabo 2.1.41.

Eratosthenes had data available as wide ranging as the observations of Pytheas,[16] those of Philon, a Ptolemaic explorer who went to Meroë on the upper Nile,[17] the reports from India of Alexander and his companions,[18] and the account of the great eastern expedition of Patrokles, who explored routes between the Caspian Sea and India for Seleukos I.[19] Thus Eratosthenes was able to create a systematic geographical overview of the world. His two baselines indicate his scope:[20] one from the Pillars of Herakles through Sicily, Attika, Rhodes, the Tauros, and to India,[21] and the other from the mouth of the Borysthenes through Alexandria to Meroë.[22] Eratosthenes also knew about Thoule from Pytheas,[23] the Caspian Sea, the rivers emptying into it, and those living beyond it from Patrokles,[24] the Atlantic coast of Europe from Pytheas or Phokaian explorers,[25] and interior India from Megasthenes, Seleukid envoy to the Mauryan kings.[26] Moreover, all these topographical data were integrated into a complex theoretical structure about the nature of the inhabited world itself. Such was the state of geographical knowledge in the late third century BC. Information about the northern and eastern extremities had made major advances in the previous century, but there was no corresponding development to the south, except toward India.

Given the wide range of Eratosthenes' knowledge, it is astonishing how little he knew about Africa outside Egypt and his home region of Kyrene.[27] He could follow the route of Pytheas to the Arctic yet seems ignorant of Euthymenes, Hanno, and Himilco. Thoule was known to him but not Kerne. His sparse comments about the Atlantic coast of northwest Africa were remembered because they were wrong,[28] although it is intriguing that he described the atmosphere of West Africa as "flat," "thick," and "misty" (πλάτυς,[29] παχύς, ἀχλυώδης), unusual vocabulary that sounds like eyewitness data from an unknown source. Eratosthenes barely knew the Nile above Meroë, hardly an advance on Herodotos 200 years earlier,[30] and showing ignorance of Dalion, who had explored the region

---

16 Strabo 2.4.2.
17 *FGrHist* #670, fr. 2 (= Strabo 2.1.20).
18 Strabo 1.2.1.
19 *FGrHist* #712, fr. 2, 5 (= Strabo 2.1.2, 11.7.3).
20 Thomson, p. 166.
21 Strabo 2.1.1; D. R. Dicks, *The Geographical Fragments of Hipparchus*, London: Athlone Press, 1960, pp. 122–3.
22 Strabo 1.4.1; Dicks (supra n. 21), pp. 146–7.
23 Strabo 1.4.5.
24 Strabo 11.7.3.
25 Strabo 3.2.11.
26 *FGrHist* #715, especially fr. 27 (= Strabo 2.1.9).
27 Strabo 2.4.2; Fraser (supra n. 12), pp. 193–4.
28 Strabo 17.3.8.
29 This can actually mean "salty" or "brackish" (Herodotos 2.108; see also Aristotle, *Meteorologika* 2.3, specifically about Africa).
30 Strabo 17.1.2; Herodotos 2.29.

for Ptolemaios II.[31] One must be cautious, for modern knowledge of Eratosthenes is filtered through secondary sources used by Strabo, as well as Strabo's prejudices and his own scant interest in Africa, but it seems evident that the events of the previous century had tilted scholarly interest toward the north and east, with the south and southwest given little consideration. That this region was in the Carthaginian sphere was certainly part of the problem, and despite the flurry of interest in circumnavigating Africa that Alexander had created, the issue became dormant with the collapse of his plans. Eratosthenes even seems to have believed that the southern regions were uninhabitable due to heat.[32] All this contributed to remarkable ignorance about the Atlantic coast of Africa in the early Hellenistic period.[33]

Between the time of Alexander and the fall of Carthage there are only two known explorations south of the Pillars of Herakles. Both are shadowy. One is the voyage of whoever wrote the ethnography of Kerne that is buried in the *periplous* of Pseudo-Skylax: as noted[34] this is a jumbled account of a Greek who visited Kerne sometime around the middle of the fourth century BC and saw the trade between the Carthaginians and the locals in action. Somehow he made it deep into territory that the Carthaginians considered their own, but came away intentionally discouraged by them and did not inspire further Greek curiosity about the region. Even more obscure is a *periplous* attributed to a certain Ophelas.[35] The sole citation, by Strabo, is predictably derogatory.[36] Ophelas was said to be one of many writers about the west coast of Africa who created fantasies (πλάσματα); all except Ophelas are unnamed. It is by no means obvious whether the two pieces of data that follow are from Ophelas or one of the anonymous others. There was a cave in the Emporikos Gulf that at high tide was filled inside for a distance of seven stadia, although an altar of Herakles at the entrance was never touched by the tide. In addition, there were 300 deserted Carthaginian settlements on the coast, destroyed by the Pharousioi and Nigritai, who lived 30 days to the south.

Despite Strabo's skepticism, these comments are far from implausible. The cave is remindful of those on the Atlantic coast just west of modern Tangier still called the Grottoes of Hercules, in a region heavily associated with the hero (Figure 19).[37] The toponym "Emporikos" implies a trading post, a typical phenomenon for this region, although the Greek name raises questions as to who was operating it.[38] This

---

31 *FGrHist* #666; Pliny, *Natural History* 6.183, 194. Eratosthenes placed the uninhabitable area of the earth 3000 (or 3400) stadia south of Meroë (Strabo 17.3.1, 1.4.2), but this does not imply knowledge of that region: it is merely putting the line far enough south to take in account Taprobane, which was known by the time of Alexander (Strabo 15.1.14–15).

32 Strabo 2.5.7.

33 Thomson, p. 139.

34 Pseudo-Skylax 112; supra, pp. 19–20, 42.

35 Ernst Honigmann, "Ὀφέλας" (#1), *RE* 18, 1939, 630.

36 Strabo 17.3.3.

37 Roller, *Juba*, pp. 154–5.

38 The name is mentioned here and immediately previously (17.3.2), in Strabo's general description of the coast. His primary source seems to be Artemidoros of Ephesos, offered as a critique of Eratosthenes (17.3.8). For possible identifications of the Emporikos Gulf see Desanges, *Recherches*, p. 134.

Figure 19 "Grottoes of Hercules", on the northwest African coast.
Photograph by Duane W. Roller.

information has been conflated with knowledge of the tidal estuaries of the northwest African coast, especially that of the Lixos (modern Leukos), itself connected with Herakles. It was here that the Garden of the Hesperides was located, and the twisting of the lower Lixos, still conspicuous today (Figure 6), was said to resemble the serpent that guarded the apples of the Hesperides.[39]

Although probably exaggerated in number, the 300 deserted Carthaginian settlements reflect the reduction in Carthaginian trade and habitation that is also apparent in the Pseudo-Skylax *Periplous*, when the Greek traveller reported the lack of a permanent settlement at Kerne: in Hanno's day, somewhat over a century earlier, this had been the greatest of the trading centers. This sense of Carthaginian decline became almost a formula: both Eratosthenes and Artemidoros reported it, as does the *Ora maritima* of Avienus.[40] Thus the environment of the *periplous* of Ophelas is reasonable: an African coast of unusual tidal phenomena, places sacred to Herakles, and a lessening Carthaginian involvement.

What is of particular interest, however, is that a reason is provided for the abandonment of so many cities and outposts. Two ethnic groups, the Pharousioi and Nigritai, were responsible. Strabo provided brief ethnographies of both.[41] The Pharousioi fought with bows and drove chariots, perhaps a confusion with the Persians, some of whom were said to have joined the entourage of Herakles when the hero came to West Africa, settling there after his death.[42] The Pharousioi were adept at desert travel and were occasionally seen in the Numidian capital of Cirta, west of Carthage. Ptolemy placed them far to the south, near Hanno's Chariot of the Gods.[43] The Nigritai, often mentioned in tandem with the Pharousioi, are somewhat more obscure, but represent a general toponym and ethnym of west central Africa, as shown in the various Niger rivers of ancient and modern times.[44] Vague as these ethnic groups are, significant is Strabo's statement that they were 30 days away from the Carthaginian settlements they destroyed. This, coupled with their proficiency at desert life and their appearance at Cirta, indicates that they were desert tribes who occasionally impacted onto the coastal settlements, another chapter in the constant tale of difficult contacts between the transhumant or nomadic peoples and settled agriculturalists, circumstances so well known in North Africa from the Roman period.[45] The suggestion that the Pharousioi used scythe-bearing chariots, even if implausible and a confusion with the Persians, shows the fearful reputation that they had among those whom they harassed. The Carthaginians, in decline and severely threatened in their heartland by the Romans, were unable to make any effective response and the West African settlements were thus abandoned.[46]

---

39 Pliny, *Natural History* 5.3.

40 Strabo 17.3.8; Avienus, *Ora maritima* 437–63 (ostensibly about the Spanish coast).

41 Strabo 17.3.7, see also 2.5.33; Pliny, *Natural History* 5.9.

42 Sallust, *Jugurtha* 18.

43 Ptolemy, *Geography* 4.6.16.

44 The word "(n)gir" means water and is common in descriptions of sub-Saharan Africa: see Thomson, p. 268.

45 Roller, *Juba*, pp. 106–14.

46 On this, see R. C. C. Law, "North Africa in the Period of Phoenician and Greek Colonization, *c.* 800 to 323 BC," *CHA* 2, 1978, pp. 139–40, which emphasized the "speculative and nebulous" nature of the evidence for Carthaginian decline.

The most obscure element in the *periplous* of Ophelas is the identity and date of its author. The context of Carthaginian decline is remindful of the information from the mid-fourth century BC in the Pseudo-Skylax *Periplous*, but the text of Ophelas may be later, even after the fall of Carthage, as there is a sense of antiquity in Strabo's description: the settlements were old and are *now* deserted. As is so often the case with Strabo, there is a difficulty as to when "now" is. It does not seem to be Strabo's own era.[47] His immediate source is probably Artemidoros, writing around 100BC,[48] which suggests the years after the fall of Carthage in 146BC, although this purely hypothetical, and the date of the *periplous* may be any time between 400 and 100BC.

Who Ophelas was is also far from certain. It was long believed that he was the companion of Alexander who was sent by Ptolemaios I to Kyrene, then to be involved in an abortive expedition against Carthage as part of the efforts of Agathokles of Syracuse, and who had plans for a great North African empire, only to be murdered by Agathokles around 309BC.[49] But there is no reason to associate this Ophellas (spelled this way) with Ophelas the author of the *periplous*.[50] Ophellas of Kyrene showed no interest in the Atlantic, well removed from his territories.[51] An Apellas of Kyrene mentioned by Markianos of Herakleia in his account of *periplooi* may suggest that this was the author's actual name.[52] There is also a certain Okelas, connected with the early wanderings of Herakles, whose travels may have come to be seen as an early *periplous*.[53] This confusion might be relieved if one could properly interpret Strabo's statement that he had already mentioned Ophelas and the unnamed other authors of *periplooi*,[54] but the name does not otherwise occur in the *Geography* and commentators can do nothing more than to look, rather futilely, for similar topics.[55] Identification of Ophelas seems impossible, because Strabo has not provided enough details.[56] The so-called *Periplous of Ophelas* may reflect a Greek traveller who went down the west coast of Africa in Hellenistic times, perhaps interested in the cult of Herakles, tidal phenomena, and the evidence of the Carthaginian decline. He may even be the same

---

47 In this passage Strabo merely used νῦν, not his key phrase of καθ᾽ἡμᾶς, which was his method of identifying events of his own time (after the Pompeian reorganization of the East in 60BC); see Sarah Pothecary, "The Expression 'Our Times' in Strabo's *Geography*," *CP* 92, 1997, 235–46.

48 The date is from the summary of *periplooi* by Markianos of Herakleia (*GGM* vol. 1, pp. 565–6).

49 The major source is Diodoros 18.21–2, 20.40–3, 70.

50 Honigmann (supra n. 35), p. 630. Nevertheless such association is still standard: see Nicola Biffi, "L'Africa di Strabone: Libro XVII della Geografia," Modugno: Edizione dal Sud, 1999, p. 379.

51 Desanges, *Recherches*, pp. 3–5.

52 *GGM* vol. 1, p. 565.

53 Desanges, *Recherches*, p. 5; Strabo 3.4.3.

54 Strabo 17.3.3.

55 H. L. Jones, the editor of the Loeb Strabo, suggested 1.1.5 (on the Blessed Isles) and 3.2.13 (on Herakles in Spain), but these seem unlikely. There is always the possibility that the citations were in Strabo's lost *History*.

56 The name, regardless of spelling, is not common; most of the handful of known cases come from Athens in the second century BC (P. M. Fraser *et al.* [eds.], *A Lexicon of Greek Personal Names*, Oxford; Clarendon Press, 1987–2000, especially vol. 2, p. 355), which might suggest the origin and date of the author of the *periplous*.

as the anonymous traveller to Kerne in the mid-fourth century BC, although this would seem to be a little early for the desolation described. His very obscurity indicates the scantiness of Greek knowledge of West Africa in the fourth and third centuries BC, a problem that was remedied after the fall of Carthage.[57]

Carthage fell to the Romans in early 146BC. Although the physical city was destroyed, the Romans were careful to remove as much as possible of its cultural heritage. Art works, in particular, were acquired, especially those of Greek origin that the Carthaginians themselves had obtained in places such as Sicily.[58] Moreover, the libraries of Carthage were saved.[59] These would have revealed the reports of Hanno and Himilco, as well as accounts of other Carthaginian explorers. Public inscriptions, such as the one that formed the basis of the extant text of Hanno, would also have been visible.[60]

Although there seems to have been no wholesale translation of Carthaginian literature,[61] the knowledge represented by the libraries had its impact on the Greco-Roman world. Scipio Aemilianus, the conquerer of Carthage, had in his entourage the historian Polybios, who already seems to have been involved in the disposition of a captured library,[62] probably that of the Makedonian king Perseus, deposed in 168BC, which Aemilius Paullus had given to his sons, one of whom was Scipio Aemilianus.[63] Polybios borrowed some books from the family, and this loan and the discussions that the books generated created the intimacy between him and the Aemilii.[64] When he was interned in Italy the following year, Polybios naturally gravitated toward the Aemilii, eventually becoming close to Scipio Aemilianus, and accompanying him to the final siege of Carthage. Thus when the Carthaginian library became available, revealing wide knowledge of the Atlantic, it was Polybios whom Scipio sent to investigate. His subsequent travels probably took place in the summer of 146BC, between the fall of Carthage and that of Corinth, at which Polybios was also present.[65] He was already known as a topographical investigator of sorts: some years earlier he had

---

57 Eratosthenes' unattributed description of the coast of West Africa (supra, pp. 94–5; Strabo 17.3.8) may also come from one of these sources, although if Eratosthenes used Ophelas, the latter must date to before ca. 200BC. See Desanges, *Recherches*, p. 50.

58 Diodoros 32.25.

59 Pliny, *Natural History* 18.22–3. The libraries were given to the Numidian kings and eventually, when the Numidian kingdom was dissolved in 46BC, passed to the historian Sallust and then probably to Juba II of Mauretania: see Roller, *Juba*, pp. 18, 27, 68.

60 Supra, pp. 32–3.

61 Pliny, *Natural History* 18.23 is specific in noting that "only" (*unius*) the treatise of Mago on agriculture was translated into Latin at this time, although nothing is said about the more probable translations into Greek.

62 The evidence for his career is summarized by F. W. Walbank, *Polybius*, first paperback edition, Berkeley: University of California Press, 1990, especially pp. 6–13.

63 Plutarch, *Aemilius Paullus* 28.11.

64 Polybios 31.23. That these were the books of Perseus is only hypothesis, but probable. See F. W. Walbank, *A Historical Commentary on Polybius*, Oxford: Clarendon Press 1957–79, vol. 3, p. 495; see also Walbank (supra n. 62), p. 8.

65 Polybios 39.2. For the date of the travels, see Walbank (supra n. 62), p. 11; Walbank (supra n. 64), vol. 1, p. 5; Desanges, *Recherches*, pp. 122–3.

retraced Hannibal's route across the Alps, attempting to correct the errors of earlier writers.[66] He knew something about Pytheas, because he was familiar with Dikaiarchos and Eratosthenes, both of whom had critiqued the Massalian explorer.[67] Massalians, perhaps present at the fall of their ancient nemesis Carthage, were questioned but were predictably uninformative, leading to suspicions about whether Pytheas had even existed.[68] However dubious, Polybios and Scipio may have had their curiosity about Pytheas stimulated at the very time that they were also learning more directly about Carthaginian explorers. Thus an extensive new world was now available to Greek intellectuals and Roman politicians, seemingly the first new information about the Atlantic since Herodotos, although there may have been some more recent rumors about the wealth of tropical West Africa, perhaps the metal trade.[69]

Polybios' reputation as an explorer is usually forgotten. Yet in antiquity it was well known: over 300 years after his time a monument to him still stood in the agora at Megalopolis in Arkadia, with a portrait and an inscription in elegiac verses recording that he wandered over the entire earth and sea.[70] He saw himself as a new Odysseus.[71] Even before the fall of Carthage, Polybios may have attempted to learn more about Pytheas, perhaps even travelling throughout Gaul as part of his quest. In addition to the Massalians, citizens of Narbo and Korbilon were questioned about the explorer.[72] Korbilon is little known but the context seems to place it at the mouth of the Liger (Loire),[73] and comments elsewhere about Narbo (modern Narbonne) imply personal knowledge.[74] If Polybios visited these places it means an extensive journey, down the Liger and along the Atlantic coast, following the ancient trade route across France.[75] He himself remarked that he had travelled on the Ocean in this region, outside (ἔξωθεν) Spain and Gaul.[76] Thus there seems to have been a circuit from the Mediterranean, probably at Massalia, up the Rhone, across to the Liger, down to its mouth near Korbilon, and along the western coast, stopping at Narbo and eventually Gades.[77] However much he was suspicious about the existence of Pytheas, he was retracing some of his route. The date of this northern journey is uncertain: it seems

---

66 Polybios 3.48.12. Walbank (supra n. 62), p. 11, dated this to 150BC.

67 Walbank (supra n. 62), p. 122.

68 Strabo 4.2.1.

69 Raymond Mauny, "Autour d'un texte bien controversé: le 'periple' de Polybe (146 av. J.-C.)," *Hespéris* 36, 1949, 47–67; Cary and Warmington, p. 68.

70 Pausanias 8.30.8.

71 Polybios 12.28.1; see also F. W. Walbank, "Polemic in Polybius," *JRS* 52, 1962, 10–11.

72 Polybios 34.10.6 = Strabo 4.2.1. The text implies these citizens reported to Scipio, not Polybios, so where they were contacted is not certain.

73 It may have been at the site of modern Nantes: see Barry Cunliffe, *Facing the Ocean*, Oxford: Oxford University Press, 2001, pp. 334–5.

74 Polybios 34.10.1–4 (= Athenaios 8.322). On the location of the toponyms in this passage see Walbank (supra n. 64), vol. 3, pp. 610–13.

75 Cunliffe (supra n. 73), pp. 331–6.

76 Polybios 3.59.8.

77 Walbank (supra n. 64), vol. 3, p. 604.

difficult to fit into the summer of 146BC along with Polybios' African expedition, and it may have occurred as early as 150BC, although some of the European coastal sailing was perhaps four years later as part of a general Atlantic reconnaissance both north and south of the Pillars.[78] At any rate nothing was learned about Pytheas, or even Prettanike, and Polybios developed the hostile attitude toward the Massalian that is so much a problem in understanding him today.[79]

For his African expedition, at least, Scipio gave Polybios a fleet, and he went into the tropics.[80] The source is Pliny, whose confused account mixes in material from the map of Marcus Agrippa, and perhaps even Hanno and Juba II.[81] Polybios' expedition is tersely described:

> Polybios, the writer of annals, received a fleet from Scipio Aemilianus during the latter's command in Africa, in order to make an exploratory voyage of that part of the world, reporting that beyond the mountain toward the west are forests full of the wild animals Africa produces.

Elsewhere Polybios demonstrated knowledge of Kerne.[82] At the very least he went beyond where the Atlas Mountains approach the coast, visited the site of Kerne and entered the forested tropics, finding wild animals. The following sentence of Pliny's summary cites Marcus Agrippa, with a confused list of toponyms, some of which can be identified on the northwest African coast. There are various distances, all in miles. Except for one reference to crocodiles in the Darat River, the information is all toponymic, as would befit the map Agrippa made. Yet after several toponyms and distances the information changes: ethnyms rather than toponyms predominate and the material is no longer totally coastal – e. g. the Gaetulian Darae who are in the interior ["in mediterraneo"] – ending with the Banbotum River, full of crocodiles and hippopotami. The next set of toponyms (Theon Ochema, in its original Greek, and the Promontory of the West), indicate that the source is Hanno; instead of miles there are sailing days. The section closes with a seeming map reference ("in medio eo spatio")

78 Walbank (supra n. 62), p. 11.

79 Supra, pp. 66–7.

80 Although scantily documented, the voyage has received extensive commentary, including P. Pédech, "Un texte discuté de Pline: le voyage de Polybe en Afrique (*H. N.*, V, 9–10)," *RÉL* 33, 1955, 318–32; Mauny (supra n. 69), pp. 47–67; R. Thouvenot, "Le témoignage de Pline sur le périple africain de Polybe (V, 1, 8–11)," *RÉL* 34, 1956, 88–92; Marijean H. Eichel and Joan Markley Todd, "A Note on Polybius' Voyage to Africa in 146BC," *CP* 71, 1976, 239–43; and especially Desanges, *Recherches*, pp. 121–47, and Walbank (supra n. 64), vol. 1, p. 5; vol. 3, pp. 633–7, where previous commentators are critiqued. See also Pliny, *Histoire naturelle livre V, 1–46*, ed. Jehan Desanges, Paris: Les Belles Lettres, 1980, pp. 106–21.

81 "Scipione Aemiliano res in Africa gerente Polybius annalium conditor ab eo accepta classe scrutandi illius orbis gratia circumvectus prodidit a monte eo ad occasum versus saltus plenos feris quas generat Africa" (Pliny, *Natural History* 5.9–10 [= Polybios 34.15.7]); see also Roller, *Juba*, pp. 188–9. Polybios referred elusively to the voyage at 3.59.7.

82 Polybios 34.15.9 (= Pliny, *Natural History* 6.199). On Kerne, see supra, pp. 37, 42.

for Mt Atlas, and a final citation of "all others" ("ceteris omnibus") who define this mountain as the limit of Mauretania.

Deconstructing Pliny is difficult and dangerous. But these two chapters of the *Natural History* seem less convoluted than many, despite the agonizing of commentators.[83] Clearly the map of Agrippa was the basis of the description, but there is an initial statement – mentioning Polybios by name – and then later a transition from the map and its use of miles to the world of Hanno, yet the actual transitional phrases are marked by names not in Hanno's text. It is probable that this section is a return to the account of Polybios, and thus the toponyms here belong to his report: the Salsum river, the tribes of the Perorsi, the Pharusii, the interior Darae, and the coastal Daratitae,[84] and the Banbotum River.[85] Then Pliny passed to Hanno's text – which may have been quoted by Polybios – and its use of sailing days. Thus it seems that Polybios went into the tropics and made a survey of the ethnic groups of the region, something that might have been of interest to the Roman government, which for the first time had acquired territory in Africa.[86] The actual extent of the expedition is not obvious, because it depends on untangling the text of Pliny. If Polybios replicated Hanno's voyage – reasonable, given the reason for the journey – he went as far as Cameroon and the Chariot of the Gods. A minimalist view is that he went no farther than the Lixos region,[87] which does not account for the tropical flora and fauna. Another suggestion is the mouth of the Dra'a, just south of the Atlas Mountains, given the prevalence in the text of similar toponyms.[88] But most commentators send him to the Senegal, often equated with the Banbotum.[89] This is the most reasonable assumption, for it allows a journey beyond the desert into the tropics, which seems implicit in the text. If so, Polybios repeated almost exactly the voyage of Euthymenes of 350 years earlier, which seems to have been unknown to him.

Polybios' voyage seems to have led to a consideration of the more southern parts of the earth, and he published a treatise titled *On the Inhabited Parts of the Earth Under the Equator*; the title appears in the *Introduction to Phenomena* of the Julio-Claudian author Geminos of Rhodes, who was noted for citing by title obscure works – he is also the only extant pre-Byzantine source to name Pytheas' treatise *On*

---

83 On the passage and its sources, see Mauny (supra n. 69), pp. 52–4; on the manuscript tradition, Walbank (supra n. 64), vol. 3, pp. 633–5.

84 On these ethnic groups, see Pédech (supra n. 80), pp. 329–31. The similar toponyms (including the Darat River, mentioned earlier) suggest the modern Dra'a, which empties into the Mediterranean south of the Atlas.

85 This name may be descriptive, from πάμβοτος, "all-nourishing," (Aischylos, *Suppliant Women* 558), the impression made by a rich tropic riverine environment (W. Aly, "Die Entdeckung des Westens," *Hermes* 62, 1927, p. 338). Although the word is rare, it is certainly an appropriate response to the lushness of the tropics. On possible identifications see Pliny (supra n. 80), pp. 117–18.

86 On the political background of the voyage, see Eichel and Todd (supra n. 80), p. 238.

87 Walbank (supra n. 64), vol. 3, p. 637–8.

88 Desanges, *Recherches*, pp. 146–7.

89 Cary and Warmington, p. 68; Hennig, vol. 1, pp. 248–51; Thouvenot (supra n. 80), pp. 88–92; Eichel and Todd (supra n. 80), pp. 237–43.

the Ocean.[90] The extract from Polybios' treatise is entirely theoretical, about the nature of climate in the tropical regions beneath the celestial equator. Other citations concern the same or similar topics.[91] The only topographical comment – that the equatorial regions are at high altitude – is itself vague. Yet this may show some awareness of the mountains of central Africa, something Polybios knew that Eratosthenes did not, reflecting the former's personal familiarity with the Atlas and other mountains of West Africa, especially the Chariot of the Gods.[92]

It is likely that Polybios' treatise was purely theoretical and that the account of his journey was a private communiqué to Scipio: hence its obscurity. Yet the travels may have influenced Polybios to include as Book 34 of his history a section on world geography, following the pattern set by Ephoros two centuries earlier.[93] But most of the fragments now printed as part of Book 34, a collation of J. Schweighäuser in the late eighteenth century,[94] are testimonia and discussions only. There are only a few comments on Africa, all preserved in the *Natural History* of Pliny.[95] Polybios, whom Pliny considered authoritative ("diligentissimus") about Africa, provided distances along the North African coast, perhaps lifted from Eratosthenes. There are some comments on elephants, quoting the Numidian king Gulussa (148–140BC), who was present at the fall of Carthage, and on lions, also in a Carthaginian context. What is significant is that practically none of these relates to West Africa. There is no further evidence in the extant fragments of Polybios' West African exploration, which further emphasizes that it may not have been published beyond a report to Scipio. It may have been discovered in the Roman archives over a century later by Marcus Agrippa when doing research for his map, and Polybios' comments may have been incorporated into Agrippa's text, which was used by Pliny. Polybios' theoretical work, *On the Inhabited Parts of the Earth Under the Equator*, also had little circulation, known only in astronomical circles and thus becoming divorced from his main reputation as an historian.

Thus the voyage of Polybios had little impact, perhaps of interest only because of the personality involved. It did not add to knowledge or influence trade,[96] although it made Roman official circles aware of the validity of the Carthaginian explorations. The report did not cause any great concern in Rome.[97] Despite the fall of Carthage, by

90 περὶ τῆς ὑπὸ τὸν ἰσημερινὸν οἰκήσεως. Geminos 16.32 (= Polybios 34.1.7). ἰσημερινὸς refers to the celestial, not earthly, equator (Aristotle, *Meteorologika* 1.7 [345a]). See also F. W. Walbank, "The Geography of Polybius," *ClMed* 9, 1947, 177–9; Walbank (supra note 64), vol. 3, pp. 573–4.

91 Strabo 2.3.1–2 (= Polybios 34.1.14–17); see also Polybios 34.1.18.

92 Polybios 34.1.16 (= Strabo 2.3.2); Walbank (supra note 64), vol. 3, pp. 575–7; P. Pédech, *La méthode historique de Polybe*, Paris: Les Belles Lettres, 1964, pp. 588–90.

93 Polybios 34.1.1 (= Strabo 8.1.1); Polybios 34.8.1, 4–10; 34.10.1–4 (= Athenaios 7.302, 8.330–2; see also Stephanos of Byzantion, "Aithale" (= Polybios 34.11.4). On Ephoros' use of geography, see supra, pp. 61–2.

94 J. Schweighäuser, *Lexicum Polybianum*, Oxford: W. Baxter, 1832; see Walbank (supra n. 64), vol. 3, pp. 563–6.

95 Polybios 34.15.6–16.3.

96 Cary and Warmington, p. 68.

97 Eichel and Todd (supra n. 80), p. 243.

the latter second century BC Greco-Roman knowledge of the Atlantic was no more than it had been two centuries earlier, and in some ways less, because of the savaging of Pytheas that effectively began with Polybios and was to continue with Poseidonios and Strabo.[98]

98 Sometime in the century after the fall of Carthage, Xenophon of Lampsakos attempted to consolidate knowledge about the Atlantic. There are three extant fragments of his *Periplous*: one is on the eastern Greek city of Latmos – although whether this is the topographical context of the citation is not clear. More interesting are the two remaining fragments: one on Pytheas and one on Hanno. This seems an impossible conflation of sources unless the Atlantic were his main topic (Valerius Maximus 8.13.ext. 7; Pliny, *Natural History* 4.95, 6.200, 7.155).

6

LATE HELLENISTIC
EXPLORATION

The explorations of Polybios represented the entry of the Romans into the Atlantic. This marks the beginning of a significant change in the ancient view of the world beyond the Pillars of Herakles. Exploration came to be driven by the unified policies of the centralized Roman state rather than the individual needs of a Greek city: Roman attitudes, in many ways, were similar to those of the Carthaginians. Yet even with the collapse of Carthage and the subsequent opening up of the west, there is no evidence of Roman exploration beyond the Pillars for a century after the reconnaissance of Polybios, despite their acquisition of much of the Iberian peninsula in the second century BC and mercantile interest in Mauretania by late in the same century.[1] The Carthaginians had done their work well: the Romans were convinced by the journey of Polybios that the world beyond the Pillars was not of interest to them. Significant is what Scipio Aemilianus learned from the Massalians: when he inquired about their explorations there was "nothing worth recording."[2] Although this became tangled with the rejection of Pytheas that pervaded the era, it nonetheless demonstrates how the Romans were diverted from the world beyond the Pillars.

Roman interests, of course, turned east. Less than two decades after the fall of Carthage, acquisition of the Pergamene kingdom extended Roman territory into Asia, setting into process a familiar series of events that saw Roman control spread toward the Levant and Egypt, where the Romans had long had allies. The Ptolemies had been involved in Roman politics since their attempt to negotiate an end to the First Makedonian War in the late third century BC.[3] It was perhaps only inevitable that Rome, increasingly involved in the East, would have little desire to explore beyond the Pillars. Yet the world outside the Pillars was to be more connected to Ptolemaic Egypt than Rome realized. Ever since the days of Ptolemaios II, explorers had moved south

---

1 On this, see Roller, *Juba*, p. 47.
2 Polybios 34.10.6 = Strabo 4.2.1: οὐδὲν μνήμης ἄξιον.
3 Polybios 11.4.1; Livy 27.30.4, 28.7.13; Erich S. Gruen, *The Hellenistic World and the Coming of Rome*, first paperback printing, Berkeley: University of California Press, 1986, pp. 677–8. Ptolemaic envoys had actually come to Rome as early as the 270s BC, in the aftermath of the war against Pyrrhos: for the sources see Gruen, pp. 673–5.

from Egypt into the Red Sea, hunting for elephants and aromatics.[4] Eventually they came into contact with Indians, whose merchants had reached west to the mouth of the Red Sea. Just as the Ptolemies had extended their diplomatic contacts to the west when they sent envoys to Rome, they also reached in the opposite direction. Ptolemaios II sent a certain Dionysios[5] to India and the Mauryan king Ashoka, who also had relations with Antiochos II, Antigonas Gonatas, Magas of Kyrene, and Alexandros, probably of Epeiros.[6] Thus for the first time the extremities of the known world came together: the wide interests of the Ptolemies extended, in theory, from the western Mediterranean to India. Aristotle had suggested that the Pillars and India were joined in some way,[7] and in the days of Ptolemaios III, Eratosthenes raised the possibility of sailing west from Iberia to India, noting that the only restraint was the distance.[8] Connecting the far west and the far east was a topical issue from the early Hellenistic period, affecting both geographical theory and political realities.

Yet for many years any proof that India could be reached through the Pillars was lacking. The early circumnavigators of Africa had shown no interest in India, and Polybios did not go beyond the West African tropics. The explorers commissioned by Alexander to define the sea routes from India to the Mediterranean had failed to do so, and the extent of the Arabian peninsula remained unknown to Greeks.[9] Indian traders were encountered at the mouth of the Red Sea, but, in the long-standing tradition, would not reveal their routes home.[10] Thus Greek seamen remained unfamiliar with large portions of the theoretical Pillars–India route, and its particulars, or whether it even existed, were a matter of geographical speculation, not seamanship.

In the last years of Ptolemaios VIII (died 116BC), the situation changed. An Indian sailor appeared at the Ptolemaic court, who had been found by the coast guard in a bay in the Red Sea, shipwrecked and the only survivor of his crew.[11] He learned Greek and eventually told how by a sudden reversal of fortune[12] he ended up in Egypt. Not

---

4 Their record is preserved by Pliny, *Natural History* 6.175–195; for other sources see Günther Hölbl, *A History of the Ptolemaic Empire*, tr. Tina Saavedra, London: Routledge, 2001, pp. 56–8.

5 *FGrHist* #717.

6 The kings are mentioned on the Thirteenth Rock Edict of Ashoka, dated to 256–255BC (Romila Thapar, *Asoka and the Decline of the Mauryas*, Oxford: Oxford University Press, 1961, pp. 40–2, 255–7). The text is in Ashoka, *Les inscriptions*, tr. Jules Bloch, Paris: Les Belles Lettres, 1950, pp. 125–32; an English translation is in Ashoka, *The Edicts*, tr. N. A. Nikam and Richard McKeon, Chicago: University of Chicago Press, 1959, pp. 27–30. The five kings appear as Antiyoka, king of the Yona, and, further west, Turamaya, Antikini, Maka, and Alikasudara.

7 Aristotle, *On the Heavens* 2.14.

8 Strabo 1.4.6.

9 *Supra*, pp. 92–3.

10 *Periplous of the Erythraian Sea* 26.

11 These events were recounted in detail by Poseidonios (fr. 28), preserved by Strabo (2.3.4–5). The only other source is Cornelius Nepos (Pomponius Mela 3.90–2; Pliny, *Natural History* 2.169), which is brief and confused.

12 The diction is interesting: the word used by Strabo – and probably Poseidonios – is περιπέσοι, connected with περιπέτεια, the technical term for reversal of fortune in tragedy (Aristotle, *Poetics* 11), which gives the tale dramatic overtones.

unexpectedly the ever-critical Strabo doubted this tale and made much of the sailor's remarkable appearance, pointing out the difficulty of getting lost in the Red Sea – a region Strabo knew personally – the suspicious disappearance of all his shipmates, and the question of how he might have sailed his ship alone. There is much validity in Strabo's suspicion: the story seems to be yet another example of a journey conveniently off course that had momentous results. But the Ptolemaic court was curious, especially when the sailor offered to guide an expedition to India, something that had never been done from Egypt.

At this point one of the more intriguing personalities of ancient exploration enters the story, Eudoxos of Kyzikos.[13] He had come to Alexandria as an ambassador connected with the rites of Persephone that were prominent in his native city,[14] and developed an intimacy with the royal court. He became an expert on remote places, especially the Upper Nile, whose exploration had been ongoing since the days of Ptolemaios II: given his later career, one suspects that he may have travelled up the Nile himself. He certainly was an educated man and as such familiar with the current state of geographical scholarship, especially Eratosthenes.[15] He gained a reputation for being particularly inclined to wonder at and admire the peculiarities of places (θαυμαστικὸν. . .τῶν τοπικῶν ἰδιωμάτων), a description by Poseidonios in almost Herodotean terms. It is therefore not surprising that Eudoxos took an interest in the stranded Indian and joined his party that was to go to India.

Presumably the Indian sailor was safely returned home. Eudoxos then led the journey back to Egypt, laden with the wealth of India, especially aromatics and precious stones, thus becoming the first Greek to make an ocean expedition all the way from India to Greek territory. But Ptolemaios VIII confiscated all the goods. There is nothing unexpected in this, and Eudoxos' annoyance apparent in the extant account may indicate the tone of his later comments to friends in Gades. A few years later the king's widow, Kleopatra III, sent Eudoxos out again. On the return he was blown off course and landed somewhere on a desolate stretch of the East African coast. He evidently learned something of the local language, and used this not only to find the way home but to inquire about a shipwreck that the locals said had come from the west. When he arrived in Alexandria, he made a futile attempt to abscond with his

---

13 The best modern discussion of Eudoxos remains J. H. Thiel, *Eudoxus of Cyzicus, Historische Studies* 23, Groningen: J. B. Wolters, n. d., originally published in 1939, supplemented by Poseidonios, *Posidonius 2: The Commentary*, ed. I. G. Kidd, Cambridge: Cambridge University Press, 1988, pp. 240–57. See also Hennig, vol. 1, pp. 271–8; Desanges, *Recherches*, pp. 151–73; and Cary and Warmington, pp. 123–8.

14 On his background in Kyzikos, see Desanges, *Recherches*, p. 156. Kyzikos, a Corinthian and Milesian foundation originally of the eighth century BC, had become a rich commercial and trading center by Hellenistic times. In Eudoxos' day it had just come under Roman control (E. Akurgal, "Kyzikos," *PECS*, 473–4). Growing up there would have well prepared him for the adventurous trading-oriented life he was to lead. His role as a religious functionary is discussed by Thiel (supra n. 13), p. 31.

15 Thiel (supra n. 13), p. 32.

Indian goods, but again had them confiscated.[16] Most notably, however, the port officials identified the pieces of the East African shipwreck as from Gades. They were astonishingly knowledgeable about sailing habits on the coasts of Africa, and, in a marvel of understatement, said that the ship was somewhat beyond its destination of the Lixos River.[17]

This inspired Eudoxos to attempt to circumnavigate Africa – he would have known something about earlier attempts, at least from Herodotos – and to create a route to India by that means, avoiding the confiscations of the Ptolemaic court. He returned home to Kyzikos[18] and set forth in a ship with all his possessions, making a grandiose tour across the Mediterranean, stopping at Dikaiarcheia on the Bay of Naples, Massalia, and eventually Gades – in other words, the great trading ports – advertising his intentions, casting the Ptolemies in the worst possible light, becoming rich through trade, and presumably putting together, in almost Argonautic terms, a crew. When he reached Gades he made his final plans, and still playing the role of Jason, built a large ship that towed two barges (ἐφόλια) full of provisions. The expedition was thoroughly outfitted with craftsmen, physicians, and especially music girls, all talents that would be useful not only on the voyage but in India.[19] He set forth, and probably reached the western tropics, since he was able to make use of a constant west wind, but evidently lost the confidence of his entourage, members of whom asked that he sail closer to shore, something Eudoxos was reluctant to do because of the power of the tides. According to Strabo the companions were tiring of the voyage – which, granted, sounds more like a strange game rather than a serious exploration – but it may have been the usual fear at being in strange places far from home.

Eventually the ships ran aground, although the provisions were saved. This was no deterent, however, as Eudoxos built a new ship from the salvaged timbers of the old ones and continued on, until he found people whom he believed spoke the same language as those he had encountered in East Africa: like Hanno, he may have had interpreters on board.[20] He also came across people so primitive that they did not

16 According to the account, Kleopatra III no longer ruled at this time. There were violent convulsions in the years after Ptolemaios VIII's death, during which she and her two sons (Ptolemaios IX and X) all ruled, separately and jointly. This ended only with the death of the queen in 101BC at the hand of Ptolemaios X, who was sole ruler thereafter (to 88BC). Thus it is impossible exactly to place Eudoxos' second voyage. Significantly, however, Strabo did not say that Kleopatra III was dead, so it was probably before 101BC. On the dating see Poseidonios (supra n. 13), pp. 247–9.

17 It may be that the Alexandrian port officials knew about a Gaderene ship that was missing: see Thomson, p. 185.

18 Nepos wrote that Eudoxos fled the Ptolemaic court by going around Africa to India (Pomponius Mela 3.90–2; Pliny, *Natural History* 2.169). This is unlikely, but may be been something that the explorer claimed. Nepos' information on Eudoxos is confused, mixing up the various voyages and claming that Eudoxos was his contemporary, when the explorer probably was a generation older, a hint that Nepos was quoting an earlier source.

19 *Periplous of the Erythraian Sea* 49; Thiel (supra n. 13), p. 37. Gaderene girls were famous in antiquity: see Martial 5.78; Juvenal 11.162–70.

20 Thiel (supra n. 13), p. 38.

know about fire. In fact, a strange ethnography reported by Pomponius Mela may be a garbled report from the explorer: there are people who cannot talk and who have no tongues, and those whose lips are stuck together except for a reed to drink with.[21] It is clear that Eudoxos felt (quite erroneously) that he was near where he had found the Gadarene wreck on the east coast. But he also learned that he was in the vicinity of the Mauretanian king Bocchus I (ca. 120–80BC),[22] and thus still in northwest Africa not far from the Pillars. Obviously the topography is quite confused, and may reflect more than one voyage. Nevertheless, at this point Eudoxos gave up on going to India and turned back to the Mauretanian coast, discovering on the way a well-watered and wooded uninhabited island.[23] On the mainland he abandoned his ship and went inland to the Mauretanian court at Volubilis.[24] There he attempted to persuade Bocchus to outfit a new expedition, but the king was not impressed and had no desire to expose his kingdom to Greek adventurers.[25] When Eudoxos heard that Bocchus planned to abandon him on an island, he escaped to the Roman mercantile communities in northwest Africa – probably at Tingis – and then to Spain.

Not to be dissuaded, however, he outfitted another expedition, again well-provisioned as a virtual colonizing force – seeds, agricultural tools, and architects are mentioned – and set forth for the island that he had discovered.[26] At this point Strabo's account breaks off; his source, Poseidonios, visited Gades, probably in the 90s BC, only a few years after Eudoxos' departure, when the explorer was still unreported but had not been given up for lost.[27] But seemingly he was never heard from again.[28] Given his ability at self-promotion and the fact that Poseidonios, obviously

---

21 Pomponius Mela 3.91, probably from Cornelius Nepos. This is perhaps a confused report of various types of facial ornamention (Walter Woodburn Hyde, *Ancient Greek Mariners*, New York: Oxford University Press 1947, p. 246). Although Eudoxos was not mentioned as the source, the passage is between Pomponius Mela's two citations of the explorer.

22 The monarch mentioned by Strabo, Bogos, can only be Bocchus I despite the orthographic problems: see Thiel (supra n. 13), pp. 38–40.

23 The Cape Verdes and Canaries were perhaps closest to his route, although the latter seem unlikely because of their visibility from the coast and the prior Carthaginian habitation (supra, pp. 47–9). One of the Madeiras is also possible but geographically remote (Raymond Mauny, "Trans-Saharan Contacts and the Iron Age in West Africa," *CHA* 2, 1978, 299). Precision is unwise.

24 Roller, *Juba*, p. 48.

25 Bocchus' distaste for Eudoxos and his plans may hint at a deeper involvement of the Mauretanian kingdom in the route to India, perhaps presuming a role as middlemen between the Greek world and the far east. See Marie Laffranque, "Poseidonius, Eudoxe de Cyzique et la circumnavigation de l'Afrique," *RPFE* 103, 1963, 217–19.

26 Witness to his preparations, perhaps, was a certain Caelius Antipater (Pliny, *Natural History* 2.169): "Caelius Antipater vidisse se qui navigasset ex Hispania in Aethiopiam commerci gratia." Eudoxos is not mentioned by name and Caelius Antipater is otherwise unknown, but this may have been the contemporary historian Coelius Antipater, who wrote on the Second Punic War. Pliny's source was not Antipater directly, but through Cornelius Nepos, who was aware of Eudoxos.

27 Poseidonios (supra n. 13), pp. 16–17.

28 For his possible fate, see Hyde (supra n. 21), p. 247. If he were attempting to find again an island that was out of sight of the mainland, he probably became hopelessly lost, perhaps even ending up in South America.

deeply interested in his fate, lived into the 50s BC, it can be assumed that Eudoxos never did return.[29]

Yet the account as rendered by Strabo has significant problems, despite its richness of detail.[30] Strabo himself, ever derisively critical, pointed many of these out. Most importantly – but unknown to Strabo – the entire tale is based on the erroneous conception of Africa shaped like a lozenge oriented east–west. This was an early idea,[31] but one that does not relate to the actual form of the continent. When Eudoxos landed in East Africa on his second return from India, he felt that he was near the Pillars of Herakles, using the ancient geographical theory that projected an African coast running straight west from its easternmost point, where Eudoxos essentially was, modern Cape Guardafui or Ras Asin, to the Niger delta. This of course is not the case, but it is a necessary component of the tale. In West Africa, correspondingly, Eudoxos felt that he was near the Somali coast. This ancient view of the shape of Africa couples with the epic and Argonautic tone of much of the tale, giving it a strange anachronistic flavor even as Eudoxos was going beyond the boundaries of contemporary knowledge. Essential also is rejection of the theorists who believed that the Indian Ocean was an enclosed sea.[32] Eudoxos used his alleged knowledge of local languages to support these ideas of the shape of Africa, but this too may have been conveniently misleading as most of the languages of southern Africa are related,[33] and his understanding may have been little more than a listing of words – a task specifically cited by Strabo – compounded by the common tendency to see similarities among languages that one does not know well.

The mysterious ships of Gades play a remarkable and strange role in the account: their shipwrecks were said to appear unusually frequently on the East African coast,[34] and the Alexandrian port officials seemed amazingly well informed about them and their routes. They are perhaps the weakest part of the tale,[35] and, as Strabo noted, a thin thread on which Eudoxos abandoned his life and headed west, although connections between Gades and the routes to India were ancient and extensive.[36] Whether the facts were correct about the Gaderene ships is of little importance: it was a pretext that allowed Eudoxos to extricate himself from the Ptolemaic court – where the regime change and his own dubious activities had diminished his influence – and to strike out on his own.[37]

---

29 Thiel (supra n. 13), pp. 15–16. Elements of Eudoxos' account are incorporated into José Saramago's *O Conto de Ilha Desconhecida*, *The Tale of the Unknown Island*, tr. Margaret Jull Costa, New York: Harcourt Brace, 1999.

30 On the contrast between the detailed and engaging nature of Strabo's account, and his dismissing of it, see Germaine Aujac, *Strabon et la science de son temps*, Paris: Les Belles Lettres, 1966, p. 46.

31 Supra, p. 41.

32 Supra, p. 24.

33 See the map in Francis Lacroix, "Les langues," in *Histoire générale de l'Afrique Noire*, Paris 1970, vol. 1, pp. 76–7.

34 Pliny, *Natural History* 2.168–70.

35 Hennig, vol. 1, pp. 276–7.

36 See, for example, Juvenal 10.1–2 and even Pliny, *Natural History* 6.175; Jean Gagé, "Gadès, l'Inde et les navigations atlantiques dans l'Antiquité," *RHist* 205, 1951, pp. 189–216.

37 Thiel (supra n. 13), pp. 22–3.

There are other obscurities. The itinerary in West Africa is confused: after a long eastern sail, which can only bring him to the Niger delta region, Eudoxos learned that he was near Mauretania, leading to the probability that existing knowledge about West African exploration has become tangled into the story of Eudoxos, or that he made several voyages in the region.

Strabo also noted the remarkable convenience of the appearance of the Indian sailor at the Ptolemaic court, having all the characteristics of a premeditated attempt to open up India to Greek shipping, and again a slender thread on which to hang subsequent events. Strabo, perhaps unfairly, made derogatory comments about the strange evolution of Eudoxos' life, from religious official to court advisor to explorer to merchant to adventurer. More reasonably, Strabo pointed out that he himself had lived a long time in Alexandria, and the activities of the port officials did not conform to his own knowledge. Yet, all in all, there is little doubt that Eudoxos did approximately what he said he did, and obviously there were people both in Alexandria and Gades quite familiar with his interesting career. As a flamboyant adventurer he would have attracted notice. But, as is often the case with such personalities, the motivations for his actions, and indeed some of those actions themselves, do not hold up to close scrutiny. The entire tale demonstrates the usual problems of oral history, with Eudoxos putting himself in the best light: he had an especially sharp mind, he was horribly mistreated by the Ptolemaic court – after serving them so well – he was a brilliant navigator, he was so daring as to stake his livelihood and all his resources on his dream, he tried unsuccessfully to save his companions from their ignorance, and he outwitted Bocchus.

The story of Eudoxos is strange, mixing epic, tragic, and comic elements. Because he was lost in the midst of his voyages, it is unlikely that he ever wrote a report, and Poseidonios and Nepos had to rely on oral reminiscences from Gades and Alexandria.[38] In a way he was a failure, never (it seems) making the journey from the Pillars to India, if this were ever his intent. Nevertheless he remains one of the greatest navigators of all time. The account of his explorations was soon published by Poseidonios in his *On the Ocean*, whose title shows its debt to Pytheas: Eudoxos became the southern counterpart to the Massalian. Most importantly, he firmly planted in the mainstream the idea that a continuous journey from the Pillars to India was possible, unlike Pytheas, who had essentially reached a dead end in his attempt to find a northern route east. Eudoxos laid the groundwork for the Roman view of the connectivity of the southern extremities of the world.

A by-product of Eudoxos' wandering was the brief involvement of the indigenous Mauretanian monarchy in the exploration of the Atlantic. This kingdom, ruling the territory that is essentially modern Morocco and Algeria, and thus a long stretch of

---

38 Pliny (*Natural History* 7.24) attributes data on the unusual size of human feet in India to a certain Eudoxos, thus hinting at a published report of his Indian travels, if this is the same person. Eudoxos' sojourn in Alexandria, his educated background, and his interest in Ptolemaic exploration suggests he might have published something, but if such ever existed it is so deeply buried in the extant material by Strabo and Pliny as to be invisible.

Atlantic coastline, had had increasing contacts with the Greco-Roman world. It had come to Roman notice as an ally of Carthage as early as the late fifth century BC,[39] and had eventually begun to receive an increasing Italian mercantile presence, especially after the fall of Carthage.[40] The first prominent Mauretanian king was Bocchus I, who, perhaps around 100BC, figured in the Eudoxos tale. He already knew enough of the Greek world to be suspicious of Greek adventurism. Some 20 years later, at the very end of his reign, he was exposed to another adventurer from the Mediterranean, this time a Roman, Q. Sertorius, who hid in Mauretania from his nemesis P. Cornelius Sulla, and then took advantage of the instability following Bocchus' death around 80BC to make himself (briefly) ruler of Tingis and its vicinity.[41] Sertorius is but a footnote to the issue of Atlantic exploration, however: he encountered some Kilikian pirates who became part of his entourage and encouraged him, unsuccessfully, to sail to remote islands in the Atlantic, probably the Madeiras,[42] which they identified as the Islands of the Blessed of myth. Although Sertorius did not take up their offer, the episode demonstrates the tangling of myth, exploration, and sailors' tales that was becoming part of the chaotic world of the first century BC. It also shows that pirates, fisherman, and other independent seamen may have had knowledge far beyond that of scholars and state-sponsored explorers.

Despite their wise distrust of the schemes of itinerant Greeks and Romans, the Mauretanian monarchs themselves, in at least one case, were not adverse to commissioning their own explorations. King Bogudes II, who reigned in the 40s and 30s BC and may have been the grandson of Bocchus I, made his own expedition into the tropics,[43] although whether by land or sea is not specified. The project had a military context, but nevertheless the king showed interest in unusual flora and sent a selection home to his wife, including reeds (καλάμοι) and asparagus (ἀσπάραγος).[44] Nevertheless this Mauretanian interest in exploration was sporadic and minimal. By 33BC the kingdom was without a ruler – Bogudes had abdicated and joined Marcus Antonius in the East – and eight years later Augustus placed two members of his household on the vacant throne. Juba II was the orphaned heir to the recently-terminated Numidian kingdom, which had been provincialized in 46BC. Around 25BC he married Kleopatra Selene, the only surviving child of Antonius and Kleopatra VII: she was heiress to another vacant and provincialized kingdom, that of the Ptolemies, and also pretender queen of the Kyrenaika. Augustus gave them the Mauretanian kingdom – all the lands west of the Roman province of Africa – but they also had claim to all the African territory east of the province. It was through the activities of these enlightened monarchs

---

39 Diodoros 13.80.3.

40 For the history of the indigenous monarchy, see Roller, *Juba*, pp. 46–58, 91–5.

41 Plutarch, *Sertorius* 7–10; Sallust, *Histories* 1.87–94 McGushin; Strabo 17.3.8.

42 Supra, pp. 45–7.

43 Strabo 17.3.5.

44 It was probably their size that made them unusual: each reed joint (γόνυ) could hold eight *choinikes*, or several liters. There is nothing inherently exotic about asparagus, although it was probably African in origin (Andrew Dalby, *Food in the Ancient World from A to Z*, London: Routledge, 2003, pp. 31–2).

that the final evolution of ancient thought about the southern part of the world took place.[45] They established themselves at their capital of Caesarea (modern Cherchel in Algeria), the ancient Carthaginian outpost of Iol, and turned it into the new Alexandria, with Egyptian art and an outstanding scholarly presence in which the king himself took the lead. Although Juba's exploration was limited and largely confined to the interior of his kingdom and issues such as the source of the Nile, he did make a detailed examination of the Canary Islands, naming the group.[46]

The most significant contribution of Juba II and Kleopatra Selene to comprehension of the world beyond the Pillars was scholarly. In his youth Juba had discovered the report of Hanno in the Carthaginian library – it had been removed to Rome – and made it available, writing his own commentary.[47] Kleopatra Selene, heiress of the Ptolemies, made the record of their explorers available to her husband. The culmination of Juba's scholarship and indeed ancient understanding of the southern half of the world, from the Pillars around Africa to India, was his two treatises, *Libyka* and *On Arabia*.[48] The former was a wide-ranging study of the mythology, natural history, and exploration of the northern half of Africa. Juba was able to bring together all the knowledge about the Atlantic south of the Pillars, from Hanno to the indigenous Mauretanian monarchs, although there is no evidence that he added to the existing data beyond his reconnaissance of the Canary Islands. Moreover, information was collated from Ptolemaic and contemporary mercantile sources to provide a summation of the eastern coast as far south as Zanzibar. The gap of several thousand miles between east and west – between Cameroon and Zanzibar – was to Juba far shorter than its reality: Juba was still beholden to the traditional view of the lozenge shape of the continent.[49]

In East Africa, *Libyka* merged into Juba's *On Arabia*. Here previous scholarship was supplemented by autopsy, as Juba was personally familiar with the vicinity of the Arabian peninsula, from when he was part of the entourage of Gaius Caesar from 2BC to AD1,[50] whose Arabian expedition reflected the Augustan desire to develop the trade routes to the East. In the century since Eudoxos, trade with India had blossomed, after a slow start in part due to the collapse of the Ptolemaic world.[51] Augustus took a personal interest, receiving Indian ambassadors in Spain in 26 BC[52] – Juba was probably present – and sending expeditions down the Red Sea.[53] Yet as trade flourished, the actual route to

---

45 For a detailed study of the monarchs and their environment, see Roller, *Juba*.

46 Supra, pp. 47–9.

47 For the extant fragments of Juba's commentary, see Duane W. Roller, *Scholarly Kings: The Fragments of Juba II of Mauretania, Archelaos of Kappadokia, Herod the Great and the Emperor Claudius*, Chicago: Ares Publishers, 2004, pp. 43–5; see also supra, p. 33.

48 Roller, *Juba*, pp. 183–211, 227–43; fragments are in Roller, *Scholarly Kings* (supra n. 47), pp. 47–103 and 107–66.

49 Pliny, *Natural History* 6.175.

50 Roller, *Juba* 212–16.

51 Strabo 17.1.13, 2.5.12.

52 Orosius 6.21; Augustus, *Res gestae* 31, stressed the frequency (*saepe*) of the Indian embassies.

53 Strabo 16.4.22–4; Augustus, *Res gestae* 26.

India was still little known; the gap in Greco-Roman knowledge of the late Hellenistic period still persisted, despite the efforts of Eudoxos, and was known to only a handful of seamen. The most recent published account of the route, astonishingly, emanated from Alexander's companions and was now 300 years old.[54] Juba was commissioned to bring this information up to date, a central part of his *On Arabia*, which included the first description of the entire sea route from Egypt to India.

Thus the idea that had been vaguely considered since the time of Aristotle now reached maturity in Juba's twin treatises. Finally, the Pillars and India were joined and the possibility of the sea route between them became more than theoretical geography. To be sure, there was still a long stretch from West Africa to Zanzibar that was unknown: the author of the *Periplous of the Erythraian Sea*, writing in the mid-first century AC, remarked that the southern African coast was still unexplored.[55] For the first time, however, the southern half of the world had been carefully defined "ab India usque Gades."[56] The Augustan concept of a world unified under Roman control[57] made this possible, although Greek and Roman seamen never actually implemented the Pillars–India route. But the explorers of early modern times did: the Indian-oriented voyages of the contemporaries Vasco da Gama and Columbus – seamen intimately familiar with the ancient sources – fulfilled the ancient concept of the unified southern half of the world.

54 Pliny, *Natural History* 6.96.
55 *Periplous of the Erythraian Sea* 18.
56 Solinus 56.6.
57 Vergil, *Aeneid* 6.792–800.

7

ROMAN EXPLORATION

Initial Roman interest south of the Pillars of Herakles was largely a result of the defeat of Carthage and did not continue, although the reconnaissance of the Canary Islands by Juba II, sometime between 25 and 2BC, is an exception.[1] Yet this was as much due to Juba's scholarly heritage as to Roman policy, and with the publication of his *Libyka* during the last decade of the first century BC, and his *On Arabia* a few years later, it was believed that all that could be said about the southern half of the world had been published. To be sure, the author of the *Periplous of the Erythraian Sea* would write in the middle of the first century AC that the southern part of Africa, the part that eventually joins the Western Ocean, was unexplored,[2] but this seemed of no concern, and the coast from Zanzibar to Cameroon was never examined in antiquity,[3] considered too far outside any area of interest for either Greeks or Romans. Roman exploration of Africa was in the interior.[4]

North of the Pillars it was another matter. During and after their conquest of central and northern Gaul, the Romans were inevitably involved in exploration of the Atlantic coasts in and beyond this region. Before that time Roman interest in the Atlantic had been occasional and sporadic. The earliest evidence of Romans north of the Pillars may, in fact, be spurious: Strabo reported on a Roman ship that was following one from Gades and was led aground to avoid its learning about the Kassiterides.[5]

---

1 Supra, pp. 47–9.
2 *Periplous of the Erythraian Sea* 18.
3 Hellenistic and Roman coins have been found throughout southern Africa, but, as is the nature of sporadic coin finds, these are probably casual removals. See Raymond Mauny, "Monnaies anciennes trouvées en Afrique au Sud du limes de l'empire romaine," in *Conferencia internacional de Africanistas Occidentales: 4ª Conferencia, Santa Isabel de Fernando Poo 1951*, Madrid 1954, vol. 2, pp. 64–7.
4 Of particular note were the expeditions across the Sahara by Suetonius Paulinus in the 40s AC (Pliny, *Natural History* 5.14–15), those of Septimius Flaccus and Julius Maternus half a century later (Ptolemy, *Geography* 1.8.5), and, at the same time, the East African explorations of Dioskouros and Diogenes (Ptolemy, *Geography* 1.9, 14). In the long-standing tradition, Diogenes attributed his contact with East Africa to being off course: it was probably he who learned about (or visited) the high mountains of interior Africa, the Mountains of the Moon, the source of the Nile (Ptolemy, *Geography* 4.8.3).
5 Strabo 3.5.11; on the Kassiterides, see supra, pp. 12–13.

A proper context for this tale is difficult to find, in part due to Strabo's vagueness, although his implication is that it was well before his own time,[6] perhaps in the early years of Roman control of Gades, which began during the Second Punic War.[7] It is doubtful that the Romans were out in the Atlantic at that date, and the story may be more anecdotal than real: Strabo pointed out that they had a persistent curiosity about the Kassiterides and had made many attempts to locate them. It may also suggest that the islands were thought to be not far from Gades. Eventually, it was said, one Publius Crassus went to them and was credited with making them generally known. Who this was is not certain, but the most likely candidate is P. Licinius Crassus (cos. 97BC), father of the triumvir,[8] who was proconsul in Hispania Ulterior from 96 to 93BC Another possibility is his grandson of the same name, who served under Caesar in Gaul.[9] But there is no evidence that he made any expedition on the Ocean, and, moreover, Strabo's account is oriented on Spain and Gades, not Gaul, and with its Gaderene connections reveals Poseidonios as the probable source, probably too early for the younger Crassus. Yet the "discovery" of the Kassiterides by the Romans was of little importance, and the islands retained their semi-mythical status.

After Crassus' expedition, there is little Roman interest in the Atlantic for half a century: Sertorius' brief dalliance in 81BC did not add to knowledge, although it had a certain cultural effect.[10]

It was only with the campaigns of Julius Caesar in Gaul that the Atlantic, particularly its northern coastal portions, became known to the Roman world. Caesar's conquest of Gaul and Roman knowledge of central Europe marks a shift in Mediterranean attitudes toward the Atlantic. No longer were the Pillars of Herakles the primary point of access to the Ocean. Pytheas had already demonstrated the viability of the overland route north, and was followed by Caesar on his visits to the British Isles in 55 and 54BC.[11] He probably made use of Poseidonios' material, which would have been misleading about Pytheas. Nonetheless there is an echo of Pytheas' tidal theory in Caesar's comment – after experiencing difficulty with the high tide in the Channel –

---

6 On Strabo's method of indicating his own time, see supra, p. 98.

7 Livy 28.37.10; see Thomson, p. 195. It has been suggested that the "Roman" ship was actually from a Greek city (Cary and Warmington, pp. 56–7), although this is not what Strabo wrote.

8 For his career, see T. R. S. Broughton, *The Magistrates of the Roman Republic, Philological Monographs Published by the American Philological Association* 15, 1952, vol. 2, 11, 579. See also Hennig, vol. 1, pp. 282–4.

9 Caesar, *Bellum gallicum* 1.52; 2.34; 3.7–11, 20–7; 8.46. The strongest proponent of this Crassus is Stephen Mitchell, "Cornish Tin, Iulius Caesar, and the Invasion of Britain," in *Studies in Latin Literature and Roman History* 3, *Collection Latomus* 180, 1983, 80–99, with a good summary of previous arguments in favor of both Crassi. Mitchell's conclusions are based on the uncertain presumption that the Kassiterides are in the British Isles.

10 Supra, p. 112. There is also the peculiar incident of the "Indians" found on the coast of Gaul in the 60sBC who had gone rather far off course while on a trading voyage (Pomponius Mela 2.45; Pliny, *Natural History* 2.170). There are obvious difficulties with this tale, and the "Indians" may have been natives of a remote part of Scandinavia, but at least it shows a sense of the Ocean as connecting the extremities of the earth. See further Klaus Tausend, "Inder in Germanien," *OT* 5, 1999, 115–25.

11 Poseidonios, *Posidonius 2: The Commentary*, ed. I. G. Kidd, Cambridge: Cambridge University Press, 1988, pp. 308–9; J. J. Tierney, "The Celtic Ethnography of Posidonius," *ProcRIA* 60c, 1960, 211–18.

that the relationship between the moon and tide was "unknown to our forces [*nostris*]", an implication that he knew about the theories but had yet to see them in practice.[12]

Caesar's interest in Britain was primarily military – evidently the locals had been supplying Gallic insurgents – but he realized that even some knowledge of the island would be important.[13] He believed that only merchants knew anything about the region, and their information was limited to the coastal areas directly across the Channel. This shows ignorance, or, more likely, dismissal of Pytheas. Caesar made a brief expedition to Britain in 55BC but the problem with the tides, the resultant damage to his ships, and a negative local response caused a prompt withdrawal. A year later there was another and longer incursion,[14] which led Caesar to make some ethnographic comments about Britain, both from personal observation and existing written sources. He believed that the island was triangular and that it was 2000 miles in circumference, over twice Pytheas' 7500 stadia. Clearly there are many sources tangled in Caesar's report, including, perhaps, differing versions of Pytheas' data and local informants. But Caesar's personal experience was limited to a small area of the southeast, and it is difficult to imagine that the locals would have been knowledgeable about the entire island. Pytheas, however garbled, seems the source for the triangular shape, at least, and probably for the statement that there are islands off Britain where the midwinter night lasts for 30 days, something unlikely to have been known to inhabitants of the Kentish coast, and in fact Caesar wrote that they could not confirm this fact. Although Caesar could claim that he carried Roman power beyond the limits of the inhabited world,[15] he did not add to knowledge of the Atlantic and its coasts. In fact, his inevitable diffidence about Pytheas, the result of over 200 years of hostility from Hellenistic geographers, meant that he was poorly informed by published information about the region. Yet his brief visits to Britain, as well as his several crossings of the Rhine,[16] set the stage for further Roman exploration of northwest Europe and the adjacent Ocean.

The convulsions of the Roman civil war meant that it was another half a century before there was any further exploration of the North Atlantic. In the late first century BC and the early first century AC there were a number of Roman expeditions that covered the coast of the Ocean from the mouth of the Rhine – believed to be the limit of previously known territory[17] – eastward, yet these are difficult to untangle. The

12 Caesar, *Bellum gallicum* 4.29. For the influence of Pytheas on the Romans in Britain, see P. C. N. Stewart, "Inventing Britain: The Roman Creation and Adaptation of an Image," *Britannia* 26, 1995, 2.

13 Caesar, *Bellum gallicum* 4.20–36. It is also possible that he was looking for sources of mineral wealth: see Mitchell (supra n. 9), pp. 80–99; R. Chevallier, "The Greco-Roman Conception of the North From Pytheas to Tacitus," *Arctic* 37, 1984, 342. Diodoros (5.21–2) wrote about Caesar and the tin mines of Cornwall in juxtaposition, although he made no connection.

14 Caesar, *Bellum gallicum* 5.7–23; Joachim Herrmann (ed.), *Griechische und lateinische Quellen zur Frühgeschichte Mitteleuropas*, Berlin: Akademie-Verlag, 1988–1992, vol. 1, pp. 465–6.

15 Plutarch, *Caesar* 23.2.

16 Caesar, *Bellum gallicum* 4.17–19, 6.9.

17 Strabo (1.4.3) placed the mouth of the Rhine opposite Kent. The error may be intentional, as it allowed him to link Caesar's explorations with those of the Augustan period.

sources – ranging from Augustus' *Res gestae* to Dio – are not clear in distinguishing who went where. Two expeditions can be identified with certainty, that of Augustus' stepson Drusus in 12BC, and that of the latter's son Germanicus in AD16.[18] A Roman fleet also sailed as far as the mouth of the Elbe in support of Tiberius in AD5. Other statements about travel along the coast, perhaps as far as the entrance to the Baltic or even beyond, may indicate further exploration. The more contemporary authors (Augustus, Strabo, and Velleius) are as vague as the later ones (Suetonius, Tacitus, and Dio). For example, Augustus' statement[19] that his fleet sailed eastward from the mouth of the Rhine into a territory that no Roman had ever seen either by land or sea may refer to Drusus, or another unspecified voyage: all that is certain is that it cannot be Germanicus' AD16 venture.

Strabo wrote that "Drusus Germanicus" sailed along the coast, conquering the islands, but was killed in the midst of the expedition.[20] This confuses events of Germanicus' voyage of AD16 with the death of his father Drusus in 9BC.[21] By the time of Tacitus, there was a tendency to see all the Roman expeditions in the North Sea and beyond as a unit and as a contest between the Romans and the Ocean.[22] This made individual accomplishments even harder to distinguish, and even mixed in data from the time of Pytheas.

In 12BC Drusus was in the second year of his campaigns on the Rhine.[23] Late in the year, he sailed down the river to the Ocean, crossing a lake, perhaps the Lacus Flevus or Flevo,[24] essentially the modern Zuyder Zee, and ran his ships aground because of the retreating tide. His new Frisian allies rescued him, and he withdrew and returned to Rome. Details of the expedition are sketchy, vague, and confused with the later movements of his son; Drusus, because he died during this campaign, may not have been able to submit a full report. Yet he was remembered as the first Roman commander to sail on the Northern Ocean,[25] and for the construction known as the Fossa Drusiana, which was still in use over a century later.[26] This canal, several kilometers long, connected the Rhine and IJssel systems near modern Arnhem and allowed

18 Thomson, pp. 239–40; see also Karl Christ, *Drusus und Germanicus*, Paderborn: Ferdinand Schöningh, 1956, pp. 36–9, 96–103.

19 Augustus, *Res gestae* 26.

20 Strabo 7.1.3; Herrmann (supra n. 14), vol. 1, pp. 511–13.

21 But see Cary and Warmington, p. 60.

22 Tacitus, *Annals* 2.23–5; *Germania* 34; see also Romm, *Edges*, pp. 140–9.

23 For the military and political context, see Erich S. Gruen, "The Expansion of the Empire Under Augustus," *CAH* 10, second edition, 1996, pp. 180–2.

24 The name is from Pomponius Mela (3.24). See also Tacitus, *Annals* 1.60, 2.8, 13.54; *Germania* 34; Dio 54.32. Tacitus has deliberately blended material from a century of North Sea exploration on the Ocean to create a mythic opponent of Roman commanders; see further, infra, pp. 125–7, and G. Neumann, "Flevum," *RGA* 9, 1995, 190–1.

25 Suetonius, *Claudius* 1.2, perhaps from a eulogy of Drusus.

26 Tacitus, *Annals* 2.8; Suetonius, *Claudius* 1.2; C. M. Wells, *The German Policy of Augustus*, Oxford: Clarendon Press, 1972, pp. 111–16; Tillmann Bechert and Willem J. H. Willems, *Die römische Reichsgrenze von der Mosel bis zur Nordseeküste*, Stuttgart: Thiess, 1995, pp. 25, 65. The expedition was noted for its engineering works: Drusus also started to build levees along the Rhine, which were only completed over 60 years later and then destroyed by Julius Civilis in AD 70 (Tacitus, *Annals* 13.53; *Histories* 5.19).

access to the Lacus Flevus and a more northerly point on the Ocean, something that would be of use to Germanicus 28 years later. Yet unlike the British expedition of Caesar, there is no evidence of even rudimentary prior research on the part of Drusus (or his son), perhaps because it was believed that there was no information available to consult.

In AD13, Augustus placed Germanicus in command of the Roman forces in Germany, a position that he held until recalled by Tiberius three years later.[27] Germanicus' situation was affected by the disaster to Quinctilius Varus in AD9 as well as Augustus' own death a few months after Germanicus' appointment. Rather than the optimistic environment of his father's expedition, there was now a pessimism that before long would assist in bringing Roman exploration of the North Sea to an end. Germanicus sailed along the coast of the North Sea[28] and allegedly conquered most of the offshore islands. These would be the Frisian Islands which today form a barrier off the coast of the Netherlands and Germany. The seafaring Frisii, whom Drusus had made Roman allies,[29] may have inhabited these islands, but only one is mentioned by name, Byrchanis, probably modern Borkum opposite the mouth of the Ems (ancient Amisa). The only other source to discuss this island (as Burcana), Pliny,[30] wrote that it was called "Fabaria" by the Romans because of its wild beans, a comment that sounds like it might have come from visiting troops. Pliny knew of 23 islands in this area, three of which he named: Austeravia, Actania, and Glaesaria, the last so called by the Romans because it produced amber.

Although these islands are clearly located by Pliny off the northwest German coast, they are part of a wide-ranging topographic list that begins in the interior Baltic – at least as far as the Vistula – and continues to the mouth of the Scaldis (modern Scheldt), betraying, as is customary for Pliny, an uncertain mixture of sources, in this case from as early as Pytheas. Significantly, Ptolemy knew none of Pliny's islands, mentioning only the three Saxonoi,[31] near the mouth of the Albis (modern Elbe), most likely Trischen, Scharhörn, and Neuwark in the Bay of Helgoland. The Romans were familiar with the mouth of the Albis – a fleet had been sent there by Tiberius in AD5[32] – and Velleius, somewhat hyperbolically, had stressed how this fleet had entered the Albis from an unheard of and unknown sea ("ab inaudito atque incognito ante mari"), demonstrating that even by the time of Tiberius' principate there was still a sense of uncertainty regarding the Roman ventures into the North Sea. Yet the vagueness about the Frisian Islands, which never entered the mainstream of Roman geographical knowledge, shows that Roman control of them was minimal.

27 Velleius 2.123; Tacitus, *Annals* 2.26.
28 Strabo 7.1.3. The name North Sea – more properly "Northern Ocean," Septentrionalis Oceanus – probably came into use at this time; the earliest extant citation is Pliny, *Natural History* 2.167, 4.109.
29 Dio 54.32.
30 Pliny, *Natural History* 4.97, 18.121. It is also listed as "Bourchanis" by Stephanos of Byzantion, whose source was Strabo. See G. Neumann *et al.*, "Burcana," *RGA* 4, 1981, 113–17. See also Herrmann (supra n. 14), vol. 1, pp. 567–9.
31 Ptolemy, *Geography* 2.11.31.
32 Velleius 2.106; see also Dio 55.28.

In the last year of his northern command, Germanicus boarded his troops onto ships – allegedly a thousand – and took them down the Amisa into the North Sea,[33] entering it at the modern Dutch–German border. Presumably this is when he "conquered" the Frisian Islands, but this was probably limited to the single island of Byrchanis/Burcana, the only one named by Strabo; if this is modern Borkum, it lies directly opposite the mouth of the river. Soon, however, disaster resulted. A major storm blew up, and the soldiers – many of whom had not been on the Ocean before – interfered with the handling of the ships. The ships began to take on water through leakage and waves breaking over them; animals, baggage, and weapons were thrown overboard. Ships sank and others were stranded on inaccessible islands, where the sailors starved. An eyewitness, Albinovanus Pedo, wrote about the events in vivid terms:

> … the one who carries immense monsters beneath its waves, who has vicious beasts everywhere and dogs of the sea, Ocean, who rises up, grasping the ships (the noise itself piles up the fear), as the ships are sinking in the mud and the fleet loses the swift wind, and they believe that an indifferent destiny leaves them to the wild sea creatures, torn apart through an unhappy fate.[34]

Germanicus' ship made it to the mainland, followed eventually by a few others; soldiers and sailors straggled in for some time, even sent back from Britain by the local kings. Germanicus was suicidal, but was eventually inspired to mount a successful offensive against various German tribes, using this prompt Roman recovery from the disaster as a potent propaganda weapon. This was the third maritime incident to strike Roman forces in this region in 30 years. Drusus had been stranded by the tides at the outlet of the Lacus Flevo. Early in his campaign, Germanicus, while sailing from the Amisa to the Rhine, attempted to avoid this problem; he had lightened his ships by sending two legions by land under the command of P. Vitellius.[35] These were caught by the tides and many were lost. Now Germanicus himself had experienced the violence of the Ocean. Tacitus was to remark that after this, attempts to investigate ("temptavit") the Ocean were abandoned.[36]

---

33 Tacitus, *Annals* 2.23–6. Hennig, vol. 1, pp. 336–43, placed this in the vicinity of Helgoland.

34 nunc illum, pigris immania monstra sub undis
    qui ferat, Oceanum, qui saevas undique pristis
    aequoreosque canes, ratibus consurgere prensis
    (accumulat fragor ipse metus), iam sidere limo
    navigia et rapido desertam flamine classem
    seque feris credunt per inertia fata marinis
    iam non felici laniandos sorte reliqui.
    Albinovanus Pedo's poem is quoted by the Elder Seneca, *Suasoria* 1.15. Pedo's service with Germanicus was noted by Tacitus (*Annals* 1.60), and he was perhaps the addressee of Ovid, *Epistulae ex Ponto* 4.10. His poetry ws praised by Quintilian 10.1.90. See further, pp. 125–7.

35 Tacitus, *Annals* 1.70. A few years later, Vitellius was to charge Cn. Calpurnius Piso with the murder of Germanicus in Syria, and then committed suicide as one of the accomplices of Sejanus. He was the uncle of the future emperor (Suetonius, *Vitellius* 2.3).

36 Tacitus, *Germania* 34.

The campaigns of Drusus, Tiberius, and Germanicus on the coast of the North Sea are the only ones of the Julio-Claudian period explicitly cited in literature. Yet there are hints of other expeditions, some of which may have been connected with these three, but which may also reflect other, more exploratory voyages. The earliest statement is that of Augustus, who, after remarking that he pacified the territory whose coasts run from Gades to the Albis, further added that "my fleet sailed on the Ocean from the mouth of the Rhine eastward as far as the lands of the Kimbri, which before that time no Roman had gone into, either by land or sea."[37] This may be Tiberius' expedition to the Albis in AD5, which Velleius, predictably, described in highly optimistic terms, but on which Dio felt nothing worth remembering (ἀξιομνημόνευτον) had happened.[38] But Pliny was more expansive: under the patronage of Augustus, a fleet went past the Kimbrian Promontory, saw a great sea, and eventually reached Skythia.[39] This implies that the fleet has rounded Jutland at Skagens Odde, but it also suspiciously reflects Pytheas.

There is no indication that the Romans knew about the Limfjord or the maze of channels through the Danish islands, and thus the report has skipped from the northern portions of Jutland into the Baltic, some distance away. Moreover, Pliny cautiously remarked that the Romans may have only heard about the great sea ("inmenso mari prospecto aut fama cognito"). Pomponius Mela described the rivers of northwest Europe from the Rhine to the Albis, and then the Sinus Codanus, an area filled with many islands and with ocean passages similar to rivers, clearly Denmark; eventually his account reaches the remote Hermiones and the Vistula, which is said to connect to the Ister.[40] Pliny's version is similar,[41] mentioning the Sinus Codanus, Scatinavia (whose natives are the Hilleriones),[42] and the Vistula, but then the account reversed direction to return to the German rivers. Mention of Pytheas is a hint of the ultimate origin of much of this material. Ptolemy's *Geography* repeats some of the toponyms,[43] including Skandia and the Vistula (Ουἰστούλα): the Vistula is cited several times as one of the definitive toponymic points. Yet his virtual juxtaposition of the Albis and Vistula shows how little was known even in his day about the world beyond the Elbe.

Significantly Strabo had almost nothing to say about the region, professing ignorance about the world east of the Kimbri, in other words, the Baltic.[44] Thus the only evidence that the Romans entered the Baltic is Pliny's qualified statement.[45] Strabo's

37 Augustus, *Res gestae* 26; Roger Dion, "Géographie historique de la France," *ACF* 65, 1965, 475–9.
38 Velleius 2.106; Dio 55.28.
39 Pliny, *Natural History* 2.167; Thomson, pp. 240–2.
40 Pomponius Mela 3.30–2.
41 Pliny, *Natural History* 4.96–8.
42 On the Hilleriones and the Hermiones see Fridtjof Nansen, *In Northern Mists*, tr. Arthur G. Chater, New York: Frederick A. Stokes, 1911, vol. 1, pp. 104–5.
43 Ptolemy, *Geography* 2.11.34–5.
44 Strabo 7.2.4.
45 But see Hennig, vol. 1, pp. 334–5, who argued for Roman penetration of the Baltic. Nansen (supra n. 42), vol. 1, p. 85, placed the Romans no farther north than the Danish islands.

silence is the proof that Pliny was correct in believing that the Romans only heard about the Baltic: Strabo was aware of Germanicus' expedition of AD16, after which, according to Tacitus, there were no further Roman expeditions on the Ocean. Most of the information about the Baltic came from Strabo's nemesis Pytheas, and rather than rely on him, Strabo professed ignorance. Some of Pytheas' material was used by Pomponius Mela and Pliny, and passed on to Ptolemy, becoming mixed with Roman reports, probably from both military expeditions and merchants, but which went no farther than the Kimbrian Promontory, or the north end of Jutland. But even here the information gathered by the Romans before AD16 was hearsay and somewhat unreliable. Nevertheless the coastal sailing of the brothers Drusus and Tiberius, and Drusus' son Germanicus, filled the final gap in knowledge of the Atlantic coast of Europe, from the vicinity of the mouth of the Rhine to the northern part of Jutland, a stretch that Pytheas may have missed because of his Arctic excursion and possible overland return to Massalia: if Pytheas did cover this coast, his data were superseded by the Romans.

These Roman expeditions may have resulted in at least one scholarly work on the northern coasts.[46] A certain Philemon provided the Kimbrian name for the frozen sea (Morimarusa, in Pliny's Latin),[47] some comments on amber,[48] and material on Ireland learned from merchants.[49] He was also a source used by Pliny in Book 10 of the *Natural History*, mostly about birds, but there is no specific reference.[50] These citations are all that is known about Philemon: when he lived is uncertain, but the context of amber and merchants in Ireland suggests a Roman date, probably after the Roman military expeditions to the North Sea. In fact, the amber trade emerged as the most significant Roman involvement in the world of the Baltic:[51] during the reign of Nero an equestrian was commissioned to obtain amber, and went from Carnuntum in Pannonia 600 miles to the coast.[52] He may have gone up the Danube and down the Rhine, which best approximates the distance, but this would not deposit him close to

---

46 For knowledge of the Baltic by Roman geographical authors, see O. A. W. Dilke, "Geographical Perceptions of the North in Pomponius Mela and Ptolemy," *Arctic* 37, 1984, 347–51.

47 Pliny, *Natural History* 4.95. This seems to be a legitimate Keltic word: see H. Reichert, "Morimarusa," *RGA* 20, 2002, 246–7.

48 Pliny, *Natural History* 37.33, 36.

49 Ptolemy, *Geography* 1.11.8.

50 Pliny, *Natural History* 1.10. On Philemon generally, see W. Kroll, "Philemon" (#11), *RE* 19, 1938, 2146–50; Serena Bianchetti, "Plinio e la descrizione dell'Oceano settentrionale in Pitea di Marsiglia," *OT* 2, 1996, 73–84.

51 On the amber trade in antiquity, with a list of literary sources, see Arnolds Spekke, *The Ancient Amber Routes and the Geographical Discovery of the Eastern Baltic*, Stockholm: M. Goppers, 1957; R. Wenskus, "Pytheas und der Bernsteinhandel," in *Untersuchungen zu Handel und Verkehr der vor- und frühgeschichtlichen Zeit in Mittel- und Nordeuropa* 1, ed. Klaus Döwel et al., AbbGött 3. ser. 143, 1985, pp. 84–108; Willy Krogmann, "Die Bernsteininsul *Basileia*," in *VII Congresso internazionale di Scienze Onomastiche: Atti del Congresso e Memorie della sezione toponmastica* 2, Florence 1963, pp. 205–20.

52 Pliny, *Natural History* 37.45; Olwen Brogan, "Trade Between the Roman Empire and the Free Germans," *JRS* 26, 1936, 199–201.

the amber regions and would hardly make his journey notable in Pliny's day. More likely he went up the Morava to near modern Ostrava where the sources of both the Oder and Vistula lie, and down one or the other to the Baltic, an ancient trade route. Once on the Baltic he travelled on the coast ("litora peragravit"), perhaps between the two rivers. Probably no account of this journey was published; Pliny seems to have talked to him personally.[53]

The Romans contributed one final chapter to the exploration of the Atlantic. When C. Julius Agricola was governor of Britain (AD77–84), he commissioned a coastal exploration.[54] The fleet was said to have established that Britain was an island, to have discovered and conquered the Orkades,[55] and to have located Thoule. It also reported that the sea was thick ("mare pigrum").[56] As was the case with the expeditions in the Kimbrian territory, the Romans again claimed to have discovered lands and phenomena that had been known to Pytheas; in fact, the ghost of Pytheas is apparent in Tacitus' comments about the powerful tides of the northern British Isles, and the ability of the ocean to force its way far up narrow channels. Tacitus' immediate source was probably Pliny.[57] Agricola's presumption that he had discovered Thoule is also a reflection of Pytheas, but by Agricola's day Thoule had already begun to wander. Knowledge of Pytheas may also be reflected in Tacitus' reference to the northern Pillars of Herakles.[58] At the very least, these northern Pillars reflect the long-standing idea that the world was defined by the wanderings of the hero, wanderings that were now superseded by the world of Augustus.[59]

There is no doubt that Agricola's fleet reached the Orkneys and went beyond; his Thoule must be Mainland in the Shetlands (Figure 20). It is possible that Pytheas was his inspiration, but the report of the Massalian was by this time little known. The *Geography* of Strabo, the principal modern source on Pytheas, was still lying in remote Amaseia, unpublished, and Agricola and Tacitus had to rely on the vague allusions of Pliny and Pomponius Mela,[60] and a growing popular vision of Thoule as

---

53 Trade items also penetrated the Baltic and Scandinavia, although these do not mean an actual Roman presence. Roman Imperial coins have been found as far north as southern Sweden, the Baltic islands of Gotland, Gotska Sandön, and Saaremas, and in mainland Estonia. Bronze vessels of early Imperial times are known from Norway (as far north as Trondheim) and southern Sweden. See Mortimer Wheeler, *Rome Beyond the Imperial Frontiers*, London: G. Bell and Sons, 1954, pp. 63–84; also Brogan (supra n. 52), pp. 195–222.

54 Tacitus, *Agricola* 38; see also Juvenal 3.160–3; Dio 66.20; Hennig, vol. 1, pp. 380–2; Cary and Warmington, pp. 59–60.

55 For the Orkneys in antiquity, see Piergiorgio Parroni, "Surviving Sources of the Classical Geographers Through Late Antiquity and the Medieval Period," *Arctic* 37, 1984, 354.

56 Tacitus, *Agricola* 10. The phrase, or its equivalent, had long been used by explorers, at least from the time of Himilco (supra, p. 27). For the suggestion that "mare pigrum" was a direct observation made by Agricola and not based on earlier sources, see A. R. Burn, "Mare pigrum et grave," *CR* 63, 1949, 94.

57 Pliny, *Natural History* 2.217.

58 Tacitus, *Germania* 34: "superesse adhuc Herculis columnas fama vulgavit."

59 Vergil, *Aeneid* 6.801: "nec vero Alcides tantum telluris obivit."

60 Pliny, *Natural History* 2.186–7, 217; 4.95, 102, 104; 37.35; Pomponius Mela 3.54–7.

Figure 20 Shetland Islands. Mainland, from the south.

Photograph by Duane W. Roller.

any remote northern place. It was perfectly reasonable for Agricola, like Caesar, Drusus and Germanicus before him, to have "discovered" lands previously visited by Pytheas.[61]

61 One of the more peculiar episodes in the exploration of the Atlantic concerns the voyage of a certain Demetrios of Tarsos, allegedly commissioned by the "king" to make a research voyage to the islands around Britannia (Plutarch, *On the Obsolescence of Oracles* 18). The context is the latter first century AC. Demetrios was a grammarian – he is often suggested to be the same as the author of the extant treatise *On Style* – and why he was chosen to make this voyage is not immediately apparent. Who the "king" was is also unclear. Plutarch's connection of Demetrios' expedition with the transatlantic fantasy island of Kronos does not inspire confidence in the reality of the situation, and it might be easily dismissed were it not for the discovery of two Greek inscriptions from York – inscriptions in Greek are rare in Britain – that are dedications by a certain Demetrios, one of which is to the Ocean. The matter remains unresolved. See R. G. Collingwood and R. P. Wright, *The Roman Inscriptions of Britain* 1; *Inscriptions on Stone*, Oxford: Clarendon Press, 1965, #662–3; H. Dessau, "Ein Freund Plutarchs in England," *Hermes* 46, 1911, 156–60; David Braund, *Ruling Roman Britain*, London: Routledge, 1996, pp. 12–20, 174. See also the intriguing argument of Carlo Marcaccini, "Giovenale, Tacito e gli studi di retorica a Tule, *Maia*" n. s. 51, 1999, pp. 247–57.

EPILOGUE

"And why do we disturb the peaceful home of the gods?" Albinovanus Pedo wrote after witnessing the disaster to Germanicus' fleet in AD16.[1] Half a millennium earlier, Pindar had expressed similar thoughts: "What is west of Gadeira cannot be crossed."[2] After hundreds of years of exploration that had revealed the Ocean from the Arctic to West Africa, attitudes had hardly changed. The Ocean was still a fearful place and there was continued divine opposition to crossing it or even entering upon it. To be sure, there had been a brief period of Roman optimism. Caesar's Parthian expedition – not pursued because of his death – was to reach the Eastern Ocean as he had reached the Western one in Britain,[3] so that the Ocean would encircle the Roman state and protect it from barbarian assaults.[4] Livy even put such a global grand design in the mouth of the consul M' Acilius in Greece in 191BC: "we mark our boundaries with the Ocean from Gades to the Red Sea."[5] Ocean as an element of imperial power was most succinctly summed up by Ovid: "the Ocean itself will be controlled by him [Augustus]."[6] And Krinagoras could write that Rome, under the confident leadership of Augustus, would not allow the Ocean to pervert its power.[7]

To some extent the role model was Alexander the Great, who had, it was believed, reached the Eastern Ocean and also showed serious interest in using it to encircle the world.[8] It was Alexander who first attempted to pass the boundaries set by the original travellers, Dionysos and Herakles.[9]

1   Seneca, *Suasoriae* 1.15: "divumque quietas turbamus sedes?"
2   Pindar, *Nemean* 4.69: Γαδείρων τὸ πρὸς οὐ περατόν.
3   Plutarch, *Caesar* 58. Allegedly, he was planning to return west across the northern edge of the world.
4   Vergil, *Aeneid* 7.100; *Panegyricus Messallae* 147–50.
5   Livy 36.17.15: "ab Gadibus ad Mare Rubrum Oceano fines terminemus."
6   Ovid, *Metamorphoses* 15.831: "pontus quoque serviet illi." See also Vergil, *Aeneid* 1.286–8. On the Ocean as an element of Roman policy and design, see David Braund, *Ruling Roman Britain*, London: Routledge, 1996, pp. 10–23, and Trevor Murphy, *Pliny the Elder's Natural History*, Oxford: Oxford University Press, 2004, pp. 174–9.
7   Krinagoras, #33 = *Greek Anthology* 9.291.
8   Diodoros 17.104; supra, pp. 59–60.
9   Quintus Curtius 8.10.1; 9.4.21; Vinzenz Buchheit, "Epikurs Triumph des Geistes," *Hermes* 99, 1971, 313–15.

In the first century BC Alexander's exploits continued to be expressed in terms of going beyond the limits set by the god and hero. Alexander came to have many imitators, who themselves attempted to cross the divine boundaries even as they emulated him. Mithradates the Great was the new Dionysos,[10] and C. Marius deliberately compared himself with the god.[11] The prime example was M. Antonius, associating himself with both Herakles and Dionysos.[12] Although these mortal intentions often came to nothing, or were used for destructive ends, they reflect an optimism that reached its peak in the early Augustan era. Yet by the late Augustan period it faded due to the military disasters. Difficulties began with Drusus in 12BC, and continued with Quinctilius Varus two decades later and Germanicus' attempts to rectify the losses of Varus. There was little talk thereafter of how divine boundaries were being crossed and the Ocean was yielding to Roman power, although Juvenal could comment that the terrors of the Ocean were worth it for the money one could obtain.[13]

The first *Suasoria*[14] of the Elder Seneca is the best surviving example of attitudes toward the Ocean in the middle of the first century AC. Seneca would have heard in his childhood about Caesar's exploits on the Ocean and been well aware of the Augustan misadventures on the North Sea. At the time of Seneca's writing, the emperor Gaius was having his strange encounters with the Ocean that resulted in his quasi-triumph.[15] Thus Seneca had ample reason to be interested in the cultural role of the Ocean. His first *Suasoria* is on the ostensible topic of whether Alexander the Great should cross the Ocean,[16] but this is merely an allegory for a more contemporary question. At the beginning of the extant text, an unknown speaker is advising Alexander not to set sail, citing the monsters and its depth, echoing Pytheas' frozen sea ("grave et defixum mare"), pointing out that the Ocean is the only infinity in the cosmos ("nihil infinitum est nisi Oceanus"), and that there is nothing beyond it. Other speakers support the same view. Dionysos and Herakles had set limits that Alexander should not cross. In another echo of Pytheas, Fabianus, Seneca's teacher, emphasized that the Ocean represents a primitive and unfinished world ("rudis et inperfecta natura"), and that even the most contemporary scientific thought was still in doubt as to its true nature.

The argument then takes a moral tone. L. Cestius Pius, a rhetorician from Smyrna, forcefully made the point that Alexander had done enough, and even if the Ocean could be sailed it should not be ("etiamsi navigari posset Oceanus, navigandum non esse"). Going further, he emphasized that it was in fact impossible to sail on it ("ne navigari quidem Oceanum posse."). There were no inhabitable lands in or beyond the

---

10 Cicero, *pro Flacco* 60.

11 Valerius Maximus 3.6.6.: "victoriae eius suas victorias compararet."

12 Plutarch, *Antonius* 60.

13 Juvenal 14.281–3.

14 A *suasoria* was a set rhetorical piece in the context of giving advice at a public meeting, used as a school exercise (Tacitus, *Dialogue* 35.4). Its value as a pedagogical tool was satirized by Petronius (6).

15 Suetonius, *Gaius* 46–7; Dio 59.25. A more politically correct view of Gaius and the Ocean was presented by Philon, *Embassy to Gaius* 10.

16 The beginning of the piece is lost: the title that appears, "deliberat Alexander an Oceanum naviget," has no tradition from antiquity, although the subject is obvious.

Ocean and even if there were, they could not be reached. An epigram of Glykon is quoted: the Ocean is essentially evil because it is at the end of the world, the oldest element in the world, where the gods originated, and too sacred for ships. Lurking behind these thoughts, although never explicitly stated, is the idea that the Ocean itself is a god. Then the *suasoria* closes with the poem of Albinovanus Pedo.[17] Its vocabulary reflects the fear and horror of maritime travel: there is a Pythean allusion to the sluggish sea ("pigris undis"), and words such as *saevas*, *fragor*, *feris*, *rumpere*, and *erepto* set its harsh, dark tone. Again there is an allusion to the sacred quality of the Ocean ("sacras aquas"), on which the gods themselves discourage travel ("di revocant").

Although inspired somewhat by the speech of Koinos, who allegedly advised Alexander not to set sail,[18] the pessimistic bombast of Pedo's poem is a fine summary of the relationship between the Greco-Roman world and the Ocean. The *suasoria* is a set piece, more interested in its rhetorical points than an accurate representation of history, yet it is replete with contemporary thought about the morality of sailing on the Ocean. Invoking the earliest travellers, Dionysos and Herakles, as the ultimate proof that such travel would be human excess, the essay dramatically demonstrates that the gain of knowledge is unimportant when divine boundaries are crossed. The Elder Seneca's son took up this cause and, in his essay on the winds,[19] outlined the dangers created by seafaring, especially cultural ones: seamanship facilitated warfare, and expansion to far distant lands would increase the chance of attack by remote peoples. Although there is a touch of optimism about the value of learning about far places ("ad ulterior noscenda"), the essay returns to the pessimism that seamanship is a force for evil ("utique alicui vitio navigatur").[20]

The vast accumulation of data in the 700 years from Kolaios to the Roman expeditions on the North Sea was perhaps of little concern when considering the essential moral question of the propriety of such voyages. The Elder Seneca's rhetoricians, while rejecting – indeed ignoring – the idea of exploration, were beholden to the results of that exploration, as the constant allusions to Pytheas demonstrate. There was to be no more sailing on the Ocean for hundreds of years until a higher cause made it possible: the opportunity to spread Christianity to the ignorant peoples beyond. Irish monks would carry the faith north, seeking Thoule, in the eighth century,[21] and Columbus well knew that in an environment of expanding Islam it was necessary to find new worlds that could be Christianized.[22] But in Seneca's day the choice was clear: "even if the Ocean could be sailed, it should not be."

17 On this, see Romm, *Edges*, pp. 142–5.
18 Quintus Curtius 9.3.3–15.
19 Seneca (the Younger), *Natural Questions* 5.18.
20 See further, Romm, *Edges*, pp. 165–71.
21 Supra, pp. 79–80.
22 Samuel Eliot Morison, *Christopher Columbus, Mariner*, New York: Mentor Books, 1956, p. 118.

APPENDIX

The *Periplous* of Hanno

The *Periplous* of Hanno is preserved in a single manuscript of the ninth century, Codex Palatinus Graecus (fol. 55r–56r); a fourteenth-century copy, Vatopedinus 655, has no independent tradition (Jerker Blomqvist, *The Date and Origin of the Greek Version of Hanno's Periplus*, Lund: CWK Gleerup, 1979, p. 57). The text has been printed several times, from *GGM* (1855) to the Oikonomides and Miller edition of 1995 (which has a facsimile of the manuscript on pp. 26–8). This is the version printed below, with some minor alterations and corrections. Section numeration is from *GGM*. The three supposed lacunae in the text – which predate the existing manuscript – have been indicated by dots. Further comments on the text are supra, pp. 29–43.

Text

(1) Ἄννωνος Καρχδονίων Βασιλέως Περίπλους τῶν ὑπὲρ τὰς Ἡρακλέους στήλας Λιβυκῶν τῆς γῆς μερῶν ὃν καὶ ἀνέθηκεν ἐν τῷ τοῦ Κρόνου τεμένει δηλοῦντα τάδε· ἔδοξεν Καρχηδονίοις Ἄννωνα πλεῖν ἔξω στηλῶν Ἡρακλείων καὶ πόλεις κτίζειν Λιβυφοινίκων· καὶ ἔπλευσεν πεντηκοντόρους ἑξήκοντα ἄγων· καὶ πλῆθος ἀνδρῶν καὶ γυναικῶν εἰς ἀριθμὸν μυριάδων τριῶν καὶ σῖτα καὶ τὴν ἄ λλην παρασκευήν ... (2) ὡς δ᾽ἀναχθέντες τὰς στήλας παρημείψαμεν καὶ ἔξω πλοῦν δυοῖν ἡμερῶν ἐπλεύσαμεν, ἐκτίσαμεν πρώτην πόλιν ἥντινα ὠνομάσαμεν Θυμιατήριον· πεδίον δ᾽αὐτῇ μέγα ὑπῆν· (3) κἄπειτα πρὸς ἑσπέραν ἀναχθέντες ἐπὶ Σολόεντα Λιβυκὸν ἀκρωτήριον λάσιον δένδρεσι συνήλθομεν· (4) ἔνθα Ποσειδῶνος ἱερὸν ἱδρυσάμενοι, πάλιν ἐπέβημεν πρὸς ἥλιον ἀνίσχοντα ἡμέρας ἥμισυ ἄχρι ἐκομίσθημεν εἰς λίμνην οὐ πόρρωδ τῆς θαλάττης κειμένην, καλάμου μεστὴν πολλοῦ καὶ μεγάλου· ἐνῆσαν δὲ καὶ ἐλέφαντες. καὶ τἄλλα θηρία νεμόμενα πάμπολλα· (5) τήν τε λίμνην παραλλάξαντες ὅσον ἡμέρας πλοῦν, κατῳκήσαμεν πόλεις πρὸς τῇ θαλάττῃ καλουμένας Καρικόν τε Τεῖχος καὶ Γύττην καὶ Ἄκραν καὶ Μέλιτταν καὶ Ἄραμβυν. (6) κἀκεῖθεν δ᾽ἀναχθέντες ἤλθομεν ἐπὶ μέγαν ποταμὸν Λίξον, ἀπὸ τῆς Λιβύης ῥέοντα· παρὰ δ᾽αὐτὸν νομάδες ἄνθρωποι Λιξῖται βοσκήματ᾽ἔνεμον παρ᾽οἷς ἐμείναμεν ἄχρι τινὸς φίλοι γενόμενοι· (7) τούτων

129

APPENDIX

δὲ καθύπερθεν Αἰθίοπες ᾤκουν ἄξενοι, γῆν νεμόμενοι θηριώδη διειλημμένην ὄρεσι μεγάλοις. ἐξ ὧν ῥεῖν φασὶ τὸν Λίξον· περὶ δὲ τὰ ὄρη κατοικεῖν ἀνθρώπους ἀλλοιομόρφους Τρωγοδύτας οὓς ταχυτέρους ἵππων ἐν δρόμοις ἔφραζον οἱ Λιξῖται· (8) λαβόντες δὲ παρ' αὐτῶν ἑρμηνέας παρεπλέομεν τὴν ἐρήμην πρὸς μεσημβρίαν δύο ἡμέρας ... ἐκεῖθεν δὲ πάλιν πρὸς ἥλιον ἀνίσχοντα ἡμέρας δρόμον ἔνθα εὕρομεν ἐν μυχῷ τινος κόλπου νῆσον μικράν· κύκλον ἔχουσαν σταδίων πέντε· ἣν κατῳκήσαμεν Κέρνην ὀνομάσαντες· ἐτεκμαιρόμεθα δ' αὐτὴν ἐκ τοῦ περίπλου κατ' εὐθὺ κεῖσθαι Καρχηδόνος· ἐῴκει γὰρ ὁ πλοῦς ἔκ τε Καρχηδόνος ἐπὶ στήλας κἀκεῖθεν ἐπὶ Κέρνην· (9) τοὐντεῦθεν εἰς λίμνην ἀφικόμεθα διά τινος ποταμοῦ μεγάλου διαπλεύσαντες Χρέτης· εἶχεν δὲ νήσους ἡ λίμνη τρεῖς· μείζους τῆς Κέρνης· ἀφ' ὧν ἡμερήσιον πλοῦν κατανύσαντες εἰς τὸν μυχὸν τῆς λίμνης ἤλθομεν ὑπὲρ ἣν ὄρη μέγιστα ὑπερέτεινεν μεστὰ ἀνθρώπων ἀγρίων δέρματα θήρεια ἐνημμένων οἳ πέτροις βάλλοντες ἀπήραξαν ἡμᾶς κωλύοντες ἐκβῆναι· (10) ἐκεῖθεν πλέοντες εἰς ἕτερον ἤλθομεν ποταμὸν μέγαν καὶ πλατὺν γέμοντα κροκοδείλων καὶ ἵππων ποταμίων· ὅθεν δὴ πάλιν ἀποστρέψαντες εἰς Κέρνην ἐπανήλθομεν. (11) ἐκεῖθεν δὲ ἐπὶ μεσημβρίας ἐπλεύσαμεν δώδεκα ἡμέρας, τὴν γῆν παραλεγόμενοι ἣν πᾶσαν κατῴκουν Αἰθίοπες, φεύγοντες ἡμᾶς καὶ οὐχ ὑπομένοντες· ἀσύνετα δ' ἐφθέγγοντο καὶ τοῖς μεθ' ἡμῶν Λιξίταις· (12) τῇ δ' οὖν τελευταίᾳ ἡμέρᾳ, προσωρμίσθημεν ὄρεσι μεγάλοις δασέσιν· ἦν δὲ τὰ τῶν δένδρων ξύλα εὐώδη τε καὶ ποικίλα· (13) περιπλεύσαντες δὲ ταῦτα ἡμέρας δύο γινόμεθα ἐν θαλάττης χάσματι ἀμετρήτῳ· ἧς ἐπὶ θάτερα πρὸς τῇ γῇ πεδίον ἦν ὅθεν νυκτὸς ἀφεωρῶμεν, πῦρ ἀναφερόμενον πανταχόθεν κατ' ἀποστάσεις· τὸ μὲν πλέον, τὸ δ' ἔλαττον· (14) ὑδρευσάμενοι δ' ἐκεῖθεν ἐπλέομεν εἰς τοὔμπροσθεν ἡμέρας πέντε παρὰ γῆν ἄχρι ἤλθομεν εἰς μέγαν κόλπον ὃν ἔφασαν οἱ ἑρμηνέες καλεῖσθαι Ἑσπέρου Κέρας. ἐν δὲ τούτῳ νῆσος ἦν μεγάλη, καὶ ἐν τῇ νήσῳ λίμνη θαλασσώδης· ἐν δὲ ταύτῃ νῆσος ἑτέρα εἰς ἣν ἀποβάντες ἡμέρας μὲν οὐδὲν ἀφεωρῶμεν ὅτι μὴ ὕλην, νυκτὸς δὲ πυρά τε πολλὰ καιόμενα, καὶ φωνὴν αὐλῶν ἠκούομεν, κυμβάλων τε καὶ τυμπάνων πάταγον καὶ κραυγὴν μυρίαν· φοβὸς οὖν ἔλαβε ἡμᾶς· καὶ οἱ μάντεις ἐκέλευον ἐκλείπειν τὴν νῆσον. (15) ταχὺ δ' ἐκπλεύσαντες παρημειβόμεθα χώραν διάπυρον θυμιαμάτων μεστήν, οἱ δ' ἀπ' αὐτῆς πυρώδεις ῥύακες ἐνέβαλλον εἰς τὴν θάλατταν· ἡ γῆ δ' ὑπὸ θέρμης ἄ βατος ἦν. (16) ταχὺ οὖν κἀκεῖθεν φοβηθέντες ἀπεπλεύσαμεν· τέτταρας δ' ἡμέρας φερόμενοι νυκτὸς τὴν γῆν ἀφεωρῶμεν, φλογὸς μεστήν. ἐν μέσῳ δ' ἦν ἠλίβατόν τι πῦρ τῶν ἄλλων μεῖζον, ἁπτόμενον ὡς ἐδόκει τῶν ἄστρων· τοῦτο δ' ἡμέρας ὄρος ἐφαίνετο μέγιστον Θεῶν Ὄχημα καλούμενον· (17) τριταῖοι δ' ἐκεῖθεν πυρώδεις ῥύακας παραπλεύσαντας ἀφικόμεθα εἰς κόλπον Νότου Κέρας λεγόμενον· (18) ἐν δὲ τῷ μυχῷ νῆσος ἦν ἐοικυῖα τῇ πρώτῃ, λίμνην ἔχουσα· καὶ ἐν ταύτῃ νῆσος ἦν ἑτέρα, μεστὴ ἀνθρώπων ἀγρίων· πολὺ δὲ πλείους ἦσαν γυναῖκες, δασεῖαι τοῖς σώμασιν· ἃς οἱ ἑρμηνέες ἐκάλουν Γορίλλας· διώκοντες δὲ ἄνδρας μὲν συλλαβεῖν οὐκ ἠδυνήθημεν, ἀλλὰ πάντες μὲν ἐξέφυγον κρημνοβάται ὄντες καὶ τοῖς πετρίοις ἀμυνόμενοι, γυναῖκας δὲ τρεῖς, αἳ δάκνουσαί τε καὶ σπαράττουσαι τοὺς ἄγοντας οὐκ ἤθελον ἕπεσθαι· ἀποκτείναντες μέντοι αὐτὰς ἐξεδείραμεν. καὶ τὰς δορὰς ἐκομίσαμεν εἰς Καρχηδόνα ... οὐ γὰρ ἔτι ἐπλεύσαμεν προσωτέρω τῶν σίτων ἡμᾶς ἐπιλιπόντων.

Translation

(1) The *Periplous* of Hanno, king of the Carthaginians, into that part of the Libyan territory beyond the Pillars of Herakles, which he set up in the sanctuary of Kronos, disclosing the following:

It was decreed by the Carthaginians that Hanno sail beyond the Pillars of Herakles and establish Libyphoenician cities. Thus he sailed in command of 60 fifty-oared ships and a great number of men and women, in the amount of 30,000, along with grain and other supplies … (2) Thus having put to sea, we passed by the Pillars and sailed beyond them for two days, and established our first city, which we named Thymiaterion. Below it was a large plain. (3) Then we put to sea, heading west, and we all came to Soloeis, a Libyan promontory overgrown with trees. (4) There we dedicated a shrine to Poseidon, and went back on board, and headed toward the sunrise for half a day until we came to a lake that was not far from the ocean. It was filled with many large reeds, and elephants were in it, and numerous other wild animals lived there. (5) Passing beyond the lake and sailing for nearly a day, we made some settlements near the ocean called Karichon Teichos, Gytte, Akra, Melitta, and Arambys. (6) From there we put to sea and came to a large river, the Lixos, flowing from Libya. Along it were a nomadic people, the Lixitai, who grazed cattle. We remained among them for some time, becoming friends. (7) Inland from here live inhospitable Ethiopians, in a land infested with wild animals and divided up by high mountains, from which, they say, the Lixos flows. Around the mountains live strangely shaped men, the Trogodytai, who were faster on a racecourse than horses, according to the Lixitai. (8) Taking interpreters from them [the Lixitai], we sailed along the desert toward the south for two days … from there back toward the sunrise for a day, and we found a small island there in the innermost part of a bay, which was five stadia around. We settled there and named it Kerne. From our *periplous* we estimated that it lay opposite Carthage, for the cruise seemed to be the same from Carthage to the Pillars as from there to Kerne. (9) From there we came to a lake, by sailing up a large river, the Chretes. The lake had three islands in it, larger than Kerne. From there we sailed for a day, arriving at its innermost point, where exceedingly high mountains stretched above it, and there were wild men dressed in animal skins who threw rocks at us in order to crush us, and prevented us from disembarking. (10) Sailing from there, we came to another large and broad river filled with crocodiles and hippopotami. We turned back from there and returned to Kerne. (11) From there we sailed south for 12 days, sailing along the coast, all of which was inhabited by Ethiopians who fled from us and did not remain. What they said was incomprehensible to the Lixitai with us. (12) On the last day we anchored at high and wooded mountains. The wood of the trees was fragrant and multi-colored. (13) Sailing around them for two days, we came to an immense gulf of the ocean, on either side of which the land was a plain. When we looked at night we saw fire rising up everywhere at intervals, sometimes larger, sometimes smaller. (14) We watered there and sailed ahead for five days, always along the land, to a great bay which the interpreters said was called the Horn of the West. There was a large island in it, and on it a sea-water lake. In it there was another island on which we landed, seeing nothing in the daytime but woods, but at night many fires were burning, and we heard the sound of flutes, cymbals, and the beating of drums, and an infinite amount of shouting. We were taken with fear, and the seers ordered us to leave the island. (15) We quickly sailed away and passed by a land that was full of burning incense, from which fiery streams flowed down to the ocean. The land was inaccessible because of the heat. (16) We quickly sailed away from here, as we were afraid, and went on for four days. At night we saw that the land was full of fire, and in the middle there was a fire that was higher than the others, seeming to touch the stars. In the daytime we could see that this was an exceedingly high mountain, called the Chariot of the Gods. (17) Three days from there, sailing past streams of fire, we arrived at the bay called the Horn of the South. (18) There was an island within it that was like the first one, having a lake on it, and another island in it, filled with wild people. Most of them were women, with hairy bodies, which the interpreters called Gorillai. Chasing them, we were unable to capture the men, since they all escaped by climbing cliffs and defending themselves with rocks, but we obtained three women, although they bit and scratched those taking them and did not want to follow them. Thus we killed and skinned them and brought their hides to Carthage … But we did not sail any farther, as we were out of supplies.

BIBLIOGRAPHY

Abel, Karlhaus. "Zone" (#1), *RE Supp.* 14, 1974, 989–1188.

Acquaro, Enrico. "Karthager in Amerika," in *Karthago*, ed. Werner Huss, *Wege der Forschung* 654, Darmstadt 1992, pp. 394–400.

Africa Pilot. 10th edition, London: Hydrographic Office, 1951.

———. 11th edition, London: Hydrographic Office, 1953–4.

Akurgal, Ekrem. "Kyzikos," *PECS*, 473–4.

———. *Ancient Civilizations and Ruins of Turkey*, tr. John Whybrow and Molly Emre, seventh edition, Izmir: Turistik Yayinlar, 1990.

Allain, Michael Lewis. "Greek Explorers in the Atlantic Ocean of the Seventh and Sixth Centuries BC," M. A. thesis, The Ohio State University, 1971.

———. "The Periplous of Skylax of Karyanda," Ph. D. thesis, The Ohio State University, 1977.

Alonzo-Nuñez, J. M. "A Note on Roman Coins Found in Iceland," *OJA* 5, 1986, 121–2.

Aly, W. "Die Entdeckung des Westens," *Hermes* 62, 1927, 299–341.

———. *Strabon von Amaseia* 4, Bonn: Rudolf Habelt, 1957.

Amiotti, Gabriella. "Cerne: 'ultima terra'," in *Il confine nel mondo classico*, ed. Marta Sordi, *CISA* 13, Milan 1987, 43–9.

———. "Le Colonne d'Ercole e i limite dell'ecumene," in *Il confine nel mondo classico*, ed. Marta Sordi, *CISA* 13, Milan 1987, 13–20.

———. "Le Isole Fortunate: mito, utopia, realtà geografia," in *Geografia e storiografia nel mondo classico*, ed. Marta Sordi, *CISA* 14, 1988, pp. 166–77.

André, Jean-Marie and Marie-Françoise Baslez. *Voyager dans l'Antiquité*, n. p.: Fayard, 1993.

Antonelli, Luca. "Aviénus et les colonnes d'Hercule," *MCV* 31, 1995, 77–83.

———. *I Greci oltre Gibilterra*, *Hesperìa* 8, Rome 1997.

———. *Il periplo nascosto*, Padua: Esedra, 1998.

Ashbee, Paul. *Ancient Scilly: From the First Farmers to the Early Christians*, Newton Abbot: David and Charles, 1974.

Ashoka. *The Edicts*, tr. N. A. Nikam and Richard McKeon, Chicago: University of Chicago Press, 1959.

———. *Les inscriptions*, tr. Jules Bloch, Paris 1950.

Atkinson, J. E. *A Commentary on Q. Curtius Rufus' Historiae Alexandri Magni Books 3 and 4*, Amsterdam: Gieben, 1980.

Aubet, María Eugenia. *The Phoenicians and the West*, second edition, tr. Mary Turton, Cambridge 2001.

Aujac, Germaine. *Strabo et la science de son temps*, Paris: Les Belles Lettres, 1966.

——. "Les traités 'sur l'Océan' et les zones terrestres," *RÉA* 74, 1972, 74–85.

——. "L'île de Thulé, mythe ou realité," *Athenaeum* 76, 1988, 329–43.

——. "L'île de Thulé, de Pythéas à Ptolémée," in *Géographie du monde au Moyen Âge à la Renaissance*, ed. Monique Pelletier, Paris 1989, pp. 181–90.

Avienus, Rufus Festus. *Ora maritima*, ed. Adolf Schulten, Berlin: Weidmann, 1922.

——. *Ora maritima*, ed. Adolf Schulten, second edition, Barcelona 1955.

——. *Ora maritima*, ed. Dietrich Stichtenoth, Darmstadt: Wissenschaftliche Buchgesellschaft, 1968.

——. *Ora maritima*, ed. J. P. Murphy, Chicago: Ares Publishers, 1977.

Bacon, J. R. "The Geography of the *Orphic Argonautica*," *CQ* 25, 1931, 172–83.

Badian, E. "A King's Notebooks," *HSCP* 72, 1968, 183–204.

Balboa Salgado, António. "Rufo Festo Avieno y su *Ora maritima*: consideraciones acerca de un sujeto y un objeto," *Gallaecia* 13, 1992, 369–98.

Banfi, Silvana Boschi. "Note sulla Tule," *NumAntCl* 5, 1976, 291–9.

Barber, G. L. *The Historian Ephorus*, Cambridge: Cambridge University Press, 1935.

Barros, João de and Diogo do Couto. *The History of Ceylon, From the Earliest Times to 1600 AD*, tr. and ed. by Donald Ferguson, *JRAS-C* 20, no. 60, 1908, 1–445.

Batty, Roger. "Mela's Phoenician Geography," *JRS* 90, 2000, 70–94.

Beaumont, R. L. "The Date of the First Treaty Between Rome and Carthage," *JRS* 29, 1939, 74–86.

Bechert, Tilmann and Willem J. H. Willems. *Die römische Reichsgrenze von der Mosel bis zur Nordseeküste*, Stuttgart: Thiess, 1995.

Behrmann, Rodrigo de Balbín *et al.* "Datos sobre la colonizacíon púnica de las Islas Canarias," *Eres (Arqueología)* 6, 1995, 7–28.

Berger, Hugo. *Die geographischen Fragmente des Eratosthenes*, reprint of 1880 edition, Amsterdam: Meridian, 1964.

Berggren, J. Lennart and Alexander Jones. *Ptolemy's Geography: An Annotated Translation of the Theoretical Chapters*, Princeton: Princeton University Press, 2000.

Bergmann, Werner. "Dicuil," *TTEMA*, pp. 151–2.

Bianchetti, Serena. "Aviено, *Ora. mar.* 80 ss.: le colonne d'Eracle e il vento del nord," *Sileno* 16, 1990, pp. 241–6.

——. "L'idea di Africa da Annone a Plinio," *Africa Romana* 7, 1990, pp. 871–8.

——. "Pitea e la scoperta di Thule," *Sileno* 19, 1993, pp. 9–24.

——. "Plinio e la descrizione dell'Oceano settentrionale in Pitea di Marsiglia," *OT* 2, 1996, 73–84.

——. "Per la datazione del Περὶ ὠκεανοῦ di Pitea di Massalia," *Sileno* 23, 1997, 73–84.

——. "Pitea di Massalia e l'estremo occidente," *Hesperìa* 10, 2000, 129–37.

——. "Cannibali in Irlanda? Letture straboniane," *AncS* 32, 2002, 215–34.

——. "Eutimene e Pitea di Massalia: geografia e storiografia," in *Storici greci d'Occidente*, ed. Riccardo Vottuone, Bologna 2002, pp. 439–85.

Bickerman, E. J. *Chronology of the Ancient World*, second edition, Ithaca: Cornell University Press, 1980.

Biffi, Nicola. *L'Africa di Strabone: Libro XVII della Geografia*, Modugno: Edizioni del Sud, 1999.

Blázquez, J. M. and J. González Navarrete, "The Phokaian Sculpture of Obulco in Southern Spain," *AJA* 89, 1985, 61–9.

Blomqvist, Jerker. *The Date and Origin of the Greek Version of Hanno's Periplus*, Lund: CWK Gleerup, 1979.

——. "Reflections of Carthaginian Commercial Activity in *Hanno's Periplous*," *OrSue* 33–4, 1984–6, 53–62.

Boardman, John. *The Greeks Overseas: Their Colonies and Trade*, fourth edition, London: Thames and Hudson, 1999.

Book of Settlements: Landnámabók, tr. Hermann Pálsson and Paul Edwards, Winnipeg: University of Manitoba Press, 1972.

Borzsák, István. "Ultimus Thules," *AAntHung* 41, 2001, 217–24.

Bosch-Gimpera, P. "The Phokaians In the Far West: An Historical Reconstruction," *CQ* 38, 1944, 53–9.

Bosworth, A. B. *A Historical Commentary on Arrian's History of Alexander*, Oxford: Clarendon Press, 1980–.

Boulakia, Jean David C. "Lead In the Roman World," *AJA* 76, 1972, 139–44.

Bousquet, Jean. "Deux monnaies grecques: Massalia, Sestos," *AnnBr* 75, 1968, pp. 277–9.

Branigan, Ciaran. "The Circumnavigation of Africa, *Classics Ireland* 1, 1994.

Bratianu, Georges I. *La mer noire, Acta Historica* 9, Munich 1969.

Braund, David. *Ruling Roman Britain*, London: Routledge, 1996.

Brincken, Anna-Dorothee von den. "Antipodes," *TTEMA*, pp. 27–9.

Broche, Gaston-E. *Pythéas le Massaliote: Découvreur de l'extrème occident et du nord de l'Europe*, Paris: Société Française d'Imprimerie et de Librairie, 1935.

Brogan, Olwen. "Trade Between the Roman Empire and the Free Germans," *JRS* 26, 1936, 195–222.

Bromwich, James. *The Roman Remains of Southern France: A Guidebook*, first paperback edition, London: Routledge, 1996.

Broughton, T. R. S. *The Magistrates of the Roman Republic, Philological Monographs Published by the American Philological Association* 15, 1952.

Brown, Truesdell S. *Timaeus of Tauromenium, University of California Publications in History* 55, Berkeley, 1958.

Buchheit, Vinzenz. "Epikurs Triumph des Geistes," *Hermes* 99, 1971, 303–23.

Bunnens, Guy. *L'expansion phénicienne en Méditerranée, Études de philologie, d'archéologie et d'histoire anciennes* 17, Brussels 1979.

Burn, A. R. "Mare pigrum et grave," *CR* 63, 1949, 94.

Burstyn, Harold L. "Theories of Winds and Ocean Currents From the Discoveries to the End of the Seventeenth Century," *TI* 3, 1971, 7–31.

Burton, Richard F. *Abeokuta and the Camaroons Mountains: An Exploration*, London: Tinsley Brothers, 1863.

——. *Ultima Thule or, A Summer in Iceland*, London: William P. Nimmo, 1875.

Carcopino, Jérôme. "Périple de Hannon," *CRAI* 1943, 137–9.

Carpenter, Rhys. *The Greeks in Spain*, New York: Longman, Green, 1925.

——. "Phoenicians in the West," *AJA* 62, 1958, 35–53.

——. *Beyond the Pillars of Heracles*, n. p.: Delacorte Press, 1966.

Cary, Max. "The Greeks and Ancient Trade With the Atlantic," *JHS* 44, 1924, 166–79.

—— and E. H. Warmington, *The Ancient Explorers*, revised edition, Baltimore: Penguin Books, 1963.

Cassidy, Vincent H. "The Voyage of an Island," *Speculum* 38, 1963, 595–602.

——. *The Sea Around Them: The Atlantic Ocean, AD 1250*, Baton Rouge: Louisiana State University Press, 1968.

——. "Other Fortunate Islands and Some That Were Lost," *TI* 1, 1969, 35–9.

——. "New Worlds and Everyman: Some Thoughts on the Logic and Logistics of Pre-Columbian Discovery," *TI* 10, 1978, 7–13.

Casson, Lionel. *The Ancient Mariners: Seafarers and Sea Fighters of the Mediterranean in Ancient Times*, New York: Macmillan, 1959.

——. *Ships and Seamanship in the Ancient World*, Princeton: Princeton University Press, 1971.

————. "Traders and Trading: Classical Athens," *Expedition* 21.4, 1979, 25–32.

Cataudella, Michele R. "Quante erano le colonne d'Ercole?" *AFLM* 22–3, 1989–90, 315–37.

Cauer, F. "Arganthonios," *RE* 2, 1895, 686.

Cavalli-Sforza, Luigi Luca. "Demographic Data," in *African Pygmies*, ed. Luigi Luca Cavalli-Sforza, Orlando: Academic Press, 1986, pp. 23–44.

Charles, J. A. "Where Is the Tin," *Antiquity* 49, 1975, 19–24.

Chevallier, R. "The Greco-Roman Conception of the North from Pytheas to Tacitus," *Arctic* 37, 1984, 341–6.

Christ, Karl. *Drusus und Germanicus*, Paderborn: Ferdinand Schöningh, 1956.

Clarke, G. W. "Ancient Knowledge of the Gulf Stream," *CP* 62, 1967, 25–31.

Clarke, Katherine. "In Search of the Author of Strabo's *Geography*," *JRS* 87, 1997, 92–110.

——. *Between Geography and History: Hellenistic Constructions of the Roman World*, Oxford: Clarendon Press, 1999.

Clavel-Leveque, Monique. *Marseille grecque: la dynamique d'un impérialisme marchand*, Marseille: Laffitte, 1977.

Colin, Frédéric. "Le récit de Sataspes s'inspire-t-il de sources egyptiennes?" *ZPE* 82, 1990, 287–96.

Collingwood, R. G. and M. V. Taylor, "Roman Britain in 1933," *JRS* 24, 1934, 196–221.

Collingwood, R. G. and R. P. Wright. *The Roman Inscriptions of Britain* 1: *Inscriptions on Stone*, Oxford: Clarendon Press, 1965.

Colón, Fernando. *The Life of the Admiral Christopher Columbus*, tr. Benjamin Keen, New Brunswick, N. J.: Rutgers University Press, 1959.

Coones, Paul. "The Geographical Significance of Plutarch's Dialogue *Concerning the Face Which Appears in the Orb of the Moon*," *TIBG* n. s. 8, 1983, 361–72.

Cordano, Federica. *Le geografia degli antichi*, Rome: Laterza, 1992.

Cunliffe, Barry. "Ictis: Is It Here?" *OJA* 2, 1983, 123–6.

——. *The Ancient Celts*, Oxford: Oxford University Press, 1997.

——. *The Extraordinary Voyage of Pytheas the Greek*, London: Allen Lane, 2001.

——. *Facing the Ocean: The Atlantic and Its Peoples, 8000BC–AD1500*, Oxford: Oxford University Press, 2001.

Dalby, Andrew. *Food in the Ancient World from A to Z*, London: Routledge, 2003.

Davin, Emmanuel. "Pythéas le Massaliote: premier grand navigateur provençal," *BAssBudé* 4. ser. 2, June 1954, 60–71.

De Anna, Luigi. *Conoscenza e immagine della Finlandia e del settentrione nella cultura classico-medievale*, Turun Yliopiston Julkaisuja ser. B, 180, Turku 1988.

——. *Thule: le fonti e le tradizioni*, Rimini: Il Cerchio, 1998.

De Beer, Gavin. "Iktin," *GJ* 126, 1960, 160–7.

De Negri, Carlo. "Considerazioni nautiche sul 'Periplo' di Annone," *MSE* 3, 1978, 33–65.

Demerliac, J.-G. and J. Meirat. *Hannon et l'empire punique*, Paris: Les Belles Lettres, 1983.

Desanges, Jehan. *Recherches sur l'activité des Méditerranéens aux confins de l'Afrique*, *CÉFR* 38, 1978.

——. "The Carthaginian Period," in *General History of Africa* 2, ed. G. Mokhtar, Paris 1981, pp. 441–64.

——. "Le point sur le 'Périple d'Hannon': controverses et publications récentes," in *Enquêtes et Documents* 6: *Nantes–Afrique–Amérique*, Nantes 1981, pp. 13–29.

——. "Des interprètes chez les 'Gorilles'. Réflexions sur un artifice dans le 'Périple d'Hannon'," in *Atti del i Congresso Internazionale di Studi Fenici e Punici* 1, Rome 1983, pp. 267–70.

——. "Le sens du terme 'corne' dans le vocabulaire géographique des grecs et des romains: à propos du 'Périple d'Hannon'," *BAC* 20b–21b, 1984–85 (1989), 29–34.

——. "Lixos dans les sources littéraires grecques et latines," in *Lixus, CÉFR* 166, 1992, 1–6.

——. "La face cachée de l'Afrique selon Pomponius Méla," *GeoAnt* 3–4, 1994–5, 79–89.

Dessau, H. "Ein Freund Plutarchs in England," *Hermes* 46, 1911, 156–60.

Dicks, D. R. *The Geographical Fragments of Hipparchus*, London: Athlone Press, 1960.

——. "Eratosthenes," *DSB* 4, 1971, 388–93.

Dicuil. *Liber de mensura orbis terrae*, ed. J. J. Tierney, Dublin: Dublin Institute for Advanced Studies, 1967.

Diehl, Erich. "Roxolani," *RE Supp.* 7, 1940, 1195–7.

Diels, Hermann. *Doxographi graeci*, Berlin: Walter de Gruyter, 1872.

Dilke, O. A. W. "Geographical Perceptions of the North in Pomponius Mela and Ptolemy," *Arctic* 37, 1984, 347–51.

——. *Greek and Roman Maps*, Ithaca: Cornell University Press, 1985.

Diller, Aubrey. "Geographical Latitudes in Eratosthenes, Hipparchus and Posidonius," *Klio* 27, 1934, 258–69.

——. "The Ancient Measurements of the Earth," *Isis* 40, 1949, 6–9.

——. *The Tradition of the Minor Greek Geographers, Philological Monographs Published by the American Philological Association* 14, 1952.

——. "Pytheas of Massalia," *DSB* 11, 1975, 225–6.

Dion, Roger. "Le problème des Cassitérides," *Latomus* 11 1952, 306–14.

——. "Géographie historique de la France," *ACF* 65, 1965, 457–89.

——. "La renommée de Pythéas dans l'antiquité," *RÉL* 43, 1965, 443–66.

——. "Où Pythéas voulait-il aller?" in *Mélanges d'archéologie et d'histoire offerts à André Piganiol*, ed. Raymond Chevallier, Paris 1966, pp. 1315–36.

——. "Pythéas explorateur," *RPhil* 3 ser. 40, 1966, 191–216.

——. "L'esplorazione di Pitea nei mari de Nord," in *Geografia e geografi nel mondo antico: guida storica e critica*, ed. Francesco Prontera, Rome 1983, pp. 203–25.

Doran, Michael F. "The Maritime Provenience of Iron Technology in West Africa," *TI* 9, 1977, 89–98.

Dupuich, J.-J. "Note sur l'*Ora maritima* de Rufius Festus Avienus," in *Littérature gréco-romaine et géographie historique, Mélanges offerts à Roger Dion, Caesarodunum* 9bis, Paris 1974, pp. 225–31.

Eichel, Marijean H. and Joan Markley Todd. "A Note on Polybius' Voyage to Africa in 146 BC," *CP* 71, 1976, 237–43.

Elter, Anton. "Das Altertum und die Entdeckung Amerikas," *RhM* n. s. 75, 1926, 241–65.

Endsjø, Dag Øistein. "Placing the Unplaceable: the Making of Apollonius' Argonautic Geography," *GRBS* 38, 1997, 373–85.

Eudoxos of Knidos. *Fragmente*, ed. François Lasserre, Berlin: Walter de Gruyter, 1966.

Euzennat, Maurice. "Thamusida," *PECS*, p. 902.

——. "Pour une lecture marocaine du Périple d'Hannon," *BAC* 12–14b, 1976–8 (1980), 243–6.

——. "Le Périple d'Hannon," *CRAI* 1994, 559–79.

Fabre, Paul. "La date de la rédaction du périple de Scylax," *EtCl* 33, 1965, 353–66.

——. "Réflexions sur les Argonautiques du Pseudo-Orphée," in *Notices d'archéologie armoricaine* 1, *Annales de Bretagne* 79, 1972, 269–313.

——. "Étude sur Pythéas le Massaliote et l'époque de ses travaux," *EtCl* 43, 1975, 25–44.

——. "Les Massaliotes et l'Atlantique," in *Océan Atlantique et Péninsule Armoricaine: Études archéologiques, Actes du 107ᵉ Congrès National des Societés Savants, Brest 1982*, Paris 1985, pp. 25–49.

——. "Les grecs à la découverte de l'Atlantique," *RÉA* 94, 1992, 11–21.

Fear, Andrew T. "Odysseus and Spain," *Prometheus* 18, 1992, 19–26.

Ferguson, John. "Classical Contacts With West Africa," in *Africa in Classical Antiquity: Nine Studies*, ed. L. A. Thompson and J. Ferguson, Ibadan 1969, pp. 1–25.

——. *Utopias of the Classical World*, London: Thames and Hudson, 1975.

——. "China and Rome," in *ANRW* 2.9, 1978, 581–603.

Fowler, Robert L. "Herodotos and His Contemporaries," *JHS* 116, 1996, 62–87.

Fox, Aileen. *South West England*, New York: Praeger, 1964.

Fraser, P. M. "Eratosthenes of Cyrene," *ProcBritAc* 56, 1970, 175–207.

—— et al. (eds.) *A Lexicon of Greek Personal Names*, Oxford: Clarendon Press, 1987–2000.

Freeman, Philip. *Ireland and the Classical World*, Austin: University of Texas Press, 2001.

Freyer-Schauenburg, Brigitte. "Kolaios und die westphönizischen Elfenbeine," *MM* 7, 1966, 89–108.

Gabba, Emilio. "True History and False History in Classical Antiquity," *JRS* 71, 1981, 50–62.

Gaffarel, Paul. *Histoire de la découverte de l'Amérique*, Paris: Arthur Rousseau, 1892.

Gagé, Jean. "Gadès, l'Inde et les navigations atlantiques dans l'antiquité," *RHist* 205, 1951, 189–216.

Garrard, Timothy F. "Myth and Metrology: The Early Trans-Saharan Gold Trade," *JAH* 23, 1982, 443–61.

Garzon Diaz, Julian. "Hannon de Cartago, periplo (Cod. Palat. 398 fol. 55r–56r)," *MHA* 8, 1987, 81–5.

Geminos. *Introduction aux phénomènes*, ed. Germaine Aujac, Paris: Les Belles Lettres, 1975.

Géographes grecs 1: *Introduction générale, Ps.-Scymnos*, ed. Didier Marcotte, Paris: Les Belles Lettres, 2000.

Germain, Gabriel. "Qu'est-ce que le *Périple* d'Hannon? Document, amplification littéraire, ou faux intégral?" *Hespéris* 44, 1957, 205–48.

Geus, Klaus. "Utopie und Geographie. Zum Weltbild der Griechen in frühhellenistischer Zeit," *OT* 6, 2000, 55–84.

Gianfrotta, Piero Alfredo. "Le àncore votivi di Sostrato di Egina e di Faillo di Crotone," *PP* 30, 1975, 311–18.

Gil, Juan. "Miscelanea critica," *EClás* 85, 1980, 135–42.

Giot, Pierre-Roland et al., *Protohistoire de la Bretagne*, Rennes: Editions Ouest-France, 1995.

Gisinger, F. "Skymnos" (#1), *RE* 11, 1921, 662–87.

——. "Pytheas" (#1), *RE* 24, 1963, 314–66.

Gómez-Tabanera, José Manuel. "Hallazgos monetarios del Mundo Antiguo en las Isles Azores y América del Norte. Un problema heurístico," *Numisma* 26, 1976, 201–8.

González Ponce, F. J. "Sobre el valor histórico atribuible al contenido de *Ora maritima*: las citas de los iberos y de otros pueblos, como paradigma," *Faventia* 15.1, 1993, 45–60.

——. *Avieno y el Periplo*, n. p., 1995.

——. "*Suda s. v.* Σκύλαξ. Sobre el título, el contenido y la unidad *FGrHist* III C 709," *GeoAnt* 6, 1997, 37–51.

——. "El corpus periplográfico griego y sus integrantes más antiguos: épocas arcaica y clásica," in *Los límites de la tierra: el espacio geográfico en las culturas mediterráneas*, ed. Aurelio Pérez Jiménez and Gonzalo Cruz Andreotti, Madrid 1998, pp. 41–75.

——. "Utilidad práctica, ciencia y literatura en la periplografía griega de época helenística," in *Los límites de la tierra: el espacio geográfico en las culturas mediterráneas*, ed. Aurelio Pérez Jiménez and Gonzalo Cruz Andreotti, Madrid 1998, pp. 147–75.

——. "La posición del *Periplo* del Ps.-Escílax en el conjunto del género periplográfico," *RÉA* 103, 2001, 369–80.

Gozalbes Cravioto, Enrique. "Algunas observaciones acerca del Periplo de Hannon" *HispAnt* 17, 1993, 7–219.

Gran Aymerich, J. M. J. "Prospections archéologiques au Sahara atlantique (Rio de Oro et Sequiet el Hamra)," *AntAfr* 13, 1979, 7–21.

Gras, Michel. "La mémoire de Lixus," in *Lixus*, *CÉFR* 166, 1992, 27–44.

Greenlee, William Brooks (tr. and ed.), *The Voyage of Pedro Álvarez Cabral to Brazil and India*, London: Hakluyt Society, 1938.

Gripp, Karl. *Erdgeschichte von Schleswig-Holstein*, Neumünster: Karl Wachholtz, 1964.

Gruen, Erich S.. *The Hellenistic World and the Coming of Rome*, first paperback printing, Berkeley: University of California Press, 1986.

——. "The Expansion of the Empire Under Augustus," *CAH* 10, second edition, 1996, pp. 147–97.

Gsell, Stéphane. *Histoire ancienne de l'Afrique du Nord*, Paris: Hachette, 1914–28.

Gusinde, Martin. "Kenntnisse und Urteile über Pygmäen in Antike und Mittelalter," *Nova Acta Leopoldina* n. s. 25, no. 162, 1962, 1–26.

Hall, J. B. "Notes on Avienius' *Ora maritima*," *RivFil* 112, 1984, 192–5.

Hamilton, J. R. C. *Excavations at Clickhimin, Shetland*, Edinburgh: H. M. Stationery Office, 1968.

Harden, D. B. "The Phoenicians on the West Coast of Africa," *Antiquity* 22, 1948, 141–50.

Harvey, F. David. "Sostratos of Aigina," *PP* 31, 1976, 206–14.

Haverfield, F. "Κασσιτερίδες," *RE* 10, 1919, 2328–32.

Hawkes, C. F. C. "Archaeology and Ancient Ideas of a Plenteous West," *UJA* 38, 1975, 1–11.

——. "Ictis Disentangled, and the British Tin Trade," *OJA* 3, 1984, 211–33.

——. *Pytheas: Europe and the Greek Explorers*, n. d., n. p.

Haywood, John. *The Penguin Historical Atlas of the Vikings*, London: Penguin, 1995.

Head, Barclay V. *Historia Numorum: A Manual of Greek Numismatics*, new and enlarged edition, Oxford: Clarendon Press, 1911.

Heichelheim, F. M. "Roman Coins From Iceland," *Antiquity* 26, 1952, 43–5.

Hemmerdinger, Bertrand. "Notes sure le *Périple* d'Hannon," *BollClass* 3. ser. 18, 1997, 51–2.

Hencken, Hugh. "Herzsprung Shields and Greek Trade," *AJA* 54, 1950, 294–309.

Hennig, Richard. *Von rätselhaften Ländern*, Munich: Delphin-Verlag, 1925.

——. *Terrae Incognitae*, second edition, Leiden: Brill, 1944.

Hermary, Antoine *et al.* *Marseille grecque, 600–49 av. J.-C.: la cité phocéenne*, Paris: Errance, 1999.

Herrmann, Joachim. "Volkstämme und 'nördlicher Seeweg' in der älteren Eisenzeit," *ZfA* 19, 1985, 147–53.

—— (ed.). *Griechische und lateinische Quellen zur Frühgeschichte Mitteleuropas*, *Schriften und Quellen der Alten Welt* 37, Berlin 1988–1992.

Hind, John. "Pyrene and the Date of the 'Massaliot Sailing Manual'," *RivStorAnt* 2, 1972, 39–52.

Hodge, A. Trevor. *Ancient Greek France*, Philadelphia: University of Pennsylvania Press, 1998.

Hölbl, Günther. *A History of the Ptolemaic Empire*, tr. Tina Saavedra, London: Routledge, 2001.

Honigmann, E. "Ὀφέλας" (#1), *RE* 18, 1939, 630.

Hyde, Walter Woodburn. *Ancient Greek Mariners*, New York: Oxford University Press, 1947.

Ingstad, Helge and Anne Stine Ingstad. *The Viking Discovery of America*, St John's: Breakwater, 2000.

Irby-Massie, Georgia L. and Paul T. Keyser, *Greek Science of the Hellenistic Era: A Sourcebook*, London: Routledge, 2002.

Isserlin, B. S. J. "Did Carthaginian Mariners Reach the Island of Corvo (Azores)?. Report on the Results of Joint Field Investigations Undertaken On Corvo in June, 1983," *RStFen* 12, 1984, 31–46.

Jacoby, F. "Euthymenes" (#4), *RE* 6, 1907, 1509–11.

——. "Kleon von Syrakus" (#8), *RE* 11, 1921, 718–9.

Jessen, Otto. *Die Strasse von Gibraltar*, Berlin: Dietrich Reimer, 1927.

Jones, Barri and Ian Keillar, "Marinus, Ptolemy, and the Turning of Scotland," *Britannia* 27, 1996, 43–9.

Käppel, Lutz. "Bilder des Nordens im frühen Antike Griechenland," in *Ultima Thule: Bilder des Nordens von der Antike bis zur Gegenwart*, ed. Annelore Engel-Braunschmidt *et al.*, Frankfurt 2004, pp. 11–27.

Karlsson, Gunnar. *The History of Iceland*, Minneapolis: University of Minnesota Press, 2000.

Keller, Otto. *Die antike Tierwelt*, Leipzig: Verlag Von Wilhelm Engelmann, 1909–1913.

Keyser, Paul T. "From Myth to Map: The Blessed Isles in the First Century BC," *AncW* 24, 1993, 149–67.

——. "The Geographical Work of Dikaiarchos," in *Dicaearchus of Messana: Text, Translation, and Discussion*, ed. William W. Fortenbaugh and Eckart Schütrumpf, *Rutgers Unversity Studies in Classical Humanities* 10, 2001, pp. 353–72.

Knaack, G. "Antiphanes von Berga," *RhM* n. s. 61, 1906, 135–8.

Knapowski, Roch. *Zagadnienia chronologii i zasięgu podróży odkrywczych Piteasa z Marsylii*, *Prace komisji historycznej* (Poznan) 18, 1958.

Konrad, C. F. *Plutarch's Sertorius: A Historical Commentary*, Chapel Hill: University of North Carolina Press, 1994.

Kristiansen, Kristian. "The Consumption of Wealth in Bronze Age Denmark. A Study in the Dynamics of Economic Processes in Tribal Societies," in *New Directions in Scandinavian Archaeology*, ed. Kristian Kristiansen and Carsten Paludan-Müller, Odense: National Museum of Denmark, n. d., pp. 158–190.

Krogmann, Willy. "Der Bernsteininsel *Basileia*," in *VII Congresso Internazionale di Scienze Onomastiche: Atti del Congresso e Memorie della sezione toponomastica* 2, Florence 1963, pp. 205–20.

Kroll, W. "Philemon" (#11), *RE* 19, 1938, 2146–50.

Lacroix, Francis. "Les langues," in *Histoire générale de l'Afrique noire* 1, ed. Hubert Deschamps, Paris 1970, pp. 73–90.

Laffranque, Marie. "Poseidonios, Eudoxe de Cyzique, et la circumnavigation de l'Afrique," *RPFE* 88, 1963, 199–222.

Lancel, Serge. *Carthage: A History*, tr. Antonia Nevill, Oxford: Blackwell, 1995.

Landi, Carolus. "Opuscula de Fontibus Mirabilibus, de Nilo etc.," *StIt* 3, 1895, 531–48.

Larsson, Sven Gisle. *Baltic Amber – A Palaeobiological Study*, Klampenborg: Scandinavian Science Press, 1978.

Lasserre, François. "Ostiéens et Ostimniens chez Pythéas," *MusHelv* 20, 1963, 107–13.

Law, R. C. C. "The Garamantes and Trans-Saharan Enterprise in Classical Times," *JAH* 8, 1967, 181–200.

——. "North Africa in the Period of Phoenician and Greek Colonization, *c.* 800 to 323BC," *CHA* 2, 1978, 87–147.

Ligi, H. "Пифей Балтийское Море," *SS* 31, 1988, 86–95.

Lloyd, Alan B. "Were Necho's Triremes Phoenician?" *JHS* 95, 1975, 45–61.

Lonis, Raoul. "Les conditions de la navigation sur la côte atlantique de l'Afrique dans l'antiquité: le problème du 'retour'," in *Afrique noire et monde méditerranéen dans l'antiquité,* Dakar 1978, pp. 147–170.

Loposzko, Tadeusz. "Ultima Thule—Północne krańce świata," *Meander* 30, 1975, 292–304.

Luce, J. V. *Lost Atlantis,* New York: McGraw Hill, 1969.

Lupher, David A. *Romans In a New World: Classical Models in Sixteenth-Century Spanish America,* Ann Arbor: University of Michigan Press, 2003.

Lynch, John Patrick. *Aristotle's School: A Study of a Greek Educational Instition,* Berkeley: University of California Press, 1962.

Maass, E. *Commentariorum in Aratum Reliquiae,* reprint, Berlin: Weidmann, 1958.

MacDonald, G. "Thule oder Thyle," *RE* 2. ser. 11, 1936, 627–30.

——. "Orcades," *RE* 18, 1939, 881–2.

Macfarlane, Roger T. "Thule," *TTEMA,* p. 602.

McGrail, Seán. *Ancient Boats in N. W. Europe,* London: Longman, 1987.

——. "Celtic Seafaring and Transport," in *The Celtic World,* ed. Miranda J. Green, London 1995, pp. 254–81.

——. *Boats of the World From the Stone Age to Medieval Times,* Oxford: Oxford University Press, 2001.

Magnani, Stefano. "Una geografia fantastica? Pitea di Massalia e l'immaginaro greco," *RivStorAnt* 32–3, 1992–3, 25–42.

——. "Le isole occidentali e l'itinerario piteano," *Sileno* 21, 1995, 83–102.

——. "Da Massalia a Thule: annotazioni etnografiche piteane," in *Dall'Indo a Thule: i Greci, i Romani, gli altri,* ed. Antonio Aloni and Lìa de Finis, Trento 1996, pp. 337–52.

——. *Il viaggio di Pitea sull'Oceano,* Bologna: Pàtron, 2003.

Maguire, Joseph. "The Sources of Pseudo-Aristotle *De Mundo*," *YCS* 6, 1939, 111–57.

Mahjoubi, A. and P. Salama, "The Roman and Post-Roman Period in North Africa," in *General History of Africa* 2, ed. G. Mokhtar, Paris 1981, pp. 465–512

Malleret, Louis. "Les fouilles d'Oc-èo (1944): rapport préliminaire," *BÉFEO* 45, 1951, 75–88.

Manfredi, Valerio. *Le Isole Fortunate: Topografia di un mito,* Rome: "L'Erma" di Bertschneider, 1966.

Marcaccini, Carlo. "Giovenale, Tacito e gli studi di retorica a Tule," *Maia* n. s. 51, 1999, 247–57.

Marcotte, Didier. "Le périple dit de Scylax. Esquisse d'un commentaire épigraphique et archéologique," *BollClass* 3. ser. 7, 1986, 166–82.

Marcus, G. J. *The Conquest of the North Atlantic,* New York: Oxford University Press, 1981.

Marcy, G. "Notes linguistiques: autour du Périple d'Hannon," *Hespéris* 20, 1935, 21–72.

Marseille, Musées de. *Phocée et la fondation de Marseille,* Marseille 1995.

Martels, E. R. W. M. von. "Orosius," *TTEMA,* pp. 462–3.

——. "Solinus, Julius Gaius," *TTEMA,* pp. 566–7.

Martin, Constance. *Distant Shores: the Odyssey of Rockwell Kent,* Berkeley: University of California Press, 2000.

Martin García, José A. "El periplo a África de Hannón," *AMal* 15, 1992, 55–84.

Masson, J. R. "Geographical Knowledge and Maps of Southern Africa Before 1500AD," *TI* 18, 1986, 1–20.

Mattes, Merrill J. *Colter's Hell and Jackson's Hole*, Yellowstone National Park: Yellowstone Library and Museum Association, 1962.

Mauny, Raymond. "Autour d'un texte bien controversé: le 'périple' de Polybe (146 av. J.-C.)," *Hespéris* 36, 1949, 47–67.

———. "Cerné l'Île de Herné (Río de Oro) et la question des navigations antiques sur la côte ouest-africaine," in *Conferencia internacional de africanistas occidentales* 2, Madrid 1954, pp. 73–80.

———. "Monnaies anciennes trouvées en Afrique au Sud du limes de l'empire romaine," in *Conferencia internacional de Africanistas Occidentales: 4ª Conferencia, Santa Isabel de Fernando Poo 1951*, Madrid 1954, vol. 2, pp. 53–70.

———. "La navigation sur les côtes du Sahara pendant l'antiquité," *RÉA* 57, 1955, 92–101.

———. "Monnaies antiques trouvées en Afrique au Sud du limes romain," *LibAE* 4, 1956, 249–60.

———. "Les navigations anciennes et les grandes découvertes," in *Histoire générale de l'Afrique noire* 1, ed. Hubert Deschamps, Paris 1970, pp. 203–18.

———. "Les contacts terrestres entre Méditerranée et Afrique tropicale occidentale pendant l'antiquité," in *Afrique noire et monde méditerranéen dans l'antiquité*, Dakar 1978, pp. 122–46.

———. "Trans-Saharan Contacts and the Iron Age in West Africa," *CHA* 2, 1978, 272–341.

Maxwell, I. S. "The Location of Ictis," *JRIC* n. s. 6, 1969–72, 293–319.

May, W. E. "Were Compasses Used in Antiquity," *JN* 34, 1981, 414–23.

Mederos Martín, Alfredo and Gabriel Escribano Cobo. "El periplo norteafricano de Hannón y la rivalidad gaditano-cartaginesa de los siglos IV-III a. C.," *Gerión* 18, 2000, 77–107.

Meek, C. J. "The Niger and the Classics: The History of a Name," *JAH* 1, 1960, 1–17.

Mercer, John. *The Canary Islanders: Their Prehistory Conquest and Survival*, London: Rex Collings, 1980.

Mirhady, David C. "Dicaearchus of Messana: the Sources, Text and Translation," in *Dicaearchus of Messana: Text, Translation, and Discussion*, ed. William W. Fortenbaugh and Eckart Schütrumpf, *Rutgers Unversity Studies in Classical Humanities* 10, 2001, pp. 1–142.

Mitchell, B. M. "Herodotos and Samos," *JHS* 95, 1975, 75–91.

Mitchell, Stephen. "Cornish Tin, Iulius Caesar, and the Invasion of Britain," in *Studies in Latin Literature and Roman History* 3, ed. Carl Deroux, *Collection Latomus* 180, 1983, pp. 80–99.

Mohr, Walter. "Des Pytheas von Massilia Schrift 'Über den Ozean'," *Hermes* 77, 1942, 28–45.

Monod, Théodore. "Les monnaies nord-africaines anciennes de Corvo (Açores)," *BIFAN* 35b, 1973, 231–8.

———. "À propos de l'Île Herné (baie de Dakhla, Sahara occidental)," *BIFAN* 41b, 1979, 1–34.

Monteagudo, Luis. "Casiterides," *Emerita* 18, 1950, 1–17.

———. "Oestrymnides y Cassiterides en Galicia," *Emerita* 21, 1953, 241–8.

Morel, Jean-Paul. "Les phocéens en occident: certitudes et hypothèses," *PP* 21, 1966, 378–419.

———. "Les Phocéens dans l'extrème occident, vus depuis Tartessos," *PP* 25, 1970, 285–9.

———. "L'expansion phocéenne en occident: dix années de recherches (1966–1975)," *BCH* 99, 1975, 853–96.

———. "Le Phocéens d'Occident: nouvelles données, nouvelles approches," *PP* 37, 1982, 479–99.

Morgan, J. R. "Lucian's *True Histories* and the *Wonders Beyond Thule* of Antonius Diogenes," *CQ* n. s. 35, 1985, 475–90.

Morison, Samuel Eliot. *Christopher Columbus, Mariner*, New York: Mentor Books, 1956.

Morrison, J. S. and R. T. Williams, *Greek Oared Ships, 900–322BC*, Cambridge: Cambridge University Press, 1968.

Mourre, Ch. "Euthyménès de Marseille," *RStLig* 30, 1964, 133–9.

Mund-Dopchie, Monique. "La survie littéraire de la Thulé de Pythéas," *AntCl* 59, 1990, 79–97.

Muhly, J. D. "Sources of Tin and the Beginnings of Bronze Metallurgy," *AJA* 89, 1985, 275–91.

——. "Copper, Tin, Silver, and Iron: The Search for Metallic Ores As an Incentive For Foreign Expansion," in *Mediterranean Peoples in Transition: Thirteenth to Early Tenth Centuries BCE*, ed. Seymour Gitin *et al.*, Jerusalem, 1998, pp. 314–29.

Murphy, Trevor. *Pliny the Elder's Natural History: The Empire in the Encyclopedia*, Oxford: Oxford University Press, 2004.

Musso, Olimpio. "Il periplo di Annone ovvero estratti bizantini da Senofonto di Lampsaco," in *Mediterraneo medievale: Scritti in onore di Francesco Giunta*, n. p., 1989, pp. 955–63.

Nakassis, Dimitri. "Gemination at the Horizons: East and West in the Mythical Geography of Archaic Greek Epic," *TAPA* 134, 2004, 215–33.

Nansen, Fridtjof. *In Northern Mists: Arctic Exploration in Early Times*, tr. Arthur G. Chater, New York: Frederick A. Stokes, 1911.

National Oceanic and Atmospheric Administration. *Tide Tables 1995: Europe and West Coast of Africa*, Washington 1994.

Nesselrath, H.-G. "Pytheas," *RGA* 23, 2003, 617–20.

Neumann, G. "Flevum," *RGA* 9, 1995, 190–1.

—— and R. Wenskus. "Codanus Sinus," *RGA* 5, 1984, 38–40.

Neumann, G. *et al.* "Burcana," *RGA* 4, 1981, 113–17.

——. "Kimbern," *RGA* 16, 2000, 493–504.

Oehler, H. *Paradoxographi florentini anonymi opusculum de aquis mirabilibus*, Tübingen: J. J. Heckenhauer, 1913.

Ó Ríordáin, Seán P.. "Roman Material in Ireland," *Proceedings of the Royal Irish Academy* 51c3, 1947, pp. 35–82.

Özyiğit, Ömer. "The City Walls of Phokaia," *RÉA* 96, 1994, 77–109.

Palaiphatos. *On Unbelievable Tales*, ed. Jacob Stern, Wauconda, Ill.: Bolchazy-Carducci: 1996.

Park, Mungo. *Travels In the Interior Districts of Africa*, ed. Kate Ferguson Masters, Durham, N. C.: Duke University Press, 2000.

Parroni, Piergiorgio. "Surviving Sources of the Classical Geographers Through Late Antiquity and the Medieval Period," *Arctic* 37, 1984, 352–8.

Pédech, Paul. "Un texte discuté de Pline: le voyage de Polybe en Afrique (*H. N.*, V, 9–10)," *RÉL* 33, 1955, 318–32.

——, *La méthode historique de Polybe*, Paris: Les Belles Lettres, 1964.

Pekkanen, Tuomo. *The Ethnic Origin of the ΔΟΥΛΟΣΠΟΡΟΙ*, *Arctos Supp.* 1, Helsinki 1968.

Pena, María José. "Avieno y las costas de Cataluña y Levante I. *Tyrichae: *TYRIKAÍ, ¿«la Tiria»?" Faventia* 11.2, 1989, 9–21.

Penhallurick, R. D. *Tin in Antiquity*, London: Institute of Metals, 1986.

Peretti, Aurelio. *Il periplo di Scilace*, Pisa: Giardini, 1979.

——. "Dati storici e distanze marine nel *Periplo* di Scilace," *SCO* 38, 1988, 13–137.

Picard, Gilbert. *Carthage*, tr. Miriam and Lionel Kochan, London: Elek Books, 1964.

Picard, Gilbert-Charles. "Le Périple d'Hannon n'est pas un faux," *Archeologia* (Paris) 40, May–June 1971, 54–9.

——. "Le Périple d'Hannon," in *Phönizier im Westen*, ed. Hans Georg Niemeyer, *Madrider Beiträge* 8, 1982, pp. 175–80.

——. "Der Periplus des Hanno," in *Karthago*, ed. Werner Huss, *Wege der Forschung* 654, Darmstadt 1992, pp. 182–92.

Pliny the Elder. *Histoire naturelle, livre II*, tr. and comm. by Jean Beaujeau, Paris: Les Belles Lettres, 1950.

——. *Histoire naturelle, livre V, 1–46*, tr. and comm. by Jehan Desanges, Paris: Les Belles Lettres, 1980.

——. *Histoire naturelle, livre VI, 2ᵉ partie*, tr. and comm. by J. André and J. Filliozat, Paris: Les Belles Lettres, 1980.

——. *Histoire naturelle, livre VII*, tr. and comm. by Robert Schilling, Paris: Les Belles Lettres, 1977.

Plutarch. *Moralia 12*, ed. Harold Cherniss and William C. Helmbold, Cambridge, Mass.: Harvard University Press, 1957.

Pomponius Mela. *Chorographie*, ed. A. Silberman, Paris: Les Belles Lettres, 1988.

——. *Pomponius Mela's Description of the World*, ed. F. E. Romer, Ann Arbor: University of Michigan Press, 1998.

Ponsich, M. "La navigation antique dans le détroit de Gibraltar," in *Littérature gréco-romaine et géographie historique* (*Mélanges offerts à Roger Dion*), *Caesarodunum* 9bis, Paris 1974, pp. 257–73.

——. "Tangier antique," *ANRW* 2.10.2, 1982, 788–816.

Poseidonios. *Posidonius 1: The Fragments*, second edition, ed. L. Edelstein and I. G. Kidd, Cambridge: Cambridge University Press, 1989.

——. *Posidonius 2: The Commentary*, ed. I. G. Kidd, Cambridge: Cambridge University Press, 1988.

——. *Posidonius 3: The Translation of the Fragments*, ed. I. G. Kidd, Cambridge: Cambridge University Press, 1999.

Posnanasky, M. "Introduction to the Later Prehistory of Sub-Saharan Africa," in *General History of Africa* 2, ed. G. Mokhtar, Paris 1981, pp. 533–50.

Pothecary, Sarah. "The Expression 'Our Times' in Strabo's *Geography*," *CP* 92, 1997, 235–46.

Pratt, Mary Louise. *Imperial Eyes: Travel Writing and Transculturation*, London: Routledge, 1992.

Pytheas of Massalia. *Pytheas von Massalia*, ed. Hans Joaquim Mette, Berlin: Walter de Gruyter, 1952.

——. *Ueber das Weltmeer*, ed. Dietrich Stichtenoth, Köln: Böhlau Verlag, 1959.

——. *On the Ocean*, ed. Christina Horst Roseman, Chicago: Ares Publishers, 1994.

——. *L'Oceano*, ed. Serena Bianchetti, Pisa: Istituti Editoriali e Poligrafici Internazionale, 1998.

Ramin, J. *Le problème des Cassitérides*, Paris: A. and J. Picard, 1965.

——. "Ultima Cerne," in *Littérature gréco-romaine et géographie historique*, (*Mélanges offerts à Roger Dion*), *Caesarodunum* 9bis, Paris 1974, pp. 439–49.

——. *Le périple d'Hannon*, BAR Supp. Ser. 3, 1976.

Randles, W. G. L. "Classical Models of World Geography and Their Transformation Following the Discovery of America," *The Classical Tradition and the Americas* 1.1, ed. Wolfgang Haase and Meyer Reinhold, Berlin, 1994, pp. 5–76.

Randsborg, Klavs. *Hjortspring: Warfare and Sacrifice in Early Europe*, Aarhus: Aarhus University Press, 1995.

Rankin, David. *Celts and the Classical World*, London: Croom Helm, 1987.

——. "The Celts Through Classical Eyes," in *The Celtic World*, ed. Miranda J. Green, London 1995, pp. 21–33.

Rasmussen, Knud. *Greenland By the Polar Sea*, tr. Asta and Rowland Kenney, London: William Heinemann, 1921.

Rausing, Gad. *Prehistoric Boats and Ships of Northwestern Europe*, Malmö: CWK Gleerup, 1984.

Rebuffat, René. "Vestiges antiques sur la côte occidentale de l'Afrique au sud de Rabat," *AntAfr* 8, 1974, 25–49.

——. "Recherches sur le Bassin du Sebou II: Le Périple d'Hannon," *BAMaroc* 16, 1985–6, 257–84.

——. "Les nomades de Lixus," *BAC* 18b, 1982 (1988), 77–86.

——. "Voyage du Carthaginois Hannon, du Lixos à Cerné," *BAC* 18b, 1982 (1988), 198–201.

——. "Les pentécontores d'Hannon," *Karthago* 23, 1995, 20–30.

Reichert, H. "Morimarusa," *RGA* 20, 2002, 246–7.

——. "Saevo," *RGA* 26, 2004, 86–8.

Richey, M. W. "The Haven Finding Art," *JN* 10, 1957, 271–6.

Rivit, A. L. F. and Colin Smith, *The Place-Names of Roman Britain*, Princeton: Princeton University Press, 1979.

Roller, Duane W. *Tanagran Studies* 2: *The Prosopography of Tanagra in Boiotia*, Amsterdam: Gieben, 1989.

——. *The World of Juba II and Kleopatra Selene: Royal Scholarship on Rome's African Frontier*, London: Routledge, 2003.

——. "Boiotians in Northwest Africa," to appear in the *Proceedings of the Tenth International Boiotian Congress*.

——. *Scholarly Kings: The Fragments of Juba II of Mauretania, Archelaos of Kappadokia, Herod the Great, and the Emperor Claudius*, Chicago: Ares Publishers, 2004.

——. "Seleukos of Seleukeia," forthcoming in *AntCl.*

——. "The West African Voyage of Hanno the Carthaginian," to appear in *AncW.*

Romm, James S. "Herodotus and Mythic Geography: The Case of the Hyperboreans," *TAPA* 119, 1989, 97–113.

——. *The Edges of the Earth in Ancient Thought*, Princeton 1992.

——. "New World and '*novos orbos*': Seneca in the Renaissance Debate Over Ancient Knowledge of the Americas," in *The Classical Tradition and the Americas* 1.1, ed. Wolfgang Haase and Meyer Reinhold, Berlin 1994, pp. 77–116.

Roseman, Christina Horst. "Hour Tables and Thule in Pliny's *Natural History*," *Centaurus* 30, 1987, 93–105.

Salama, P. "The Sahara in Classical Antiquity," *General History of Africa* 2, ed. G. Mokhtar, Paris 1981, pp. 513–32.

Santini, Carlo. "Il prologo dell'*Ora maritima* di Rufio Festo Avieno," in *Prefazioni, prologhi, proemi di opere tecnico-scientifiche latine* 2, ed. C. Santini and N. Scivoletto, Rome 1992, pp. 937–47.

Saramago, José. *O Conto de Ilha Desconhecida: The Tale of the Unknown Island*, tr. Margaret Jull Costa, New York: Harcourt Brace, 1999.

Savage, Thomas S. "Notice of the External Characters and Habits of *Troglodytes gorilla*, a New Speices of Orang From the Gabon River," *Boston Journal of Natural History* 5, 1847, 417–26.

Schönfeld. "Scadinavia," *RE* 2. ser. 2, 1921, 340–2.

Schmid, W. "Antiphanes" (#19), *RE* 1, 1984, 2521–2.

Schmitt, P. "A la recherche du Char des Dieux," in *Littérature gréco-romaine et géographie historique*), *Mélanges offerts à Roger Dion*, Caesarodunum 9bis, Paris 1974, pp. 473–9.

Schulten, Adolf. *Tartessos: Ein Beitrag zur ältesten Geschichte des Westens*, second edition, Hamburg: Cram, De Gruyter, 1950.

——. "Die 'Säulen des Herakles'," in Otto Jessen, *Die Strasse von Gibraltar*, Berlin 1927, pp. 174–206.

Schwabacher, Willy. "Die Azoren und die Seefahrt der Alten," *SchwMbll* 12, 1962–3, 22–6.

Schweighäuser, J. *Lexicon Polybianum*, Oxford: W. Baxter, 1832.

Scullard, H. H. *The Elephant in the Greek and Roman World*, Cambridge: Thames and Hudson, 1974.

Seel, Otto. *Antike Entdeckerfahrten*, Zürich: Artemis, 1961.

Segelhandbuch für den atlantischen Ozean, third edition, Hamburg: L. Friederichsen, 1910.

Segert, Stanislav. "Phoenician Background of Hanno's Periplus," *MélBeyrouth* 45, 1969, 501–18.

Selkirk, Raymond. *The Piercebridge Formula*, Cambridge: Patrick Stephens, 1983.

Shetelig, Haakon. "Roman Coins Found In Iceland," *Antiquity* 23, 1949, 161–3.

Sitwell, N. H. H. *The World The Romans Knew*, London: Hamish Hamilton, 1984.

Soren, David *et al. Carthage: Uncovering the Mysteries and Splendors of Ancient Tunisia*, New York: Simon and Schuster, 1990.

Spann, Philip O. "Sallust, Plutarch, and the 'Isles of the Blest'," *TI* 9, 1977, 75–80.

——. *Quintus Sertorius and the Legacy of Sulla*, Fayetteville: University of Arkansas Press, 1987.

Spekke, Arnolds. *The Ancient Amber Routes and the Geographical Discovery of the Eastern Baltic*, Stockholm: M. Goppers, 1957.

Stefansson, Vilhjalmur. *Ultima Thule*, New York: Macmillan, 1940.

Stephens, Susan A. and John J. Winkler (eds.). *Ancient Greek Novels: The Fragments*, Princeton: Princeton University Press, 1995.

Stewart, P. C. N. "Inventing Britain: the Roman Creation and Adaptation of an Image," *Britannia* 26, 1995, 1–10.

Stichtenoth, Dietrich. "Pytheas von Marseille, der Entdecker Mittel- und Nordeuropas," *Das Altertum* 7, 1961, 156–66.

Strabo. *Géographie*, vol. 1, part 1, ed. Germaine Aujac and François Lasserre, Paris: Les Belles Lettres, 1969.

——. *Géographie*, vol. 1, part 2, ed. Germaine Aujac, Paris: Les Belles Lettres, 1969.

——. *Géographie*, vol. 2, tr. François Lasserre, Paris: Les Belles Lettres, 1966.

——. *Strabonis Geographika* 1, ed. Stefan Radt, Göttingen: Vandenhoeck and Ruprecht, 2002.

Strang, Alastair. "Explaining Ptolemy's Roman Britain," *Britannia* 28, 1997, 1–30.

Svennung, J. *Skandinavien bei Plinius und Ptolemaios*, Uppsala: Almqvist and Wiksell, 1974.

Szabó, Árpád. "Strabon und Pytheas – die geographische Breite von Marseille – Zür Frühgeschichte der mathematischen Geographie," *Historia scientiarum* 29, 1985, 3–15.

Tartessos: Arqueología protohistória del bajo Guadalquiver, ed. María Eugenia Aubet Semmler, Barcelona: Editorial AUSA, n. d.

Tausend, Klaus. "Inder in Germanien," *OT* 5, 1999, 115–25.

Taylor, E. G. R. "The Oldest Mediterranean Pilot," *JN* 4, 1951, 81–5.

——. "The Navigating Manual of Columbus," *JN* 5, 1952, 40–54.

——. *The Haven-Finding Art: A History of Navigation From Odysseus to Captain Cook*, London: Hollis and Carter, 1956.

Taylor, John W. "A Nigerian Tin Trade in Antiquity?" *OJA* 1, 1982, 317–24.

Thapar, Romila. *Asoka and the Decline of the Mauryas*, Oxford: Oxford University Press, 1961.

Thiel, J. H. *Eudoxus of Cyzicus, Historische Studies* 23, Groningen: J. B. Wolters, n. d.

Thomas, Charles. *Exploration of a Drowned Landscape: Archaeology and History of the Isles of Scilly*, London: Batsford, 1985.

Thompson, L. A. "Eastern Africa and the Graeco-Roman World (to AD641)," in *Africa in Classical Antiquity: Nine Studies*, ed. L. A. Thompson and J. Ferguson, Ibadan 1969, pp. 26–61.

Thomson, J. Oliver. *History of Ancient Geography*, Cambridge: Cambridge University Press, 1948.

Thouvenot, R. "Le témoignage de Pline sur le périple africain de Polybe (V, 1, 8–11)," *RÉL* 34, 1956, 88–92.

Tierney, James J. "Ptolemy's Map of Scotland," *JHS* 79, 1959, 132–48.

——. "The Celtic Ethnography of Posidonius," *ProcRIA* 60c, 1960, 189–275.

Todd, Malcolm. *The South West to AD1000*, London: Longman, 1987.

Treister, M. Yu. *The Role of Metals in Ancient Greek History, Mnemosyne Supp.* 156, 1996.

Vallet, Georges and François Villard. "Les Phocéens en Mediterranée occidentale à l'époque archaique et la fondation de Hyélè," *PP* 21, 1966, 166–90.

Van Raalte, Marlein. "The Idea of the Cosmos as An Organic Whole in Theophrastus' *Metaphysics*," in *Theophrastean Studies* 3, ed. William W. Fortenbaugh and Robert W. Sharples, New Brunswick 1988, pp. 189–215.

Villalba i Varneda, Pere. "El text crític de l'*Ora maritima* d'Aviènus," *Faventia* 7.1, 1985, 33–45.

———. "La «qüestió avienea»," *Faventia* 7.2, 1985, 61–7.

———. "'Sed in Pyrenen ab columnis Herculis' (*Ora Maritima* 562)," *Actas del Congreso Internacional "Historia de los Pirineos" Cevera 1988*, ed. Eduardo Ripoll Perello and Manuel F. Ladero Quesada, vol. 1, Madrid 1991, pp. 411–17.

Vinland Sagas: The Norse Discovery of America, tr. and intro. by Magnus Magnusson and Hermann Pálsson, London: Penguin, 1965.

Vivenza, Gloria. "Altre considerazione sul *Periplo* di Annone," in *Economia e Storia* 2. ser. 1.1, 1980, pp. 101–10.

Wackernagel, H. G. "Massalia" (#1), *RE* 14, 1930, 2130–52.

Walbank, F. E. "The Geography of Polybius," *ClMed* 9, 1947, 155–82.

———. "Polybius on the Pontus and the Bosphorus," in *Studies Presented to David Moore Robinson*, ed. George E. Mylonas, St Louis 1951–3, pp. vol. 1, 469–79.

———. *A Historical Commentary on Polybius*, Oxford: Clarendon Press, 1957–79.

———. "Polemic in Polybios," *JRS* 52, 1962, 1–12.

———. *Polybius*, first paperback printing, Berkeley: University of California Press, 1990 .

Wallinga, H. T. "Phoenicische en Griekse verkenning ter zee in het Westen voor Alexander," *Lampas* 26, 1993, 194–205.

Warmington, B. H. *Carthage*, revised edition, New York: Praeger, 1969.

Weinman, Edward. "Life Takes Root," *Iceland Review* 41, 2003, 28–33.

Wells, C. M. *The German Policy of Augustus*, Oxford: Clarendon Press, 1972.

Wenskus, Reinhard. "Pytheas und der Bernsteinhandel," in *Untersuchungen zu Handel und Verkehr der vor- und frühgeschichtlichen Zeit in Mittel- und Nordeuropa* 1, ed. Klaus Döwel *et al.*, *AbbGött* 3. ser. 143, 1985, pp. 84–108.

——— and K. Ranke, "Abalus," *RGA* 1, 1973, 5–6.

West, M. L. *The Orphic Poems*, Oxford 1983.

West, Stephanie. "'The Most Marvellous of All Seas': The Greek Encounter With the Euxine," *GaR* 50, 2003, 151–67.

Wheeler, Mortimer. *Rome Beyond the Imperial Frontiers*, London: G. Bell and Sons, 1954.

Whitaker, Ian. "The Problem of Pytheas' Thule," *CJ* 77, 1981–82, 148–64.

Whittaker, C. R. "The Western Phoenicians: Colonisation and Assimilation," *PCPS* 200, 1971, 58–79.

Wijsman, H. J. W. "Thule Applied to Britain," *Latomus* 57, 1998, 318–23.

Wolska-Conus, Wanda. "Cosmas Indikopleustes," *TTEMA*, pp. 129–31.

Woodward, Kesler E. *Sydney Laurence: Painter of the North*, Seattle: University of Washington Press, 1990.

Wüst, Ernst. "Pygmaioi," *RE* 23, 1959, 2064–74.

Zimmermann, K. Review of Bianchetti, *Pitea, CR* n. s. 50, 2000, 28–30.

Zubov, N. N. *Arctic Ice and the Warming of the Arctic*, tr. E. Hope, Moscow: Northern Sea Route Directorate, 1948.

LIST OF PASSAGES CITED

Italicized numbers are citations in ancient texts; romanized numbers are pages in this volume.

GREEK AND LATIN SOURCES

Aelian, *Diverse History 3.18*, 52n; *5.3*, 15n
Aetios, *3.17.2*, 77n; *3.17.3*, 66n; *3.17.6*,
  77n; *FGrHist #647, no. 2*, 16n
Aischylos:
  Persians 496, 85n
  Prometheus Bound 349–52, 2n
  Suppliant Women 558, 102n
Albinovanus Pedo, 120n
Ammianus Marcellinus *18.6.1*, 79n
Androsthenes of Thasos (*FGrHist #711*), *fr.*
  1–5, 92n
Anonymus Florentinus (*FGrHist #647, no. 1*),
  16n
Antonius Diogenes, *The Unbelievable Things*
  Beyond Thoule, 53n
Apollonios of Rhodes, *Argonautika*
  4.507–684, 68n
Appian, *Italika 8.1*, 60n
Aristeides *36.85–95*, 16n; *48*, 33n
Aristotle:
  Constitution of Massalia, 7n, 64
  History of Animals 5.15, 64n; *7(8).12*, 21n
  Metaphysics 1.3, 85n
  Meterologika 1.5, 72n; *1.13*, 17n; *2.1*, 1n,
    20n, 59n; *2.3*, 94n; *2.5*, 25n, 51n, 64n,
    92n
  On the Heavens 2.14, 51n, 64n, 106n
  Parts of Animals 4.5, 64n
  Poetics 11, 106n
  Politics 5.5.2, 64n; *6.4.5*, 64n; *7.13.1*, 9n
[Aristotle]:
  Mechanika 7 (851b), 32n

On Marvellous Things Heard 37, 30n; *84*,
  45n, 57n; *87*, 64n; *89*, 64n; *136*, 30n
On the Cosmos 3, 52n
Arrian:
  Anabasis 2.15.6–24.6, 58n; *2.24.5*, 59n;
    5.26.1–2, 59n; *7.1*; 59n; *7.1.4*, 60n;
    7.15–16, 60n; *7.16*, 59n; *7.20.7–8*, 92n
  Indika 43.9, 93n; *43.11–12*, 31n, 33n, 41n
Athenaios *2.44e*, 24n; *3.83*, 48n; *3.93*, 92n;
  7.302, 103n; *8.322*, 100n; *8.330–2*,
  103n; *12.540*, 64n; *13.576*, 7n, 64n;
  14.655, 64n
Avienus:
  Descriptio orbis terrae 760, 68n
  Ora maritima 42–50, 10n, 27n; *80–145*,
    68n; *90–102*, 70n; *96*, 10; *102*, 11;
    108–9, 11; *108–29*, 28n; *110–12*, 11;
    114–15, 29n; *117*, 10n, 27n, 49n;
    117–29, 27n; *120*, 11; *129–45*, 11n;
    130–3, 29n; *137–9*, 11; *139–42*, 11;
    147, 11; *164–5*, 46n; *176–7*, 11; *182*,
    11; *183*, 11; *225*, 11; *267*, 11; *275–83*,
    10n; *284–5*, 11; *303*, 11; *319*, 11;
    336–74, 90n; *341*, 11; *364–5*, 27n;
    375–89, 27n; *380–9*, 57n; *383*, 10n,
    27n; *402–13*, 27n; *406–13*, 20n, 57n;
    412, 10n, 27n; *414–15*, 27n; *437–63*,
    97n; *440–3*, 22n; *459–60*, 22n; *460–1*, 11;
    491, 11; *519*, 11; *545*, 11; *572–3*, 11; *587*,
    68n; *623*, 11; *631*, 11; *689*, 11; *704*, 11
Augustus, *Res gestae 26*, 113n, 118n, 121n;
  31, 113n

149

OTHER PRE-MODERN SOURCES

INDEX

Generally there is no distinction in this index between toponyms (e.g. Massalia), ethnyms (e.g. Massalians) and the ethnic adjective (e.g. Massalian). Not every variant of every toponym is listed. Greek, Roman, and Carthaginian authors appear only in the List of Passages Cited (pp. 149–53) unless they are actual players in the events.

INDEX

Scatinavia 88, 121
Scharhörn Island 119
Schweighäuser, J. 103
Scilly Isles 13
Scipio Aemilianus, P. Cornelius 43, 62,
  99–101, 103, 105
Scotland 71, 75, 77n, 83
Sebou, Oued 34, 37
Seine River 69n
Sejanus, L. Aelius 120n
Seleukids 27, 94
Seleukos of Seleukeia 77
Seleukos I 94
Seneca, L. Annaeus (the elder) 126–7
Senegal River 18, 38, 41, 102
Septimius Flaccus 115n
Sertorius, Q. 46–7, 49, 112, 116
Seyðisfjördur 83
Shetland Islands 74–6, 78–9, 84, 87, 91n,
  96
Sicily 1n, 26n, 94, 99
Siggjo 89n
Skagens Odde 90n, 121
Skaggerak 89
Skandia 121
Skanör 87
Skansen (Stockholm) 86n
Skarðsfjörður 81
Skylax (Pseudo-) 28, 47, 49n
Skylax of Karyanda 8–9
Skymnos of Chios 6n
Skythia 61, 87–8
Soloeis 34–5, 129–32
Solomon, Israelite king 5
Somalia 25
Sostratos of Aigina 4n
South Foreland (Kent) 70
Smyrna 6
Spain 2, 22n, 45, 51, 100, 109, 116; coast
  of 4, 10–11, 13, 46, 58, 61, 97n
Spartel, Cape 15n, 34–6
Statius Sebosus 47n, 48n
Strabo of Amaseia 104, 107, 110
Sububus 34
Suetonius Paulinus, C. 38n, 115n
Suiones 89
Sumerians 44n
Surtsey 87
Sweden 87, 89n, 123n
Syria 120n

tacking 32

Tamesa/Tamesis River 67n
Tamousida/Tamousiga 34
Tanagra 14
Tanais 67–9
Tanatis 67n
Tangier 34, 95
Taprobane 95n
Tariq, Jebel 1
Tarraco 11
Tarshish 5
Tartaros 5
Tartessos 4–7, 11, 13–14, 28–9, 58
Taruga 42n
Tauros 94
Temara 14n
Tenerife 47n
Thales of Miletos 16
Thames, River 67n
Thanet 67n
Theon Ochema: see Chariot of the Gods
Theophrastos of Eresos 64
Thoule 65, 68n, 70n, 73, 78–88, 91n, 94,
  123–4, 127
Thrinke 30n
Thule: see Thoule
Thymiateria/Thymiaterion 34–5, 129–32
Tiberius (emperor) 118–22
tides 17–18, 61, 72, 74, 76–7, 86n, 95, 98,
  117, 123
Timaios of Tauromenion 65
Timbuctu 21
Timosthenes of Rhodes 93
tin 12–14, 29, 41–2, 72, 117n
Tingis 34–5, 109, 112
Toulouse 68
Trischen Island 119
Trogodytai 129–32
Trojan War 5
Trondheim 123n
Turnus xvi
Tylos 80, 92
Tyre 58–9, 80
Tyrrhenia 7

Ultima Thule 79–80
Ursa Minor 74n
Ushant 29n, 69

Vectis 73n, 74
Veii 60n
Vendyssel 89
Vert, Cap 39

Related titles from Routledge

Britannia
The Creation of a Roman Province
John Creighton

In the late Iron Age two kings held dominion over much of Lowland Britain: Cunobelin and Verica. Just before AD43 the rule of both of them ended – one died and the other fled – and Rome, under the Emperor Claudius, took the opportunity to invade.

Within a few generations the ceremonial centres of these Iron Age kings had been transformed into the magnificence of Roman towns with their monumental public buildings. This book looks at the interface of these two worlds, Iron Age and Roman, to see how much each owed the other.

Britannia: The Creation of a Roman Province offers a complete re-evaluation of both the evidence for and the interpretation of the rule of the kings of Late Iron Age Britain on the eve of the Roman conquest, and their long-lasting legacy in the creation of the Roman province of Britannia. Among topics considered are:

- the links between Iron Age kings of Britain and Rome before the Claudian conquest
- the creation of the towns of Roman Britain
- the many different natures of 'Roman Identity'
- the long lasting influence of the kings on the development of the province
- the widely different ways that archaeologists have read the evidence.

Hb: 0-415-33313-X

Available at all good bookshops
For ordering and further information please visit:
www.routledge.com

Related titles from Routledge

Globalizing Roman Culture
Unity, Diversity and Empire
Richard Hingley

What is Romanization?

Was Rome the first global culture?

Romanization has been represented as a simple progression from barbarism to civilization. Roman forms in architecture, coinage, language and literature came to dominate the world from Britain to Syria. Hingley argues for a more complex and nuanced view in which Roman models provided the means for provincial elites to articulate their own concerns. Inhabitants of the Roman provinces were able to develop identities they never knew they had until Rome gave them the language to express them.

Most work that has been done in this area has concentrated on specific areas or provinces. Hingley draws together the threads in a sophisticated theoretical framework that spans the whole Roman Empire, and provokes intriguing comparisons with modern discussions of 'Coca-colaization' and resistance to American cultural domination.

Hb: 0-415-35175-8
Pb: 0-415-35176-6

Available at all good bookshops
For ordering and further information please visit:
www.routledge.com

Related titles from Routledge

Hannibal's Dynasty
Dexter Hoyos

Hannibal has always been the most famous member of the Barcid dynasty, which dominated Cathage and its empire in Africa and Spain in the latter half of the third century BC. However, Dexter Hoyos' revealing study makes it clear that Carthaginian success was founded on the military and political skills of more than one member of this remarkable family.

It was Hannibal's father, Hamilcar Barca, who relaunched Carthage as an imperial power after disastrous wars; Hamilars' son-in-law, Hasdrubal further developed the new *imperium* in the face of Roman suspicion and opportunism. Only then was Carthage's historical zenith reached by Hannibal and his two remarkable brothers in the war with Rome from 218–201BC.

Hb: 0-415-29911-X
Pb: 0-415-35958-9

Available at all good bookshops
For ordering and further information please visit:
www.routledge.com

Related titles from Routledge

Ancient Greece
Social and Historical Documents from Archaic Times
to the Death of Socrates
Matthew Dillon and Lynda Garland

In this revised and updated edition Matthew Dillon and Lynda Garland present a wide range of documents on Greek social and political history from 800 to 399 BC, from all over the Greek World. *Ancient Greece* includes:

Source material on political developments in Greece, including colonization in the Mediterranean and the Black Sea, Athenian democracy, the constitution of Sparta and the Peloponnesian war.

Detailed chapters on social phenomena, such as Greek religion, slavery and labour, the family and the role of women.

Clear, precise translations of documents taken not only from historical sources but also from inscriptions, graffiti, law codes, epitaphs, decrees, drama and poetry, many of which have not previously been translated into English.

Concise, up-to-date bibliographies and commentaries for each document and each section.

Hb: 0-415-21754-7
Pb: 0-415-21755-5

Available at all good bookshops
For ordering and further information please visit:
www.routledge.com

Related titles from Routledge

Mycenaeans
Life in Bronze Age Greece
Rodney Castleden

Following on from Castleden's best-selling study *Minoans*, this major new contribution to our understanding of the crucial Mycenaean period clearly and effectively brings together research and knowledge we have accumulated since the discovery of the remains of the civilization of Mycenae in the 1870s.

In lively prose, informed by the latest research and using full bibliography and over 100 illustrations, this vivid study delivers the fundamentals of Mycenaean civilization including its culture, hierarchy, economy and religion. Castleden introduces controversial views of the Mycenaean palaces as temples, and studies their impressive sea empire and their crucial interaction with the outside Bronze Age world before discussing the causes of the end of their civilisation.

Providing clear, easy information and understanding, this is a perfect starting point for the study of the Greek Bronze Age.

Hb: 0-415-24923-6
Pb: 0-415-36336-5

Available at all good bookshops
For ordering and further information please visit:
www.routledge.com

Related titles from Routledge

War and Society in Imperial Rome, *c.*31BC to AD280
Brian Campbell

This well-documented study of the Roman army provides a crucial aid to understanding the Roman Empire in economic, social and political terms. Employing numerous examples, Brian Campbell explores the development of the Roman army and the expansion of the Roman Empire from 31BC to AD280.

Dealing with issues such as the financial implications of supporting a professional army in war and peace, Brian Campbell explores the wider significance of the army and warfare in Roman life and culture. This superbly researched survey provides readers with an invaluable guide to this important and much neglected subject.

Hb: 0-415-27811-3
Pb: 0-415-27882-1

Available at all good bookshops
For ordering and further information please visit:
www.routledge.com

eBooks – at www.eBookstore.tandf.co.uk

A library at your fingertips!

eBooks are electronic versions of printed books. You can store them on your PC/laptop or browse them online.

They have advantages for anyone needing rapid access to a wide variety of published, copyright information.

eBooks can help your research by enabling you to bookmark chapters, annotate text and use instant searches to find specific words or phrases. Several eBook files would fit on even a small laptop or PDA.

NEW: Save money by eSubscribing: cheap, online access to any eBook for as long as you need it.

Annual subscription packages

We now offer special low-cost bulk subscriptions to packages of eBooks in certain subject areas. These are available to libraries or to individuals.

For more information please contact webmaster.ebooks@tandf.co.uk

We're continually developing the eBook concept, so keep up to date by visiting the website.

www.eBookstore.tandf.co.uk